Leathers Publishing, Co.
3840 West 75th Street
Prairie Village, Kansas 66208
(913) 384-2625

Library of Congress Catalog Number: 95-081403
ISBN: 0-9646898-2-0
Printed in the United States of America
FIRST EDITION 1995

FRONT COVER: Kansas City Skyline at Dusk
BACK COVER: Portrait of Jerry Cohen
Both photographs by Gerald W. Crabtree,
Studio of Visual Images, Kansas City, Missouri
Book design and production: Pat Whalen

CONTENTS

Cookingham quits; in 1963, after four years of wrangling, Bartle cannot win reelection.

Jacobson, a successful investment broker, in to help run company; Jerry is named sales and marketing executive for 1981 in Kansas City in elaborate ceremonies at the Allis Marriott Hotel; on the 50th anniversary of the founding of the Tempo Co., Jerry announces he is merging with an American duplicating giant, Danka Industries, as an independent entity.

CITIZEN JERRY COHEN

FOREWORD

I f you've been a resident of Kansas City for any length of time it is strongly possible that you have run into an ebullient, good-natured dynamo named Jerry Cohen. In 1993, Jerry Cohen looked back on his 81 years in Kansas City and decided he wanted to work on a book that would leave a written record of his enjoyment of his life in this great city, a life that has traditions. The life of Cohen needs to be told because his story is that of hundreds of other Jews who overcame anti-Semitic prejudice and other obstacles it left in its trail to make the United States a better nation from their very presence. Cohen is proud of his heritage and is at the same time grateful for the American way of life that allowed him the freedom to make the major contributions of his life to his community. Perhaps best known as the spirit of Christmas at Kansas City in his role of 40 years as chairman of the Mayor's Christmas Tree Fund, a fund-raising effort held annually during the holidays to help make the season a little cheerier for the less fortunate of the city, he left his mark on the countless other activities from the Starlight Theater to a variety of children's charities. Cohen and his wife, Jeannette, are products of the great floodtide of Jews who left Russia and Eastern Europe in the 1880s and 1890s to escape persecution and become a part of the American dream of instant riches for those who had the drive and intelligence.

"The New Covenant," a book published by the University of North

Carolina in the late 1980s, is the story of these Jewish immigrants and what they have meant to America and is written by Samuel B. Girgus, an American collage professor. In the book, Professor Girgus writes: "The history of the Jews in America is to a considerable extent the history of an idea. It is the story of how Jewish history was transformed by the idea of America and how, in turn, Jewish writers, intellectuals, artists and public figures helped to sustain and modernize this idea. While the American idea altered the modern Jewish experience, Jewish thinkers often led the effort to make the idea of America relevant to the needs of an urban, industrial and even post-industrial age. The work of such Jews served to keep the American idea meaningful in a time of competing authoritarian and totalitarian ideologies. By the American idea I mean the set of values, beliefs and traditions of freedom, democracy, equality and republicanism that are known as the American way and give America a unique identity in history. For the Jews that idea included the concept of emancipation. It has been noted that only in America did emancipation precede Jewish life. In the context of the American idea, emancipation meant that Jews could be treated as individuals as a basis of equality with all other individuals. This new freedom inspired a devotion to the American Way that paralleled and for many even strengthened the devotion to God and to people." What Professor Girgus wrote in a way is an articulate capsule of the life of Jerry Cohen in his more that 80 years of service to his religion, his community, his fellow citizens and his nation.

Both of the parents of Cohen were a part of the late nineteenth century floodtide of Jews coming to this country to seek refuge. His father was born in the city of Vilna in Lithuania into a poor family and taught himself how to read and write. His mother was born in Hungary and came to Kansas City at the behest of her sister who had immigrated here earlier. Cohen says his earliest memories are of seeing his father meeting with other immigrants who followed him here, giving them lessons in English and helping them with other matters in connection with getting settled in a new country. His early memories are also full of stories of how poor the families of his mother and father had been in Europe because of religious persecution and how they labored long hours in fields to get enough to eat and survive. He recalls them telling of how Jewish women frequently had their babies while in the fields to work because of difficult times. Always such stories were accompanied by reminders of how lucky they were to be in the United States and how they must work to better themselves and their community because of the opportunities they had been given.

As soon as he could, Cohen started his own modest business in 1938, selling stencils for the old mechanical duplicating systems in the Kansas City trade territory. From that humble beginning, Cohen used the lessons learned from his father to build a multi-million-dollar business in duplicating equipment. Much of his success is due to his shrewdness in becoming associated with the old Minnesota Mining and Manufacturing Company, an innovator in developing new duplicating methods and now known world wide as the 3M Corporation. In his work with 3M and other corporations in the duplicating equipment world, Cohen showed a willingness to enter into partnership with the firms in introducing new equipment and working with them in refining the products. His office in downtown Kansas City is a museum of awards he has received from the industry for his entrepreneurial skills.

As his personal fortune grew, Cohen never forgot his humble beginnings and showed a willingness to share his earnings with those less fortunate than himself through all kinds of charitable works. He credits a well-known Kansas Citian, the late H. Roe Bartle, a former regional Boy Scout executive who became mayor of the city in the tumultuous 1950s, with being one of his principal mentors in the charitable field through the years. It was Bartle that got him involved by appointing Cohen as a member of the Kansas City Parks and Recreation board.

The story of Jerry Cohen is the Horatio Alger American success story about which his ancestors had dreamed in European ghettoes. It is a story for the world today in which the struggle by minorities continues because Cohen never let prejudice hinder him. When he was confronted with anti-Semitism, as he frequently was, he simply went another way to overcome such prejudice. He never let the fact that he came from an economically depressed background hinder him because, as he said, "I don't think we ever realized we were poor." He credits much of his success in him to the discipline of a public school education in the U.S. before World War II and the instilling in him by his immigrant parents of the great desire of such new Americans for their children to do well in their new-found system of freedom. His story is worth telling as an example that the American dream of 218 years is still alive and working.

JERRY COHEN WITH HIS MOTHER AND FATHER — *Jerry Cohen is shown as a small boy at the upper left in this photograph with his mother and father, Helen Silverstein Cohen, left, and Reuben Cohen. Standing in the back row with Cohen are his two brothers, Harry and Bernard. Another brother, Robert Cohen, right, stands beside his father while the only girl, Rose Cohen, at left by her mother. The youngest brother, Albert Cohen had not yet born.*

I

To America, Brothers!

The seeds that led to the impact of Jerry Cohen on Kansas City began in the Russian pogroms against the Jews which reached a crescendo in the 1870s and early 1880s. In Lithuania, a small boy, named at the time Reuben Zagarorski, saw the rising unrest among the Jews over the Russian persecution and the waves of Jewish refugees coming out of deeper in Russia with what few belongings they could bring with them in an effort to try to reach the United States. As a small boy watching the chaos, he, too, began to develop a dream of reaching the promised land across the sea. Near Budapest in Hungary, Helen Silverstein, younger than Reuben, was undergoing the same kind of pressures. Her sister, Annie, left Hungary first for the U.S. and landed in Kansas City where she met and married Abe Lebrecht when she was 16. The Russian czar and his family and associates, including the leaders of the Russian Orthodox Christian church, had been publishing anti-Jewish tracts through the 1870s to divert attention from the growing hunger and unemployment that was spreading throughout Russia at the time. Finally in the 1880s, barefoot brigades of peasants in Russia began attacking the Jews in their communities in Kiev and Odessa, murdering, burning and looting, and the violence spread throughout Russia. Before it was over, the rioters had attacked 160 Jewish communities in Russia, including near Vilna, where Jerry's father lived. They had killed hundreds of Jews, leaving thousands homeless, destroying millions of dollars in property and leaving more than 100,000 Jews reduced to the most abject poverty.

At the time, there was a Jewish writer and educator, Abraham Cahan, living in Vilna who wrote graphically for the Jews living in the area, including the family of Jerry's father, about an incident about which he heard and which had occurred in Kiev during the rioting there in 1881. Cahan wrote that the Kiev Jewish quarter was filled with the debris of destroyed homes and crowds of terrified persons. Cahan went on to write about how some of the Jews had gone to their synagogue to seek refuge when a group of Jewish students from the University of St. Vladimar entered the synagogue. Cahan described one of the students saying with tears in his eyes: "Brethren...we are a committee of the Jewish students of the University, sent to clasp hands with you and to mingle our tears with your tears. We are here to say to you: 'We are your brothers; Jews like yourselves, like our fathers. We have striven to adopt the language and manners of your Christian fellow countrymen; we have brought ourselves up to an ardent love of cultures and of progress. We have tried to persuade ourselves that we are children of Mother Russia. Alas! We have been in error. The terrible events which have called forth our tears have aroused us from our dream. The voice of the blood of our outraged brothers and sisters cries unto us that we are only strangers in the land which we have been used to call our home, that we are only stepchildren here, waifs to be trampled upon and dishonored. There is no hope for Israel or Russia. Let us go beyond the seas to land which knows no distinction of race or faith, which is mother to Jew and gentile alike... To America, brethren! To America!' "

Thus in the land of the forefathers of Jerry Cohen, Cahan had set in the tinder of Russian Jewry the sparks of immigration. Under such circumstances began one of the greatest migrations in history, of thousands of Jews from Russia as depicted in the great American Broadway musical, "Fiddler on the Roof," persons who were giving up everything to go to that great land across the sea, the United States.

As the Jews fanned out of Russia across Eastern Europe, they also kindled the flame of migration in the hearts and minds of other Jews in that part of the world such as Hungary where the family of the woman who was to become the mother of Jerry Cohen was living. Cohen recalled his father had told him that his family in Lithuania had built a small row boat to row passengers across the river at Vilna on their trek as part of an effort by the family to get money to join the migration. Like all other Jews in that part of Europe from the mid-1880s until the early 1900s, they began to make plans to get to that great promised land, the United States, as quickly as they could. Finally in 1890, at the age of 17, Reuben Zagarorski had gathered enough money to pay his passage across the Atlantic and set off for the great haven. Because he had taught himself English, the youth believed Zagarorski would be too difficult for Americans and changed his name to Cahan in tribute to his fellow Lithuanian who had penned the essay that may be considered the spark for the migration from the Lithuanian section of Russia. Cahan in 1882 had been forced to migrate to the U.S. for the essay and became famous as a writer and publisher here. In immigration, however, the name Jerry's father had taken for himself became Cohen.

From the first time the first Jews arrived in North America in what is now New York in 1654, the number had grown to only 250,000 Jews living throughout the nation by 1880 when the Russian and Eastern Europe migrations began.

By the time it was over, the migration brought an additional three million Jews, many whole communities and provinces. The great migration of the Jews was not without its problems, however. The Jews in the United States, who had played an integral part in the nation from its beginnings, were starting to become concerned about how these thousands of new Jewish immigrants were going to effect the relationships of the Jews who were already here with their fellow Americans.

One indication of the negative impact on some American Jews of these immigrants such as Reuben Cohen and Helen Silverstein was reflected in this statement at the time by the United Hebrew Charities of Rochester, N.Y.: "They are a bane to the country and a curse to the Jews. The Jews have earned an enviable reputation in the United States but this has been undermined by the influx of thousands who are not ripe for the enjoyment of liberty and equal rights, and all who mean well for the Jewish name should prevent them as much as possible from coming here. It is no relief to the Jews of Poland, Russia, etc., and it jeopardizes the well-being of the American Jews." Not all the immigrants found the new world to their Jewish liking either. Some of them wrote back to their families who were still in Europe urging them not to come because it was not good for the Jews. The correspondence included such warnings as these: "The abundant freedom which is practiced in America can sometimes be like the flood from the ever-swelling breach in the wave of freedom, which destroys its foundations." "In America, they have no synagogue, they have no Shochet (a ritual slaughterer) and neither expect or seek one; they do not teach children Torah and with neither Torah nor Derech Eretz (proper manners) they are growing up wild." "Who is the man who wants to be free of God? Let him go to America, a land which collects all those who forget God and abandon religion, a land which devours the faith of its inhabitants."

But these kinds of negative comments failed to stop Jerry's father and thousands of other Jews from coming to the promised land. Jerry Cohen remembers his father telling another story which drove him to the U.S. and also resulted in his adopting the Cohen name. The father felt that he had been told that his family to which he belonged was a part of that select group of Jews known as Kahane, a race of longtime Jewish priests who were almost invincible. That was another reason he wound up as Reuben Cohen of the U.S. and not his original name of Zagarorski — in addition to the Cahan of the writer from Vilna was this Jewish tradition of Kahane. Jews in the migration who arrived in New York such as Reuben found themselves under pressure from such groups as the Jewish Alliance of America to move into the interior of America. The Jewish Alliance at the time was handing out materials to established Jewish residents who were trying to deal with the immigration tide. The materials read in part: "It may be stated beyond question that the greatest evils attending the present tide of immigration, both in regard to the immigrants and the community at large, may be directly traced to the massing of the newcomers in the great centers of population... The immediate purpose to be kept in view is the settlement of small Jewish communities in the towns and villages in the interior throughout the country. It is manifest that if two or three families could be settled anywhere in self-supporting conditions, they would soon become the nucleous of further growth through the accession of relatives and friends for whom the first comers would have more or less adequate provisions."

Fortunately, however, the Eastern Europe and Russian Jews were also getting more positive, sage advice from American Jewish intellectuals such as Jacob Riis, the writer, who told the immigrants such as Reuben

Cohen: "Hold fast. This is most necessary in America. Select a goal and pursue it with all your might. No matter what happens to you, hold on. You will experience a bad time but sooner or later you will achieve your goal. If you are neglectful, beware, for the wheel of fortune turns quickly. You will lose your grip and be lost. A bit of advice to you: Do not take a moment's rest. Run, do work and keep your own good in mind. Do not say 'I cannot; I do not know how.'" Reuben took heed of such advice and tried to instill it in the minds of his children such as Jerry Cohen. With such advice Reuben began the journey from New York to Kansas City. When he arrived in Kansas City, Reuben Cohen became a protege of a wealthy and well-established Jew in Kansas City, Jacob L. Gold. Gold introduced Reuben Cohen into the world of buying and selling jewelry, a profession to which Reuben Cohen was to devote his life in America and Kansas City. For a time, he worked for a Kansas City jewelry store, Striker Jewelry Co., near Seventh and Main Streets. Later, with experience, Reuben Cohen moved up to join the staff of the Oppenstein Brothers Jewelry Company. In 1911, Cohen opened his own jewelry store and pawn shop at 1423 Grand Avenue, a business he continued to operate at that location until he retired in 1956 after 45 years of running his own business.

While Reuben Cohen settled in Kansas City, a pretty young woman named Ilona Silverstein was anxiously waiting in Hungary to join the Jewish exodus and make her way to Kansas City. The young girl, who Americanized her name to Helen Silverstein when she arrived in America, had targeted Kansas City as the place she was headed because her sister, Annie Silverstein, had made her way there with another family as part of the Russia-Eastern Europe exodus. Within a short time after she had arrived in Kansas City, Annie, at the age of 16, had married another Kansas City Jewish immigrant, Abe Lebrecht, who for years operated one of the largest red meat butcher shops on 12th Street. As soon as Annie and Abe Lebrecht were able to save up enough money to pay her passage, they sent for Helen Silverstein to come to Kansas City. Once Helen arrived in Kansas City, the Lebrechts arranged for her to meet Reuben Cohen, who had never married. Reuben was 13 years older then Helen, having been born in Lithuania in 1873 compared to the birth of Helen in Hungary in 1884. Nevertheless, the two took to each other and shortly after that were married. Jerry Cohen's parents set up housekeep-

9

ing at 3716 Park, a house they were to occupy all of their married life and one that was not far from where the Lebrechts lived at 3820 Troost Avenue. Not long after Annie and Helen Silverstein had arrived and set up housekeeping in Kansas City, their little sister, Serena Silverstein, arrived and was married. For the Silverstein daughters, it was a time for having and rearing children with all its attendant problems of illness, feeding and clothing the children and ensuring that the children got the kind of education the immigrants never had. Reuben and Helen Cohen began almost immediately having children. The first was Harry, and Jerry and his sister remember their mother telling them later in life that he was born nine months and nine days after she and her husband were married, adding with a sense of humor, "Thank goodness for those extra nine days." Bernard was born following Harry and then came Jerome Cohen, on October 9, 1913, to be followed by Bob, Rose and Al, in that order.

Life was not kind to Jerome Cohen immediately after his birth and for a time his parents despaired of his ever growing to be anything but a infant. He developed exczema shortly after he was born and his tiny body was covered with scabs from the rash, scabs that often opened when he was sleeping and left him to be found in his bed bleeding. While his parents were going through that trauma with him, Jerry Cohen also contracted high fever from an epidemic of typhoid fever that was a sweeping the area at the time. Cohen remembers that his mother told him in later life that the physician whom his mother and father brought in to treat him finally told them one night that all hope was gone and Jerry would probably not make it through the following day. He told the distraught parents their was nothing more he could do and that the child should be allowed to die in peace. He said that even if he survived the fever that he would grow up hideously scarred from the exczema. After he left a nurse that had been called in to help Mrs. Cohen with the infant told the distraught mother: "Mrs. Cohen, I don't know anything about Christian Science but I do know that many people have turned to it in such cases and it has helped them. I know it's a last resort but why don't you call one of the practitioners and see if it might not help. It certainly won't hurt." Reared as a Jew, the distraught mother struggled with the problem until finally she decided to make the effort in desperation. Reuben Cohen did not object and so a Christian Science practitioner was summoned and came.

For whatever reason, the Christian Science practitioner seemed to relieve the suffering child. Jerry Cohen said of the incident: "I don't know what he did but my mother told that almost immediately I got better. She said my skin began to clear up and continued to improve. I don't have any kind of scars left." Whatever happened, the fact that Jerry Cohen was able to recover was enough for her. She joined the Christian Science movement, becoming a member of the Second Church of Christ Scientist then located at Thirty-first Street and Troost Avenue. His father remained true to his faith, however, and served as secretary of his synagogue in Kansas City for years, getting the job at first because he was one of the few men in the congregation at the time who could write fluent English for the correspondence and minutes. It was not as far-fetched for Mrs. Cohen to become a member of Christian Science as a Jew at the same time in the 20th century since Mary Baker Eddy had founded the concept in the 1860s on the basis that Jesus was not the Messiah as the Christians believed. As Jerry Cohen later recalled, members of the Christ Scientist faith did not celebrate Christmas or Easter so that Mrs. Cohen's membership did not conflict with the fact that his father remained a Jew. As Mrs. Eddy, the founder had written: "God is indivisible. A portion of God could not enter a man; neither could God's fullness be reflected by a single man, else God would be manifestly finite, lose the deific character and become less than God. Jesus is the man and Christ is the divine idea; hence duality of Jesus the Christ." Mrs. Cohen moved on from the Second Church to the First Church at Ninth Street and Forrest Avenue. It was there that Jerry Cohen remembers attending Sunday School and being taught by two men who had been reared as Jews. He said the two former Jews "were an inspiration to me for the good things they did." One of them was a man who was to have a greater impact on Jerry Cohen in a few short years, a man named Jerome Joffee, who was later to become a Missouri state senator.

While Jerry Cohen did not attend the synagogue as a child, he did not lose touch with the religion of his forefathers. He remembers taking walks with his father during which his father discussed with him and the other sons the tenets of Judaism. He also remembers sitting in his father's jewelry store on Grand Avenue after school, listening to his father talking about his religion to other Jews who came to visit him at the store and helping the immigrants by reading their English mail and interpreting the meaning to them. He helped them with financial matters and other things as they adjusted to their new life in America. He was also an excellent penman. During the walks, he said his father was also telling him about the how hard things were for the Jews in Eastern Europe and Russia when he and his wife were growing up there. He said the experience there made him grateful for the opportunities the United States had given him and other Jews as well as other immigrants. He said it was difficult for him to understand why so many Americans failed to truly appreciate the kinds of freedoms under which they were living. Jerry Cohen remembers how his parents were always reminding him and his brothers about not wasting food. As Jerry Cohen recalls it: "When we would sit down at our table at night to eat supper, my father would tell us to 'Take whatever you want, but don't take more than you can eat. What we throw away from our table in America at meals would feed the people in the town where I come from.' So he always taught us to be thoughtful, and my mother was the same way. 'Enjoy your food but don't take more food than you can eat, don't waste it.' "

2

Public School Values

Jerry Cohen firmly believes that any success he had in later life here in Kansas City is due to the discipline and skills he learned in the city school system at Horace Mann Elementary and Central High Schools in the 1920s and having to work at odd jobs in the neighborhood to earn money to help his family with his education and that of his brothers and sisters. Because of the discipline and the affection and interest the teachers showed in each of their students, Cohen still remembers elementary and high schools as pleasant places to attend and where learning for the future was the order of the day. He remembers a second grade teacher "who if we didn't behave in school... had no qualms about taking a ruler and cracking us right across the knuckles." He went on: "I can still remember our principal, Alva R. Hamilton, at Horace Mann School. She was a very strict disciplinarian. She also insisted that we all have exercise and we would go out in the halls and we would exercise. I can also remember that we had strict discipline in everything. If you didn't behave, you were sent into the cloak room and you stayed there until you could learn how to behave in class." There were pleasant memories of the halls of Horace Mann as well. He remembers being enamored with arithmetic and mathematics that stood him in good stead in his business career. He fondly recalls learning to spell and the challenge of competing with other kids in spelling bees. A fourth grade teacher formed an Audubon Club with some of the students so they could meet after school to learn to appreciate being kind to animals, the development of a lifelong interest that was to serve him in good stead in supporting the Kansas City Zoo at Swope Park. There was support for the school and for the children with parents taking pride in being present on parent nights to help the rooms of their children win prizes for having the greatest percentage of parent participation. When Cohen was in public schools, teachers were not allowed to be married. He felt that without children of their own, the teachers had a tendency to treat the students as their own children. His memories may be idyllic to some extent but he makes no bones about the comparison of the situation then and today: "The schools were not the kinds of places they are today with all the troubles but places where parents, teachers and children cooperated in trying to give a good education. It was a real pleasure to go to school in those days. I would hope the schools of today can develop a similar atmosphere, an atmosphere in which children can work together in a spirit of cooperation for the children."

Those were halcyon days for children growing up in Kansas City and Cohen has fond memories of his childhood. On hot summer nights when there was no air conditioning, he and members of his family would go to Swope Park to a band concert or other outdoor entertainment to remain until the daytime temperatures cooled down in the nighttime darkness. There were trips to an amusement park called Electric Park and he remembers one such trip when the family cheered for his brother, Harry, who entered a cake eating contest there. There was another amusement park called Fairyland Park and one of his favorite attractions there was the Annual Grocers Picnic, a special promotion where local food merchants gave out free food samples to the spectators as a means of advertising. As he grew older, Jerry Cohen would walk with his friends to the Young Men's Hebrew Association to swim and take lessons, paying a nickel each time to get a clean towel. For longer trips, the family would go in the car of his uncle, Abe Lebrecht, to a place called Winnwood Beach where they could swim and have other summer amusements. His uncle also hired him at 50 cents a time to walk from his house on Park to the Lebrecht house on Troost to mow the lawn. A next-door neighbor to the Lebrechts, Dr. Anna Stoeltzing, liked his work so well she hired him to mow hers as well. An exciting moment for Cohen in his boyhood days was when the famed Electric Park caught fire and he remembers going with members of his family to the grounds of a nearby mortuary to watch the massive flames that destroyed the landmark. He also had memories of going with a family friend to one of the early automobile racing tracks located near 85th and Holmes Street where he would aid the man in selling balloons and other novelties to the race spectators.

Cohen takes pride in the fact that he has had a most-legible, Spenserian-style handwriting and credits one of his teachers at Horace Mann, Anita Grimes, for drilling him in penmanship with a variety of writing exercises such as making ovals and what was called "push-pull" hand movements with pen on paper. This same teacher, who taught him in sixth grade, was responsible for the fact that Cohen was able to skip the seventh grade at Horace Mann and enroll that fall directly into the brand-new Central Junior High School. As he recalls: "She made arrangements with the school board to hold special classes for me and five other students she had chosen to enable us to skip the grade and make the transition directly to junior high school. That experience made it possible for me to enter the upper grades when I was only 12 years old and gave me a pride and a sense of discipline over what I had been able to do." He recalls that there was a new athletic field between the Central Junior and Senior High Schools when he started that fall at 32nd Street and Indiana Avenue. It was about one and one-half miles from his home at 3716 Park to the new school and he walked the distance twice a day, regardless of weather. He would meet fellow students near 35th and Park and together they would make their way to Central. As he recalls: "We would walk to and from the school in snow, rain or whatever the weather. It never seemed to be a chore and I am sure we were all healthier for this. I am proud to say that I never missed a day of school and had perfect attendance at Central Junior and Senior High Schools as well as Horace Mann, for that matter."

At Central, life began to change for Jerry Cohen as he moved on with his schooling. Perhaps, according to Cohen, one of the things which had the greatest impact on his life from his years at Central was being involved in the Reserve Officer Training Corps — ROTC — which was a big part of high school life in Kansas City for years. He had always had an interest in sports but since at Central he weighed less than 120 pounds and was only five feet, three inches tall he was too small for the other major high school interest of the time, football. In those years, a requirement for graduation was that boys take physical education classes or ROTC. As he said: "Since I didn't feel that I was a great athlete or had the potential for becoming one, I enrolled in the ROTC program." When he made the decision, he said he had not realized how much it would help his family in one way. That was that he was required to wear uniforms provided by the ROTC three days a week to school. The uniforms meant that his parents, who were trying to rear six children, did not need to buy him as many clothes as otherwise might have been necessary. There were annual competitions between the high school ROTC units of Central, Manual, Westport and Northeast, and young men took pride in their attempts to do well in these competitions. Cohen gives his ROTC instructor at Central, Staff Sgt. Frank L. Bowling, credit for giving him a sense of discipline and the value of obeying the rules as well as other facts of life. He said he remembered being made corporal and attending a session for non-commissioned officers conducted by Sergeant Bowling. As Cohen recalls: "He let us know in no uncertain terms that if we were ever seen smoking in uniform we would be stripped of our ranks. I was not a smoker but if I ever got any desire I always remembered this admonition. I was so proud of those stripes no one could have forced me to smoke. I am happy to say I have never smoked." One other aspect of the ROTC training which Cohen felt had a positive effect on the hundreds of youths throughout their lives was their experience in dealing with firearms, learning from marksmanship training on shooting ranges and the fundamentals of shooting as well as the danger of careless handling of all firearms.

Cohen has always been an optimist but having teachers in other areas recognize his abilities at Central helped him reinforce this feeling. He was especially fond of mathematics and he recalls a geometry teacher, W. H. Templeton, telling him in class when he was always raising his hand in answer to questions posed by the teacher, "Jerome, put your hand down and let some of the older kids have a chance." Classes in manual training were still required of upper school students, and one such course under J. M. Lukens, the teacher, impressed him. He recalls: "The course taught me how to design and read construction plans but, more important to me in later years, I learned to print well and this has been very useful to me." He learned the value of applying himself in all areas from a history teacher, Maude Compton, who told him, "You have a great mind and it is too bad you don't use it to your fullest ability in all areas such as history. You need to spend more time reading and studying in everything you do." It was at Central that he first ran into discrimination personally and he reacted to it in the same way he did whenever he encountered it during the rest of his life. He wanted to join a fraternity at the school for the social life but was denied admission because he had a Jewish background. Not letting the rebuff get him down, he organized other youth at the school into a chess club and the members sharpened their social skills while learning to improve their chess playing skills. For the rest of his life, he was to take a different tack toward the same goal without brooding whenever he was faced with a discrimination barrier raised against him because of his Jewish heritage. At Central, he also learned typing and filing, skills he thought would be useful in business later.

In a large family with limited resources, Cohen learned the value of working to get additional funds while he was a student at Central to meet extra expenses. Thanks again to his mother's brother-in-law, Abe Lebrecht, Cohen got the job which gave him the greatest income during his high school career, working Saturdays at the Hanlon Poultry House on Troost at Thirty-third Street. Cohen would show up for the job there at 7 a.m. Saturdays and work until 9 p.m., carrying out whatever duties. He was paid $5 for the 14-hour day and would use part of the money to buy a chicken wholesale for the Sunday family dinner with the rest going for personal expenses. When the chickens were sold, they were tagged and dropped down a chute to the basement where they were killed, dressed and all the feathers were removed. When that was done, the chickens were brought back upstairs. There the tags would be used to match each chicken with the correct customer. The chickens would then be wrapped. As he learned the business, Jerry would fill in as cashier and wrap purchases for customers. As he recalls: "I also learned to cut up a chicken so that I could do it when a customer would ask for the service. The customer would give me a nickel or dime tip. I really wasn't supposed to do it but Mrs. Hanlon would say: 'It's, okay Jerry. We're not busy now. Go ahead and help the lady.' " For lunch, he would slip over to a nearby White Castle Hamburger stand and get a bag of six hamburgers for 25 cents. On Sunday, Cohen also had a part-time job working for the owner of the Odessa Kosher Meat Market at 39th and Park. The owner would pick up Jerry at 7 a.m. on Sunday to help him deliver meat orders. He would drive the car and Jerry would take the meat to the customer's door. For his work on this job, he got a small amount of change and a cut of meat for his mother to use in family dinners. During summer, he got a job part-time filling in as a soda clerk, making sodas and sundaes, at a drug store located at 37th and Brooklyn. Of that experience, he remembers also serving children there behind the candy counter while they took forever to decide which piece of penny candy they would finally take. He got 15 cents a day for lunches at school from his father and sometimes Jerry and some of his friends would skip lunch in order to go immediately after school to a drug store across the street from Central for something called a "Central Winner," a giant sundae made up of three dips of ice cream, chocolate, strawberry, and vanilla, with all kinds of toppings, nuts and whipped cream. As Jerry recalls: "I guess you would say we were poor by the standards of today but we never realized it because everybody else was as poor as we were. We were having a good time."

Finally, the high school days came to an end for Jerry Cohen when he was graduated at the age of 15 from Central High School as a part of the class of 1929. There were 523 graduates in the 1929 class, a class that was to run into immediate economic difficulties with the great stock market crash that year. There was no gloom and doom among the graduates and their parents, grandparents, brothers, sisters and other relatives. In those days, each of the high schools held their annual commencement exercises separately in the old Convention Hall in downtown Kansas City. The hall was crowded for the music and ceremony, pictures were taken of the graduates and there was much celebrating of a milestone event in the lives of many American families of the day.

With the high school graduating ceremonies behind him, Jerry Cohen was encouraged by his family to try to continue his education. That summer he enrolled in the Kansas City Junior College, specializing in accounting and mathematics courses. Cohen had also taken some accounting and bookkeeping courses at Central. In the fall of 1929, Cohen had persuaded a friend of his father, Harry Kushner, to let him keep his books. Kushner had come to the United States as a part of the Jewish immigration that also brought Reuben Cohen to the Kansas City area. Reuben had befriended Kushner, when he first arrived in Kansas City from Europe, reading and writing his letters for him and helping him get started in business. He was a good tailor and a hard worker and began a shop making uniform caps for the Craddock Uniform Co. of Kansas City as a sub-contractor. Craddock made military and office uniforms for which Kushner made the caps. It was with this business that Jerry Cohen got his start as a bookkeeper. The reputation for speed and accuracy in keeping the books and writing the checks which Cohen developed with the Kushner enterprise got him additional customers. Within a short time, he was keeping the books for another firm in addition to the one owned by Kushner, that of the Katz Hat Co., a hat manufacturing company operated by two brothers, Lou and Ben Katz, at 929 McGee Street. They were brothers-in-law of Cohen's older brother. At the same time, he was continuing to sharpen his skills in business management and office operations in school, attending Kansas City Junior College for 18 months, then the Huff Business School and finally the Central Business College. In addition to keeping Kushner and the Katz brothers as bookkeeping clients during this time, he picked up a third and even more interesting client, Tommy Manzello, the operator of the American Cab Co. With the free and open days in Kansas City during the time under the free-wheeling days of Tom Pendergast, the political boss, a cab operator named Manzello was bound to involve Cohen in experiences that opened his barely 20-year-old eyes even wider. As he got into it, Cohen decided that stage of the bookkeeping business was a little more than even an ambitious young man such as himself could handle. He decided he would try the retail business in selling shoes.

Cohen began his selling career which was eventually to make him a wealthy man by signing on as an extra at Burt's Shoe Store on Petticoat Lane, now 11th Street downtown between Main and Grand. Cohen recalls that the store he joined sold the most economical shoes on the street at $1.95 a pair. Burt's ran in competition with two other shoe stores on the street, Baker's, which sold shoes at $2.95 a pair, and Chandler's, the elite store, with shoes starting at $3.95 a pair. Being an extra in those days, according to Cohen, meant you didn't get a salary but were paid a commission on the shoes sold of six percent. Salesmen took turns serving customers and restocked the shelves while waiting for a turn. As Cohen recalls: "We had a procedure we were directed to go through with each customer. After trying three pairs of shoes on a customer without a purchase, we were to turn them over to a second salesman by saying, 'Ma'am, I'm not as familiar with the stock as Mr. Jones is, so would you come over here, Mr. Jones, and see if you can help this lady?' If Mr. Jones couldn't sell her, he was instructed to go through the same procedure with a third salesman. We always tried to turn over a customer three times before we would let them out of the store without a sale. If we sold them a pair of shoes, we were to try to sell them a buckle to be added, for which we got a 5-cent commission, and a bottle of shoe polish, for which we got another 5-cent commission. For selling two pairs of shoes to a customer, the salesman got a 10-cent bonus and for selling three pairs, a 20-cent bonus."

Cohen said he learned a valuable lesson about sales while serving as a salesman on extra at the store. He recounted the story of a large black woman with rather large feet who came into the store and was turned over to him as the junior man because none of the others wanted to serve her. They knew the store only carried up to size eight shoes, and it looked as though she wore at least a size 10. Cohen said he went up to her and started to remove her shoe to measure her foot as was the custom. As Cohen recalls the incident: "She told me, 'Don't bother to take off this shoe, son. I want nine pairs of shoes and here are the sizes. I'm here for a fashion show and we need these right away.' I even sold her extra buckles. That taught me a valuable lesson about sales that I continue to teach to this day. Never judge a customer by appearance or what you think the customer wants or can afford. You don't know and you'll never know until you try to serve them. I learned that if you treat a person right, they'll treat you right."

In the 1930s, the federal government enacted the National Recovery Act — NRA — which required that the store pay the salesman a minimum wage of 30 cents an hour or $12 a week in addition to commissions. Cohen recalls that the store would want the salesman to work two nights a week to trim windows, put up store displays and restock. The NRA officials, however, said they had to pay overtime for such required work over 40 hours a week. Cohen said: "I remember that rather than pay overtime they decided to give me the title of assistant manager and that meant I got a flat salary of $18 a week and had to come back two nights a week to take care of the duties without being paid overtime."

It was about this time that fate stepped into the picture to bring a new approach to life for Cohen.

3

A Missouri Civics Lesson

t was in these years when he was struggling to learn the ways of the business world immediately following his graduation from Central High School at the age of 15 that two events that were to have a lifelong influence on him occurred for Jerry Cohen. By far the most important was his first date with the woman who was to become his wife of more than 60 years, Jeannette Baier, when he was barely 16 years old. The second was his acquaintance with Frank "Dad" Land, the prominent Kansas City member of the orders of Freemasonry, who was also the founder of the Order of DeMolay, an organization of youths 16 and older, in Kansas City on February 9, 1919. These meetings were the result of the fact that Cohen had had two longtime chums with whom he remained friends following their graduation from Central in 1929, Leo Schultz and Mason Hemphill. The two were older than Cohen and were into dating while Cohen, being younger, was too busy trying to get on with his education after graduation. They had already met Land and joined the Order of DeMolay, now in its 10th year, and told Cohen that dances the DeMolay had with a girls' organization were a good way to meet girls. When he turned 16 on October 9, 1929, the minimum age for joining DeMolay, he became a member, starting a relationship with the orders of Freemasonry that was to last a lifetime.

That fall was also the time when he met the woman he was subsequently to marry, Jeannette Baier. He met her as a result of a blind date arranged by a friend both of hers and Cohen, Violet Brauer. It was a result of one of those things sometimes referred to as "small world" items. An older brother of Jerry Cohen, Bernard Cohen, had married Gladys Brauer, a sister of Violet. Gladys Brauer Cohen was arranging a birthday party for her sister and as a result Violet invited both the future bride and groom as dates. Miss Baier was the daughter of a Kansas City theater owner who owned the Lindbergh Theater at 40th Street and Troost Avenue. As Cohen recalls their courtship after that first blind date: "I would walk from my house over to the theater there at Fortieth and Troost and Jeannette, whose family lived at 6940 Brooklyn Avenue, would come to the theater with her father and meet me there. We would get to see the movies for free. Her mother, Rosa Baier, was the cashier at the theater. Mr. Baier would drive me over to my house and then take Jeannette on home." In addition to the dates at the family movie theater, Jeannette and Jerry would go to the various DeMolay social functions.

The longstanding relationship with the DeMolay founder, "Dad" Land, gave Cohen a support that was to last until Land died in 1959, some 30 years after Cohen first met Land in 1929 when Cohen was initiated into the order Land had founded. In 1954, when Land was installed as the imperial potentate of the Mystic Shrine of North America at the international convention in Atlantic City, Land remembered his relationship with DeMolay in his address marking his installation: "Progress brings new responsibilities. We have to learn to live with each new invention. This fact has been brought home forcibly to me in my work with the Order of DeMolay. That's because DeMolay's major goal has been the training of young men to become the type of leaders we must have to safeguard and protect our future. The world's greatest need always has been outstanding leadership. To insure our future depends on what we do today in the matter of providing better leadership." Cohen was to say later that that kind of emphasis on training young men to be good citizens by Land provided Cohen with a sound background to try to be of service during the remainder of his lifetime. Almost immediately after joining DeMolay, Cohen took a leadership roll in the Mother Chapter by helping to form a marching unit for the youth organization. The unit was called the DeMolay Cadets and its members wore uniforms patterned after the ones worn by the West Point Military Academy cadets, including the high Shako hats. His experience in the ROTC at Central stood Cohen in good stead in turning more than 30 youths from the Mother Chapter into a superb marching unit. They wore attractive matching uniforms and began appearing in parades, first in Kansas City and later at Midwest DeMolay conventions in various states. Cohen remembers going with the marching unit to Springfield, Ill., with Land in a parade honoring Abraham Lincoln in his hometown.

As a result of his work with Land in the Mother Chapter of the Order of DeMolay in the early years, Cohen developed an early interest in being active in other units of Freemasonry, including work in the Blue Lodge, the Scottish Rite and Ararat Shrine, eventually achieving the highest honor Freemasonry has to offer, that of Thirty-third Degree Mason. Land provided Cohen with spiritual leadership and guidance when Cohen tasted the first bitter fruit of anti-Semitism within the Lodge ranks. Always interested in close order marching drills from his experience with the ROTC at Central and as one of the founders of the DeMolay marching unit, it seemed only natural to Cohen that he would lend his marching skills to the Shrine Temple Patrol, an elite marching unit of the Ararat Shrine Temple when he joined. After some hemming and hawing, a friend of Cohen told him he would not submit his name for the drill team because he said "you're too good a friend of mine to have you black-balled (rejected) for membership in the Patrol because you're Jewish." That was in 1944, 15 years after he joined DeMolay, when America was in the midst of World War II. Cohen went to his mentor in Masonic affairs, Dad Land, and told him what had happened. Land said: "Well, let's form a new Ararat Shrine Temple unit. We will call it the Sentinels and it will be made up of Shriners who are former DeMolay members. One of its first projects will be to serve as an advisory council for the Mother Chapter of DeMolay here in Kansas City." Among the initial members was Charles Price, who was later to become U. S. ambassador to Great Britain along with Cohen.

Among the other Kansas Citians who were charter members of the newly formed Sentinels of Ararat Shrine Temple were Jack Abshier, Seymour Asher, Harold J. Arlund, Harold C. Bergstresser, William E. Briece, Charles W. Chaney, Harry Cohen, Harold Crow, George J. Davidson, George A. Dearing, Sam Eddy, Vernie G. Fisher, Jr., Floyd Frank, Gerald Gore, Adolph Koch, Loren Lundy, Gordon F. McCulloch, Richard Manning, Al Shipley, E. D. Sold, Morris M. Stern, John H.

Bishop, George W. McChristy, Robert Goulden, Herman Major, Jr, and Claude Reichel. Cohen remembers that the Sentinels became a sensation as they marched in Shrine parades as a unit in tuxedos, their Shrine fezzes, red spats and carrying swagger sticks. They met in the Shrine offices of the old Continental Hotel downtown, as Cohen recalls, and one of their functions early was to sponsor the meetings of the Mother Chapter of DeMolay, parties that would feature leading American entertainers who were appearing at a downtown night spot called Eddy's and providing refreshments for the young men. After about three years of operations of the Sentinels, Land came to them again and suggested they might want to form another marching unit for Ararat Shrine Temple, as well. Land said it was to be called the Oriental Band of Ararat Shrine Temple and was to be a part of the Association of the Shrine Oriental Bands of the Imperial Council. The members came from the Sentinels and were limited to 25 members and a drum major originally. Both units were to be carried on from the beginning without costing Ararat Shrine any money. Cohen remembers soliciting $9 from each member of the new band to be used to buy cloth wholesale for the uniforms. Wives of the original members made the uniforms which consisted of bright green knickers resembling bloomers with a gold stripe, and red blouses and capes and green turbans with bright paste jewels. Members could not be trained musicians and played music on their instruments on the basis of charts of numbers instead of notes.

It was a proud moment in July 1954 for the men of Ararat Shrine Temple Oriental Band and the Sentinels, two marching units Land himself had formed 10 years earlier in 1944 when Cohen called the first whiff of anti-Semitism in the Shrine to his attention, when they received places of honor in the parade of Ararat Shrine marching units in the 42,000 seat Atlantic City Convention Center when Land was installed as the imperial potentate of the Shrine of North America. The marching units of Kansas City were a part of an hour-long telecast of the ceremonies done under direction of Hugh Beach, assistant in charge of special events for the then-burgeoning CBS-TV. Leon Loneidoff, senior vice-president and producer of the famed Radio City Music Hall, provided the music and staging and Thomas Mitchell, the actor, portrayed Land in his younger years on the telecast. Noble Anderson, deputy secretary of Defense and Navy secretary under President Dwight D. Eisenhower, presented the official fez of office for Land. Sen. Stuart Symington, of Missouri, gave him the official jewel of office and read a message from Harry Truman when the former president became ill just before the ceremonies. Kansas Gov. Edward F. Arn, a DeMolay, presented Land his gavel of office and said that no matter what other titles and honors Land might achieve he would always be known as "Dad" Land to his boys in the order Land had founded. Through it all, Jerry Cohen was a smiling, dedicated spectator and participant for Land and for his Masonic teaching.

Cohen said later in life that the influence of Land and the DeMolay order had been partly responsible for his personal attitude toward life of trying to give back to Kansas City as much as he had gained in profits from business operations which he operated to such financial success throughout his life. This kind of a philosophy of Land was shown in all his speeches as quoted in a biography of Land called "Hi, Dad" written by the Rev. Herbert Duncan, a Congregational minister and long-time friend of Land. In the remarks, Land said: "I will enumerate some of the things I believe we must build our future on. I cannot pick them up with my hand as I would a piece of paper, book, or glass of water. They are imponderable things — like the sunlight — they slip through your fingers on the air that brushes so close to you but which you never see. I like to call them the invisible things of life; the things our mothers taught us from the time we first knelt at her knee — honesty, integrity, truth, beauty, freedom, goodness, clean thinking, love of God, love of home and love of country. You cannot pick up any of these virtues and hide them from the eyes of men and women. They are free to everyone who accepts them. They are the anchors to which we must tie if we are to live beauteous and righteous lives... But the greatest of all of these qualities is character. Ability and personality may open doors but it's character that keeps them open. It is built on the strength of a slow, steady, continuous growth. No matter what you do, you must have character to endure, even as you must have ability and personality to achieve. As you contribute character, it flows back to you in strength and inspiration. Since our character exists only in the estimation of others, it must be constantly guarded and fostered and not allowed to waste itself in thoughtlessness or selfishness." They were words which would stand Jerry Cohen in good stead throughout his life.

DeMolay was one of a series of factors in the years since Cohen

first met the attractive Jeannette Baier in 1929 that were inexorably drawing them closer together. There were many DeMolay parties and social
events that drew them together as they dated each other through the
years following their first meeting. Another was the Jewish background
of her and her family, a Jewish tradition to which Cohen had remained
loyal through his father even in spite of his mother's participating in the
Church of Christ Scientist following Cohen's recovery from severe ill-
nesses as an infant. As they dated, Cohen struggled with attending the
old Kansas City Junior College and the Huff and Central business colleges as well as taking care of the books for his three clients, helping his
father at his jewelry store from time to time and selling shoes on Petticoat Lane in downtown Kansas City. The great stock market crash had
happened in 1929 when Cohen was graduated from high school but, as
in most economic trends, it took a while for the backlash of that to reach
Kansas City. By 1933 and the early part of 1934, the City had joined the
nation in the depths of what was subsequently to be known as The Great
Depression. It was then that a ray of light in the economic gloom struck
Cohen, thanks to his mother having taken him to Sunday School first at
the Second Church of Christ Scientist and then at the First Church downtown where he had Jerome Joffee as a Sunday School teacher. Joffee had
befriended the young Cohen then and when Joffee was elected to the
Missouri Senate in 1934 he asked Cohen, whom he knew had skills in
typing, shorthand, bookkeeping and filing, to accompany him to the state
capital in Jefferson City as his secretary. Cohen, seeing a steady salary
and experience that would serve him for the rest of his life, immediately
accepted.

   With things starting to look up for him with the new job, Cohen
immediately asked his sweetheart, Jeannette Baier, to marry him and she
readily accepted. They set their wedding date for November 25, 1934.
With the Jewish background of both sets of parents, it was natural that
they would decide to hold a Jewish wedding ceremony. The wedding
ceremony and reception were held at the Roof Garden of the Ambassador Hotel, 3650 Broadway. Cantor Sidney Rothblatt from Beth Shalom
Synagogue conducted the ceremony. It was a typical Jewish service, replete with the traditional silk canopy and the ritual smashing of the wine
glasses. With that return to his traditional Jewish heritage, Jerome Cohen never strayed from the Biblical faith of his fathers again. When they

moved to Jefferson City for his new job with Senator Joffee, they joined a small synagogue in the Missouri state capital. They attended services regularly with Mrs. Cohen playing piano at regular intervals as accompanist for the services. Since the congregation had no rabbi at the time, various members took turns conducting the services, including Jerry. He remembers that when he and his new bride went to Jefferson City, they rented second floor rooms in a personal residence and had to go downstairs to use the bathroom. They lived in these quarters for a short time until they were able to locate a regular small, second floor apartment in an apartment building.

In a short time as secretary to Senator Joffee, Cohen got a quick lesson in how Missouri state government really worked. Cohen said he went remembering from a Central High civic class how state laws were made, but said when he got to the state capital he learned quickly "that what I had leaned in the civics class was not the way laws were really made." Cohen said working with Senator Joffee showed him in no time at all that three powerful senators from Kansas City and St. Louis made the decisions on what the Missouri General Assembly would pass during a session. The three senators, he said, would caucus in a suite of rooms at the Central Hotel in downtown Jefferson City nightly during the session to go over bills which had been introduced. They would then decide among themselves which ones would move ahead and which ones would not and that's the way they went. Cohen said he also quickly learned about lobbyists from serving with Senator Joffee. He said he recalled one particular occasion when lobbyists for the insurance industry were trying to get the Missouri General Assembly to pass some special interest legislation to help the industry. As Cohen recalls one incident related to this effort: "Three lobbyists brought in this gorgeous set of luggage and said 'This is for Senator Joffee.' I said 'Fine, I'll tell him about it. Give me your names. Thank you.' When Senator Joffee came back from the session, he said 'Give those back!' I said: 'Heck, if you don't want them, I'll take them.' He said firmly, 'We don't take bribes. You call that man and tell him to come get them.' That gave me a whole new perspective on things. Here I am working for an honest guy who practices what he always taught me in Sunday School."

These were the days when the old Democratic political machine was still riding high in Kansas City and this was to give Cohen another lesson in the practical side of how machine politics worked. He remembers being in Kansas City for one of the elections while he was working as secretary to Senator Joffee and being taken to a local polling place by a Missouri member of the House. The polling place was located in the courtroom of a Jackson County judge and faction leader, Casimir (Cash) Welch. In the regular polling place, voters were coming in and voting in regular fashion. The representative took Cohen to a back room of the polling place and showed him where the election judges had stored a duplicate set of ballot boxes there already filled with ballots and locked and sealed. As Cohen recalled: "They had the election rigged the way they wanted it. It was all over. They were going through the motions. I don't know whether it was that way all over the city but it made me realize what was happening." As a result, when Cohen got a chance to join the reform movement later under the influence of The Kansas City Star and the rabbi of his synagogue in Kansas City, Rabbi Samuel Mayerberg, he took it.

In Jefferson City, the Missouri legislators were struggling with the deepening economic depression and how to cope with it. As one measure of trying to help the economy and provide some kind of economic assistance to needy citizens in those days before the federal government had entered into massive welfare programs, Cohen's employer, Senator Joffee, and a senator from Springfield, Sen. Allen McReynolds, wrote a bill to provide a pension of $10 a month to all persons in Missouri over 65 years of age. The two were able to get the bill through the legislature and it was signed into law by Gov. Lloyd Stark, giving Missouri one of the first old-age assistance programs in the nation. The legislature, however, could appropriate only enough to pay the $10 monthly pension to 10,000 of the aged rather than the 100,000 who were estimated to be eligible. Largely because of his respect for Senator Joffee, Governor Stark called Cohen to his office and asked his help to set up the state old-age assistance program. After talking to Senator Joffee, Cohen took the job and was sent to Des Moines, Iowa, by Governor Stark to study the Iowa program already in existence. Cohen came back to Jefferson City with his knowledge and set up the state program for Missouri. He was named chief clerk of the assistance program under Allen Thompson as director. One of his first problems, he discovered, was that there were no state facilities for writing and mailing 10,000 checks a month. He had to improvise and he called in Harry Straight, an area representative of the International Business Machines Co., to provide assistance in trying to meet the need. The result was an automated punch card system that printed and addressed 10,000 checks a month, the first such IBM computer system in Missouri. As Cohen explained how the whole system worked: "We would punch one card with the name of the person, a second with his address and a third one with the amount and the date; and then we would use a sorting machine to sort the cards alphabetically and then finally we would use a printing tabulator operated by the punch cards. We could write all the checks in one day." Suddenly the state treasurer was faced with the redeeming all these thousands of additional checks and had to install a similar IBM system, introducing Cohen for the first time to what office automation was beginning to be.

Cohen learned one other valuable experience out of the whole thing. Kansas City political leaders came to him to get recipients moved up on the old-age assistance lists and Cohen said he would do it because he thought he was helping his fellow Kansas Citians. Then he learned to his chagrin that the same faction leaders were charging the recipients $10 apiece to get their names moved up on the list. He was to say later that his experience with the elderly poor and later with the other needy of the 1930s was to make him dedicate himself to helping others as much as he could for the rest of his life. His experience with various aspects of machine politics such as manipulating the welfare recipient lists, the cronyism and the stuffed ballot boxes "made me vow that I was going to work for good government wherever I could for the rest of my life."

HIS WIFE OF OVER 60 YEARS — *Jerry Cohen, left, was married to Jeannette Baier, whose parents owned a Kansas City theater, the Linwood, on November 25, 1934. They moved to Jefferson City so Jerry could serve as secretary to a Missouri state senator, Jerome Joffee.*

JERRY COHEN AS A DEMOLAY CADET — *With his marching experience gained in the Reserve Officer Training Corps at Central High School in Kansas City, Jerry Cohen started the DeMolay Cadets, a marching unit, in whose uniform he is shown here, for the Mother Chapter of DeMolay, a young men's Masonic organization founded in Kansas City by Frank S. (Dad) Land. Land became a longtime mentor of Cohen.*

4

Jerry Begins Business Career

By 1937, the Congress at the urging of Franklin D. Roosevelt had passed the Federal Emergency Relief Act, rolling old age assistance, aid to dependent children and other aspects of the welfare program to help the needy under one federal agency administered by the states. Cohen had done such and admirable job in setting up the Missouri Old Age Assistant Department since it was a created in 1935 and was acquainted with Kansas City political leaders through his work with that agency that Governor Stark and Senator Joffee asked Cohen to move back to Kansas City to establish the Jackson County Welfare Department as its chief clerk under the new federal programs. By that time after three years in the Missouri capitol in Jefferson City, Cohen and is wife, Jeannette, were eager to move back to Kansas City where both their families still lived. Cohen remembers opening the welfare offices in an old public school building at Nineteenth and Wyandotte Streets. A staff was hired to administer various aspects of the new federal programs, a part of which were designed to provide temporary employment for the growing number of unemployed rising out of the worsening economic conditions. Cohen himself administered the employment part of the program because it was the source of the most difficulties. As Cohen remembers the situation then: "As word spread about what we were trying to do about jobs, we had men spending all night in the school yard to be first in line for what ever jobs were available. We could only process about 100 applications a day so we had to have security guards on hand to keep order. I still remember the bonfires in the school yard when I'd come to open up in the morning. We'd get the staff ready and then I'd go down to open the door to begin letting them into the office. I'd stay there until we had counted off the first 100. Then we'd tell the rest of them to come back tomorrow and we'd shut the door. We developed all kinds of makeshift jobs for them to do, counting trees on city streets and other miscellaneous jobs."

As the days rolled by, Cohen became more frustrated with the way things were going. While the programs were having some effect, there were never enough federal and state funds to meet the need. Hundreds were given parttime jobs at $15 a week but more jobs were needed. As 1937 ground into 1938, Cohen began to decide that if he was ever going to get into business for himself, the time was now. It had always been his goal to start his own business and after discussing the situation with his wife he decided to quit the frustrating job and strike out on his own. From his experience with the government agencies, it seemed to him that a growing field for the future would be to get into the copying business for all the new paper the growing number of federal and other government agencies were going to require. A cousin of his wife, Nathan Wedlin, talked him into going into business with him. Wedlin had been working for Stanley Sargent a Kansas City company that had been selling stencils from a manufacturer in Denver and he thought the stencil business had a growing future that would make another such company profitable. He convinced Cohen of the possibilities and each of them borrowed $300 to go into business for themselves. They opened a tiny office in room 209 of the City Bank Building located at Eighteenth Street and Grand Avenue directly across the street from The Kansas City Star. In starting the new company, Cohen showed a willingness to take a chance on the new development in the duplicating field, a trait that was to stand him in good stead for the rest of his successful business career. At that point in 1938, the stencil duplicating machines were still using an old cellulose stencil that had company secretaries tearing out their hair. They were required to type the stencils on a waxed surface and the wax on the stencils caused the keys on their typewriters to become clogged so that they would not print properly unless they cleaned their keys after typing six or seven lines.

Cohen and his partner in the new venture were offered a newly-patented film stencil that did not have the wax buildup problems and the two new entrepreneurs quickly snapped it up for their main product line. The new film stencils were manufactured by a firm called the Milo Harding Co. and was called Tempo, thus giving Cohen a name to be associated with him for the remainder of his business career, the Tempo Sales Co. Cohen and Wedlin set up a 6-state sales territory of Kansas, Missouri, Iowa, Arkansas, Oklahoma and Texas and divided it up between them as the only fulltime employees of the new firm to make the sales. They paid themselves a salary of $15 dollars a week each plus travel and expense allowances. Mrs. Cohen was employed on a fulltime basis to handle office operations and fill the orders as well as many other duties she was assigned. She generally worked five days a week and on the weekends, for which she was paid $3 a week. Cohen thought of making sales in country towns and county seats so he and his partner called on the schools primarily in towns of 200 or more and the courthouses in the county seats. Because they needed operating capital for the business, Cohen hit on the idea of selling customers couponbooks for stencil orders. Quires of stencils sold for $3.50 each. Cohen gave them the opportunity to buy books of 12 coupons at $3.15 a quire. The customer got the advantage of mailing in a coupon instead of going through a purchasing order route and check paying for each. The company owners got the cash for large orders up front while the coupon system kept them from having to maintain a large inventory of product on hand. By the end of the first year, Tempo had generated $25,000 in sales, not bad for a couple of barefoot entrepreneurs just starting out in their own business. In the second year of the operation, Cohen was already starting to look around for new products to add to the line.

World War II had already begun in Europe when the Germans invaded Poland on September 1, 1939, violating the treaty Neville Chamberlain had negotiated on behalf of England and France, promptly causing the British and French to declare was on the Germans. Since 1936, a new wave of Jewish immigration from Europe had swept across the United States, including the Kansas City area, as the Nazis stepped up its persecution of Jews. What Cohen had no way of knowing at the time was that the welfare programs and the burgeoning World War II would create a new tide of record keeping that would require new methods of duplication of countless documents with an accompanying growth of new techniques that would cause his business decision to be a far-reaching one. By 1940, Cohen had added two new products to the line of the business, the first silk-based typewriter ribbons which greatly improved the quality of printing and length of life of such products and plastic laminated carbon paper that was to end some of the ink mess that soiled the hands of earlier secretaries. Both of the products were the result of research by a firm called Buckeye Ribbon and Carbon Co. As war production grew and more money came into circulation in the Kansas City area, the business Cohen had started with his partner began to grow, causing the two partners to add a fulltime salesman to service the metropolitan area exclusively. By early 1941, the aircraft industry and other war-related businesses began to step up the economy in Kansas City as the U.S. took on the role President Franklin D. Roosevelt had outlined as the "arsenal of democracy". Wedlin wanted to pursue other business interests and Cohen brought him out for $4,000. Jerry's brother, Bernard, who had been an accountant in Kansas City, then joined the company as a partner and office manger. As business boomed, there was a need for more space and the company was moved from its original location with 225 square feet of floor space to a larger location of 500 square feet on the fifth floor of the City Bank Building at Eighteenth and Grand.

His marriage, his experience in taking part in synagogue services in Jefferson City when he was working as secretary to Senator Joffee and his return to Kansas City with greater frequency of conversations with his Jewish father caused Cohen to re-establish his ties with the Jewish community. He and his wife, Jeannette, were soon active in the congregation of Temple B'Nai Jeuhdah where Rabbi Samuel Mayerberg, a leading figure in efforts to reform Kansas City, was serving. Cohen already had accepted the idea, from his experience in state government and with local Kansas City political figures, that the system was corrupt and that there was a need for reform and this was reenforced by the activities of Rabbi Mayerberg. The young business executive quickly became associated with the reform movement for a city charter and a change in city government from the old machine political spoils system. By the 1940 city election Cohen was active in the efforts by the reform movement, eventually to be known as the Citizens Association, in attempting to elect

John B. Gage, a prominent lawyer, as mayor over the machine-backed democratic candidate. Cohen was in good company in the reform movement in addition to Rabbi Mayerberg with the Kansas City Star and other leading business and professional men aligned with the movement as well. When the votes were counted in that 1940 election, Gage had been elected mayor by the reform movement by a majority of 20,159 votes, garnering 94,192 votes to 74,033 for the Pendergast machine candidate. The strength of the reform movement of which Cohen was a part was shown in the fact that its members were able to elect candidates to seven of the other eight city council positions leaving only the old First District where Alderman James Pendergast had started the whole thing years ago in the hands of the remnants of the old Democratic machine. For Rabbi Mayerberg, the victory was a personal triumph, since he had been fighting the Pendergast machine and its underworld allies for eight years since 1932, only four years after he had arrived from Detroit to became rabbi of Temple B'Nai Jehudah in 1928.

In his immensely popular history of the Pendergast machine, "Tom's Town", William H. Reddig, a Kansas City writer, credits Rabbi Mayerberg with being the catalyst for lighting the fires of reform and says the incident might have gone unnoticed except for an enterprising reporter for The Kansas City Star, Alvin S. McCoy. Reddig writes that Mayerberg was to speak before a group called the Government Study Club, a women's organization, at a luncheon at a downtown hotel. Reddig wrote that McCoy, a cub reporter at the time, saw the rabbi going to the meeting. He goes on to write: "Ordinarily, a session of the club was not something a newspaperman made a point of attending but the cub took a chance because he had heard the rabbi speak on cultural matters and was impressed by his erudition and eloquence. What he heard this time was a flaming assault on the machine. Reporter...McCoy, later a political writer and later a war correspondent for The Star, got the details right and his story made a smash in the afternoon edition. 'You've turned your city over to a gang and given it into the hands of crooks and racketeers because you are asleep.' Mr. Mayerberg informed the Government Study Ladies. 'The time had come for action. The time for study has passed.' One of the rabbi's main points was that the city manager had violated Section 124 of the city charter, which made it illegal to solicit a member of a political party for campaign funds or to discharge city employees because of their affiliations. Repeated violations of that section had been made in the 'lug' openly placed on city employees for campaign funds and in the wholesale firing of Republicans from the police department. Penalty for the violation was a fine of fifty dollars to a five hundred dollars and sentence of up to six months in jail." Cohen recalls that Rabbi Mayerberg was subjected to all kinds of threats by the machine. He was given a body guard and bullet proof glass placed in his car which was fired on once. He got pre-dawn telephone calls making all kinds of whispered accusations.

Attacks on such an entrenched political organization as Rabbi Mayerberg was carrying on was bound to cause difficulties for him within his own congregation and Temple B'Nai Jehudah was no exception. Cohen, as a majority of the synagogue members supported Mayerberg, however, as Mayerberg said: "While I hold firm conviction that ministers should never engage in partisan political activities, I also cherish the unwavering belief that, where iniquity runs rampant, when depraved and selfish men prey upon a community, it is not only the right but also the compelling duty of the minister to lead in the movement to eradicate such evil powers from his community. If one holds the fearless, God-intoxicated prophets of Israel as his human ideals, as I do, one is compelled by his conscience to enter the fray with all the courage and strength he can summon." How Cohen and other members of the congregation felt was best stated by a Jewish author, Albert Vorspan, in a book, "Giants of Justice", published by the Union of American Hebrew Congregation, in which Vorspan devoted an entire chapter to Rabbi Mayerberg, putting him in the same status with other Jewish giants included as Louis Brandeis, Stephen Wise, Albert Einstein, David Dubinsky and Herbert Lehman. In the Book, Vorspan wrote thus of the actions of Rabbi Mayerberg: "So stormy a career as Rabbi Mayerberg's is bound to provoke controversy. Not a few, even of Mayerberg's friends and admirers, have raised questions about some of his actions. For example, it had been suggested that, when a rabbi plunges into a bitter and protracted political controversy in the community, the inevitable divisions and conflicts set in motion within the congregation must, at the same point, endanger the congregation itself... Rabbi Mayerberg had the staunch support and cooperation of his temple's Social Action Committee...Somebody once said that God will not look us over for medals and ribbons but for our well-earned scars. Both Mayerberg and B'Nai Jehudah can wear their scars with prideful honor."

Needless to say, Rabbi Mayerberg survived the overthrow of the old machine politicians and the beginnings of the Citizens Association, continuing to serve at Temple B'Nai Jehudah until he retired as rabbi in 1960. Cohen continued to lend his efforts to honest government throughout his life. Although he may not have said it as exquisitely, Cohen expressed sentiments about how he tried to run his life similar to those of Vorspan in his book, "Giants of Justice", in the introduction: "Whatever definition of the Jew in conjured up, one soon comes face to face with a characteristic which amounts almost to one of the stigmata of the Jew: A passion for justice. Judaism gave the world not only monotheism but ethical monotheism. All the major religions of the world, and democracy itself, have felt the impact of the sublime prophetic tradition. 'Justice, justice shalt thou pursue'—this ancient injunction has weighed upon the shoulders of the Jew as a special yoke from God, the universal mission of the Jew through all time. Jacques Maritain, noted Roman Catholic philosopher, described Judaism as 'like as activating ferment injected into the mass, it teaches the world to be discontented and restless as long as the world has no God— it stimulates the movement of history'...The messianic dream has become, for the Jew, a kind of incurable social disease. This dream permeates his literature, religious and secular. It motivates Jewish organizations in their work for brotherhood and democracy and social justice. It afflicts Jews with a painful sensitivity to social evil and compulsive need to correct every injustice".

When Cohen returned to synagogue life with his wife, Jeannette, in Kansas City in 1938, they were part of a movement in which Jews across the nation who had come as a part of the great immigration from Eastern Europe to escape persecution such as Reuben Cohen, the jeweler, and his wife, Helen, Cohen's parents, were doing the same thing. As one report said: "Profound socio-economic changes in the makeup of American Jewry in general made themselves felt at a greatly-accelerated pace in the prosperous years of the forties and early fifties. That period brought to fruition the reservoir of economic advantage which Jews had built in earlier years through superior education and experiences in business. The American Jewish community became as prosperous as some of the longest-established elements of the population in the United States. This prosperity brought a social homogeneity as pronounced, perhaps, as it had been before 'the great migration' from Eastern Europe. It also influenced hundreds of thousands to enter the synagogue fold, many of them for the first time." At the time of the 1940 city elections, the populations of the metropolitan Kansas City area for Jews was approximately 21,400 of whom 10,000 lived in Kansas City, Missouri, representing five percent of that city's population. Only about one-third of that total of Jews were foreign-born when 1940 dawned compared to a large majority of the Jews living there in 1941. Cohen had grown up in the area in which six out of every ten Jewish families with children lived, a middle-income area in which Cleveland and Troost avenues represented the east and west boundaries respectively and from Linwood Boulevard on the north to Forty-seventh Street on the south.

Since 1933 and the rise of Adolph Hitler and the National Socialist party with its anti-semitic doctrines in Germany, Kansas City Jews began to become concerned about the plight of Jews in Germany and Austria as well. By mid-1933, the German Nazis under Hitler had vowed "to eliminate the Jews from the German life." Cohen was too busy trying to make a living at that point in 1933 but he was concerned just as other young Jews in Kansas City as Hitler called for a National Boycott Day for the Germans to refuse to do business with firms operated by Jews and legislation was introduced in Germany to ban Jews from the civil service and to deprive them of their right to higher education. Reuben Cohen, still remembering the pogrom days in Eastern Europe, was more concerned in his conversations with his friends. Rabbi Mayerberg, in a sermon before his congregation on the eve of the Hitler-sponsored National Boycott Day, called the Nazi methods "a program of extermination" of Jews and ranked the effort with " the most awful pogroms in history." In his sermon, the rabbi declared: "The Spanish Inquisition with its horrors were not equal to the situation in Germany today. The inquisition came in an age of violence when men were trained to expect bloodshed. Jews did not attempt to establish themselves. They had nothing to lose but their lives." He added he felt confident "the Jews of America will not look quietly on the extermination of some 600,000 of their co-religionists in Germany."

Efforts to help German Jews to emigrate from Nazi persecution were supported in the early stages but it was not until Cohen returned to

Kansas City from Jefferson City that a program of size to help the German Jews came to the United States and got off the ground in 1938. Irvin Fane, a longtime friend of Cohen, had helped form the first Temple Brotherhood at B'Nai Jehudah in the winter of 1935-37. Cohen was to become active in the Brotherhood and eventually became its president. As an outgrowth of the formation of the Brotherhood, every member of its board in 1938 pledged himself to get Jews to sign affidavits of sponsorship for German or Austrian Jews who had no relatives in the U.S., agreeing to serve as their American relatives in bringing them here. A Kansas City Placement Council was formed to direct the operation with two women of Temple B'Nai Jehudah, Ruth Kander and Mrs. Maurice Stiefel, serving as its staff. Miss Kander was the granddaughter of the Rabbi Elias Epstein, who had sought local job opportunities for the first contingents of Jewish refugees from the Russian pogroms more than 50 years earlier. Temple B'Nai Jehudah members led the community in bringing the greatest number of Jews from Nazi Germany. the new immigrants experienced many of the difficulties that Rueben and Helen Cohen had found earlier. The German Jews found synagogue worship here strange, meager in using Hebrew, lacking in ceremonial and having many of the choral responses set to Protestant hymns rather that traditional melodies.

HE STARTED DUPLICATING COMPANY IN 1938 — *Jerry Cohen, seated left, is shown in an early-day trade show booth promoting the company, Tempo Sales Company, which he founded in 1938 to sell duplicating supplies. The company went on to become a multi-million-dollar firm.*

COHEN BECOMES A TELEVISION STAR — *Jerry Cohen, center under the microphone, is shown on the set of KCMO-TV, now known as KCTV-5, where he did duplicating equipment commercials live on the nightly newscasts for his new dry process duplicating machines, the 3M Thermofax Copier.*

5

Business Is Booming

During the years of 1940 through 1945 of World War II, Jerry Cohen was subjected to the ups and downs of life that had forged the lives of his religious forebears, the prophets of Israel, in the flames of experience. He and his wife, Jeannette, were subjected to tragedies much in the manner of the Jewish prophet, Abraham, and his wife, Sarah, in the Bible, but they did not lose their faith in God any more than did their spiritual ancestors. In early 1940, there was joy in the Cohen household when their first child was born, a little boy who was given the name of Ronald Cohen. Ronald was a good-natured little boy who was the light of his grandparents on both sides as well as Cohen and his wife but he was not a strong little lad. When he was four years old in 1944, the child fell ill with a massive fever and infection. As Cohen was later to recall: "Jeannette and I came to view what happened as having lost our son to World War II. The family doctor we had who had brought him into the world and treated the family was called into military service and we had to get a new physician. He didn't know us as well and there were so few physicians left at home to take care of the patients because of the demand by the military for doctors. When Ronnie seemed to take a turn for the worse, one night after midnight, we tried to get in touch with the doctor but he was out on call. He finally called back and said that he would get there as quickly as he could but by the time he got there, our boy had died." The Cohens were grief-stricken but they never lost their faith in God. The doctor told them it would be best for them if they were to have another child as quickly as possible. Their oldest daughter, Rosalyn Cohen, had been born two years earlier in the spring of 1942 and she was a source of comfort to her parents. It was not until January of 1948, however, before their youngest daughter, Elaine Cohen, was born. In the meantime, tragedy again struck the Cohen family in the spring of 1944 when Jerry's mother, Helen Silverstein Cohen, died at the age of 60 from cancer. The bright young woman who had come to Kansas City at the turn of the century from her home near Budapest in Hungary at the behest of her older sister, Annie Lebrecht, had been a tower of strength to Cohen, his brothers and his sister as well as her husband, Reuben Cohen. Cohen remembered that his mother "was always urging each of us to be the best that we could. I remember her telling me many times: 'Jerome, you can be anything you want to be if you only try.' " She worked diligently keeping her children clean and fed and well cared for while his father spent long hours earning a living with his jewelry store and helping other Jewish immigrants like himself. Like so many other members of her generation of older European immigrants, Helen Cohen had a fear of going to a hospital. Cohen remembers her telling him even after she knew her illness had been diagnosed as cancer: "Don't let them take me to the hospital because I know I'll never come home alive. I want to die at home when it is time." In February 1944, death came to Helen Cohen. To the last, she retained her deep faith in God, a faith she passed on to Jerry and her other children. For their father, Reuben Cohen, the death of his beloved wife brought grief and a sense of loss. He had married Helen Silverstein 40 years earlier in 1904 when he was 31 and she was only 20. Now when she died at age 60, he was much older at 71. Fortunately, the business Jerry had started in 1938 had continued to grow and prosper and had outgrown the larger space to which it had moved in the bank building at Eighteenth Street and Grand Avenue. The result was that Jerry Cohen had purchased the building at 1423 Grand Avenue in which Reuben Cohen operated his jewelry store and had moved his business into the rest of the building shortly before his mother died. This gave Cohen and his brothers an opportunity to keep an eye on their aging, grieving father as he continued to operate his jewelry shop.

Whatever else may be said, Jerry Cohen showed a sixth sense in business acumen when he decided in 1940 to begin a business associated with the production of business documents. The beginning of the growth of the federal government which started in the late 1930s under the guise of helping the poor created by the Great Depression of 1929 gave no indication of the eventual insatiable appetite for documents it would spawn in the years ahead. It was the beginning of an unbelievable avalanche of paper copying that was given impetus further by World War II as the federal government struggled to keep track of millions of Americans under arms across the world and their dependents as well as the construction of billions of dollars worth of military installations and war production facilities were spawning. Cohen had himself strategically placed with the latest in duplicating stencils and inks with exclusive rights in Iowa, Nebraska, Missouri, Kansas, Oklahoma and Texas. Within two years, Cohen had added the first silk typewriter ribbons and plastic laminated carbon papers for further ease in duplicating giving him a complete line of the latest in duplicating supplies except a new offset process that was developing. To get into this field, Cohen negotiated an agreement with a firm known as Rapid Roller Co., a leader in developing synthetic rubber printing rolls and blankets when the old natural rubber was coming into war-produced shortage. Since Cohen had bought out his original partner in 1941 for $4,000, brought in his brother, Bob Cohen, who had been working as department manager in a women's clothing department, for the ever-increasing copy products that now included the famous Copywrite spirit and gelatin duplicating supplies. A third brother, Harry Cohen, joined the firm in 1941 as a salesman.

As the need for men grew after the United States entered World War II following the Japanese bombing of Pearl Harbor, the brothers in the firm were called into the military and Jerry kept the firm going during those years in the new location at 1423 Grand. With his ROTC training at Central High, Jerry began working with the home guard companies that were being organized by the army as an adjunct to the U.S. military service in World War II. After months of difficult times for the nation, World War II ended in 1945, first in Europe in May against the Germans and later in August against the Japanese in the Pacific. The Cohen brothers were reunited in the business as fast as they came out of military service in 1946. The youngest of the Cohen brothers, Al, came into the firm, now known as the Tempo Company. It was now that the vision of Jerry in getting into the duplicating business in 1940 really began to pay off. From his move into the field of artificial rubber printing rolls and offset press blankets from Rapid Roller Company in Chicago in 1942 as a foot in the door for his growing company into the offset field, Jerry Cohen had made a decision that would lead to two additional developments that were to have long lasting and successful effects on the long-range future of the company. These developments got him fully into the use of presensitized printing plates that were to be the future of the duplicating business to which Cohen had hitched his business star. Because Cohen had been successful in being willing to pioneer with the artificial rubber printing rolls and press blankets, he was approached by another innovative company, Lithomat Corporation of Boston. Lithomat had successfully developed a paper presensitized offset plate and was looking for distributors in the duplicating field across the nation. Cohen and his firm took the offer and began greatly expanding sales of Lithomat plates until the firm was sold in 1947 to the A.B. Dick Co., one of the largest U.S. manufacturers of office duplicating equipment with whom unfortunately the Cohen company did not have an agreement.

Not one to let momentary adversity get him down, Cohen was quickly looking around for another pioneering firm. His experience with Rapid Roller of Chicago and Lithomat of Boston had convinced Cohen of a business axiom he was to quote to associates for the rest of his career. His axiom: "If it don't eat or it don't drink, we don't want it." A translation of that was explained as: "If it doesn't consume paper or ink in its processes, we don't want it." He had already learned the valuable lesson that the business was much more lucrative if you could sell duplicating machines that continually use paper, ink and duplicating supplies and that you could make a lot more money than simply selling duplicating supplies. Almost immediately, Cohen located a successor for Lithomat, Kueffel & Esser, in 1947 through Ed Fritz, the Lithomat sales manager. Kueffel & Esser had come up with a presensitized plastic plate for offset accompanying supplies. By now Cohen had gained a reputation in the duplicating industry nationwide as a man who was willing to take a chance on a new product if it appeared capable of making a profit for his company. When he lost the Lithomat account when it was sold to A.B. Dick, Cohen was asked to join Kueffel & Esser in its pioneering efforts. As executives of Kueffel & Esser were to say later "Tempo Company played an important part in the marketing and developing of the Kueffel & Esser Presensitized Plastic Plate." Kueffel & Esser joined the other lines of products which had become staples of the Tempo Company and the business continued to grow and expand as part of the increasing demand created by the avalanche of copies being required by American business and industry in the postwar period.

At that moment, Cohen had no idea that the best was yet to come. Although he was not aware of it at the time, that bright future that was just around the corner in late 1947 was related to an event which took place in 1938, the year Cohen returned from a stint in Jefferson City and started his own business. It took place on a second floor above a bar in the Astoria section of Queens in New York City. A 32-year-old physicist, lawyer and inventor, Charles Carlson, was taking a step that was to later make a fortune for Cohen, beginning in 1948 10 years later. In the New York bar building, Carlson handed his assistant a glass microscope slide on which Carlson had written "10-22-38-Astoria," the date and place of the experiment, in India ink. Laying the glass aside for a moment, the assistant takes a sulfur-coated metal plate which he rubs briskly with a cotton glove to charge it with static electricity. As Carlson watches, the assistant puts the glass slide and the metal plate together under a blazing light bulb. After a few seconds under the light, the plate is removed by the assistant and separated from the glass. He sprinkles the metal plate with powder and then blows away the surplus powder. Carlson and the assistant are delighted to see "10-22-38-Astoria" transformed to the plate from the slide. They hold their breath as the assistant presses a piece of wax paper against the metal plate and then peels it away. They read on the paper "10-22-38-Astoria," feeling instant jubilation. The jubilation quickly turns to celebration as they are able to repeat the process with different words several times. Although Cohen and the world did not know it on that day in 1938, a new revolutionizing copying process had been born. Carlson originally called the process electrophotography, a name he was later to change to xerography.

It was 10 years after Cohen had formed the company in 1938 that incidents began to happen which would cause the Tempo Company to grow and prosper beyond the wildest dreams of the founder. A company called Minnesota Mining and Manufacturing Company, now known worldwide as the 3M Company, had been working on a presensitized aluminum offset printing plate, the first such metal plate in history, to be used in document copying. It was a process that had been fully developed by its 3M inventor, Cliff Jewett, and the company was looking for someone with experience in the duplicating field who was willing to gamble on a product. They had heard of the work of Cohen with Lithomat, Rapid Roller and Kueffel & Esser in Kansas City and he looked like a logical choice since they were a Midwest company based in St. Paul and Cohen was in the Midwest. The result was that Jewett came to Kansas City with Ray Herzog, who was later to become chairman of the board of 3M, and Ernie Boverman, a 3M vice president. They offered to give Cohen and Tempo exclusive control of the new presensitized plate output of the 3M laboratory for a year to evaluate the salability of the product and develop markets for it. Cohen had been working with a chemist to develop a plate washing technique for such a product and the 3M offer looked like a good one to him. Because of his own work in the field and suggestions he made, the 3M Company got new patents for the process, with Cohen getting his name on one of the 3M patents. As a 3M executive said later of the events: "Our plate of aluminum, which is now the standard of the industry, proves to be the first successful one in the printing industry, thanks in a large part to the pioneering efforts of the Tempo Company."

In many respects, the joining of forces by Cohen and the 3M Company was a marriage made in heaven. There were many similarities between the giant 3M Company and Cohen on a smaller scale. Both companies were started on a small investment and both companies had shown a willingness to gamble on new product lines during their company lives. Minnesota Mining & Manufacturing Company, the predecessor of 3M, was started in 1902 to mine a natural abrasive, carborundum, to be made into grinding wheels for industry. It was started by a lawyer, a meat market operator, two railroad executives and a doctor with a $200,000 investment put up by a St. Paul plumbing company owner, Lucius Pond Ordway. The carborundum turned out to be of poor quality for grinding wheels so the company tried making sandpaper. The company was about to go under in 1907 when Ordway put up another $35,000 and brought in a bookkeeper, William Lester McKnight, an ambitious young man who proved to be a business genius. Quickly embarking on a sales program for the company, McKnight showed many of the qualities Cohen

had brought to good use with his company. McKnight bypassed purchasing agents and sold the sandpaper direct to plant foremen, the people
who actually supervised the use of sandpaper in factory production. A
near disaster seven years after McKnight took over the faltering company showed him to be a man with a willingness to experiment similar to
that displayed later by Cohen. The problem came in 1914 when 3M
sandpaper began to lose its abrasiveness in large quantities. The source
of the problem was difficult to trace but McKnight traced it to a load of
garnet imported from Spain to meet the fast growing 3M demand. Spanish olive oil had been stored in casks in the hold of the freighter with the
garnet for 3M and the casks ruptured during a heavy storm at sea, spilling the olive oil into the garnet and putting an invisible coating on it that
caused it not to stick permanently to the sandpaper adhesive. McKnight
talked the 3M owners into developing a laboratory for quality control
from which sprang many innovations, including Scotch brand transpar-
ent tape and the presensitized aluminum printing plate among many other
products. By 1954, the $235,000 investment by Ordway was worth
$272 million in 3M stock with McKnight still serving as chairman of
the 3M board.

Breaks continued to come the way of Jerry Cohen, even while he
was handling the 3M presensitized aluminum offset printing plate along
with his other duplicating supplies. Agfa Ansco Film Company, a German film producer second only to Eastman Kodak, had developed a pho-
tocopying process called Copease and had offered Cohen a dealership
for the process in 1948. Cohen again showed his gambling flair and took
on the Copease process. Under his guidance, Tempo continued to do
well with the Copease process until 1960, then years later, when the dry
copying process took over the duplicating business. You may remember
that Cohen had suffered one minor reversal in 1947 when Lithomat sold
its presensitized offset plate which Cohen had been handling to the A. B.
Dick Co., another large duplicating firm which already had a Kansas
City regional dealership, freezing Cohen out of one of his lucrative lines.
The circle came full round with A. B. Dick Co. in 1949, however. A. B.
Dick had entered into a cartel agreement with Gestetner Company of
England to keep it out of the U.S. market. That agreement with Gestetner,
the originator of the stencil process and the largest stencil duplicating
company in the world, expired in 1950. A. B. Dick and the Gestetner

Company had entered into a cartel agreement which barred Gestetner from entering the U.S. market and kept Dick out of the rest of the world. Gestetner was preparing to enter the U.S. market in a big way and once again the willingness of Cohen to gamble with new duplicating processes surfaced with Gestetner executives, including Sir Sigmund Gestetner, the company founder. Cohen was selected as one of the five original Gestetner dealers in the U.S. with exclusive rights to all Gestetner products in western Missouri and the state of Kansas. As Cohen was to say later: "This was really the turning point for growth for Tempo. The agreement with Gestetner marked the first time Tempo had had a complete line of duplicating machines and the supplies that they required from one company, a company which had developed sales worldwide. We had to change the sales philosophy of the company from concentrating primarily on duplicating machines and thereby creating a market for Gestetner supplies."

In the meantime, 3M Company had been experimenting with paper coatings that would lead to better duplicating machines. By 1953, 3M came up with the first dry thermographic duplicating process to challenge Kodak, whose so-called wet silver halide system called Verifax, was the hottest thing in the office copier field at the time. Once more, Herzog, Boverman and Bert Cross, the 3M corporate president, came to Cohen and offered him the new dry copying machine which 3M was calling Thermofax. Dry copying was a major breakthrough in the duplicating field at the time since the wet process used by Kodak was basically a simplified photographic process by which a negative paper is exposed with the original, passed through a liquid developer together with the positive sheet which dries after they are peeled apart. Kodak had improved the process with Verifax but it was still slow and used a liquid developer which required drying. Thermofax, the dry process copier Cohen was undertaking to sell for 3M, eliminated the liquid developer and the need for drying as well as speeding up the process. In Thermofax the original was passed through an infrared light together with a special heat-sensitive copy paper in a one-step process that sped up the time for making copies from around two minutes per copy for the old wet process to four seconds on Thermofax. The first Thermofax copiers were console models that were quite heavy, one of which Cohen still keeps as a museum model in the lobby of his headquarters. The improved process and the speed of copying, however, caused the new machine to be a big seller for Cohen and 3M. Despite its success with the new dry copying machine, 3M continued to develop an improved dry copier of desktop size it called the Secretary.

During one of the visits by 3M company executives to Kansas City in the 12 months of 1948, Cohen said he wanted company officials to talk to his customers because he said "they know what they need in this business and I want you to hear it from them personally." The 3M officials agreed and later told Cohen the meetings with customers were one of the most valuable they held in trying to learn what they needed to do to improve their duplicating processes. Cohen said a Lawrence executive told the 3M representatives, "If you can make these new offset plates big enough to fit our presses we can revolutionize the industry." The 3M officials got it done and once again the Cohen magic had worked.

It was the dawning of a new era and the new smaller, improved machine took off like a rocket. In 1955, television was still an infant, but it had already demonstrated its power as an advertising medium. The Kansas City Star had entered the field in 1951 with WDAF-TV and Kansas City was agog over this new broadcast novelty of pictures and sound as was the rest of the nation. Always innovators, the officers of 3M company recognized how much television could do to introduce their new desktop copiers with the improved process and offered their area dealers such as Cohen lucrative shared-time television promotion programs. The results were to make Cohen a household word in the Kansas City area as he appeared nightly on KCTV-5, Channel 5, then known as KCMO-TV, as the sponsor of the nightly news 11 to 11:15 p.m. demonstrating the new copiers for his company, Tempo Co. Those were the days before taped television and Cohen was on live with his machines. Much of Kansas City watched. As a result, Cohen had one of his most embarrassing moments on live television. As he recalls the incident: "I made my pitch about the speed and success of the machine and then pushed the button to get the machine going for the demonstration. Someone had forgotten to plug the machine in and nothing happened. There I am and nothing is happening. It was the talk of Kansas City for months, especially among friends. It certainly didn't hurt our sales any, though. It probably helped because people felt sorry for me." It certainly didn't because Cohen salesman were marketing the machines by the hundreds those first few months. As popularity of the weather, sports and news casts grew for television, the telecasts were moved, first to 10:30 p.m. and then to 10 p.m. As they moved, Cohen moved with them, sponsoring the 30-second introduction, the 30-second closing and the two 2-minute commercials during the newscasts. Cohen credits an advertising executive, Al Coleman, of the Potts-Woodbury Agency, with talking him into making his debut in television advertising. Working with him on the program details was another member of the advertising agency staff, Gene Miller. It was the first time office equipment had been sold through television advertising in Mid-America, manufacturers who supplied him said.

6

From Racers to Israel

While the Tempo Company was beginning its phenomenal growth with its contacts with the 3M Company through the leadership of Jerry Cohen in its 10th anniversary year in 1948, Cohen was not forgetting his long commitment to bettering Kansas City as well. When World War II ended, Cohen began a career of community service that was to cover more than 50 years into the early 1990s, touching every aspect of city life from the parks to charitable organizations and his help to the underprivileged. One of the things that helped catapult him into the forefront of community service began in 1946 through his association with Ararat Shrine Temple and its sponsorship of a youth activity for boys, the Soap Box Derby, originated by the Chevrolet Division of General Motors to interest grade school boys in cars. The other was his assisting the rotund, bombastic Boy Scout executive for the Kansas City Council, H. Roe Bartle, future mayor after whom the sprawling Bartle Convention Center in downtown Kansas City is named, in 1948 in founding an organization conceived by Bartle, the American Humanics Foundation, designed to develop leadership for American volunteer youth organizations such as Boy Scouts, Girl Scouts, Campfire, YWCA and others. Throughout the life of Bartle and following his death, Cohen contributed his time and money as an officer of the foundation for more than 35 years, succeeding in 1994 in helping to obtain a $1.4 million grant from the Kellogg Foundation to rejuvenate the American Humanics Foundation. Bartle was always grateful for such efforts and was quick to reward his friends for their loyalty to him whenever he could. Both his experience in serving for 17 years as the general chairman of the Soap Box Derby for Ararat Shrine Temple and as a personal confidante to Bartle succeeded in opening many doors for Cohen.

Just as he did everything he approached, Cohen put his heart and soul into seeing that hundreds of boys had the opportunity to race their homemade wooden cars down the hill in Swope Park for a shot at being declared the champion and getting a chance to go on to Akron, Ohio, with their cars to compete in the national championships. For the 17 years he served as general chairman of the Soap Box Derby, Cohen made the event into one of the most popular summertime attractions in Kansas City, pulling hundreds of spectators at the park on a Sunday afternoon to watch the boys race. The races were colorful spectacles with the Ararat Shrine parade units and bands parading down the raceway with each of the boys entered as drivers in that year's race marching as a unit, a celebrity race with mayors, television celebrities and others racing down the course in the first race in special cars and then the boys vying for the championships. Cohen, showing the organizing acumen that caused his business to grow, organized every detail of the races to perfection. Other organizations showed a willingness to cooperate with Cohen in the races such as the 4676th Air Defense Group which was stationed at Grandview Air Force Base, later named Richards-Gebaur, which provided its mobile machine shop to help the boys with the last-minute repairs or adjustments to their cars on race days. One of his lasting memories of those Soap Box Derby Days was his development of a lasting friendship with a super motivator such as himself, William G. (Bill) Power, the national advertising manager for Chevrolet who was responsible for organizing Soap Box Derby meets such as the one in Kansas City across the nation as well as the national meet in Akron, Ohio. It was from Power that Cohen got a phrase he often used: "You can't spell youth without you." As Power said in an article about him in The Indianapolis Star Magazine, where he was born and reared: "Sometimes in a boy's early years, he has to learn that the basketball or the baseball or football doesn't belong to him alone. He must develop early respect for other people's rights and property. He has to learn that it takes the help of others to do the job right — and to get that help and cooperation, he has to earn it." These were precepts Cohen took to heart.

As Power said in letters to Cohen during the 17 years he served as chairman of the Soap Box Derby: "The fine job you are doing for the boys of Kansas City through your work in promoting the Soap Box Derby is appreciated by all of us, as I am sure it is by the people of Kansas City. I am looking forward to seeing you at Akron." "It was swell visiting with you at the Derby and having a chance to thank you personally for the great job you are doing in heading up the Soap Box Derby promotion in Kansas City. Your personal interest is certainly a great contributing force that makes the derby such a big event in your city. I have enjoyed our visits together at Akron and appreciate your ideas and suggestions that add so much to the effectiveness of the overall program." How Kansas City felt about the annual event under the direction of Cohen for those 17 years was expressed in one of the numerous proclamations issued annually by the city government about the derby: "The youth of our city will compete in the spirit of true sportsmanship in this important race of homemade, gravity-propelled racers built according to national rules. This event is outstanding in this community for bringing together many civic organizations, all working for the welfare of the youth, developing a splendid spirit of friendship, goodwill and cooperation in the city. Stimulation of ingenuity and enterprise among the youth of our city, and throughout the nation, is one of the principal purposes of this event." For the 17 grade school boys who won the Kansas City championship under the direction of Cohen, it was an experience that would mark their lives forever and ever.

An illustration of this was shown in this wire sent by General Motors from Akron to the news department of The Kansas City Star about the 1955 winner, Johnny Evans. "Johnny Evans, Kansas City's 1955 Soap Box Derby champ, arrived in Akron this morning and was greeted at the station by a Soap Box Derby convertible and motorcycle escort. He was escorted through Akron to derby headquarters at the Mayflower Hotel. Dressed in a Kansas City Athletics uniform and carrying a box of Kansas City steaks, he was welcomed at the entrance by the Akron Soap Box Derby band whose members played 'Everything is Up to Date in Kansas City!' He walked up the golden stairs in front of the hotel where he was greeted by W. G. Power, general manager of the All American Soap Box

Derby, and Johnny presented Mr. Power and other officials with the Kansas City steaks. Johnny was then officially registered and left for four days of fun at Derby Town where all champions will live during their stay in Akron... Johnny was accompanied on his trip to Akron by his parents, Mr. and Mrs. John Evans; Cohen, general chairman of the Kansas City derby, and Russ Gentzler, assistant chairman, representing the Ararat Shrine Temple." As Cohen said: "That's the way it was every year we went. It was the thrill of a lifetime for those boys who got to go from Kansas City to the nationals. It had an impact on them that was beyond measure. Many of them came back to become some of our most prominent citizens in subsequent years. One of them was Whitney Kerr, who has become one of the leading real estate developers and civic leaders here."

Despite all of his work with the Soap Box Derby that started in the late 1940s, Jerry Cohen probably was to receive more exposure in civic affairs in Kansas City in addition to that stemming from his drive to succeed in business from his association with H. Roe Bartle. Bartle had come to Kansas City to work for the Boy Scouts of America in 1928, the year before Cohen was to graduate from Central High School in 1929. From the time Cohen first met Bartle in the mid-1930s, Cohen found the two of them had many things in common, including an affection for DeMolay, the young men's organization, and its founder, Frank Land, also a Kansas Citian; a sense of humor that brought loud guffaws and a bombastic approach to life at times; a sense of salesmanship that Cohen demonstrated in business dealings and Bartle demonstrated as a motivational speaker and the concept that God placed human beings on earth to help their fellow human beings in service. What Bartle said in a newspaper interview at one point in his life could also apply to Cohen's approach to life: "I'm happiest when I'm doing a lot of things. I just can't stop going. Nervous energy is a part of me. When I'm not busy, I'm not good. Inactivity affects my mental processes, my body. Under those circumstances, I'm fortunate that the demands on me right now are great — from so many phases of life and living." Bartle and Cohen probably drew closer to each other in 1948 when they began to share an interest that was to last the remainder of their lives. As a Boy Scout executive in Kansas City, Bartle had seen a growing demand for young leaders for American youth groups following World War II and had found no recognition of this growing need at the college level across the country. He had originally hatched the idea for a college humanics program in 1925 and was instrumental in getting the national council of the Boy Scouts of America, with which he was by then associated, to adopt curriculum standards for the program with the help of educators. The problem was that no college or university was immediately interested in implementing the proposed program.

Never one to turn down a request for assistance, just as Cohen always did in civic life, Bartle had accepted a request to help a small struggling Missouri school of higher education, Missouri Valley College, to stay afloat during World War II by becoming chairman of its board. With the war over and students returning, Bartle, while continuing to serve as the Kansas City Boy Scout council executive, had taken over the presidency of the college on an interim basis. During the period as president of Missouri Valley, Bartle was able to implement his dream of having a college program devoted to training youth leaders under the humanics concept as well as getting the small college started on a program of building construction. With the appointment of a fulltime president, Bartle was back in Kansas City and had conceived the idea of the American Humanics Foundation to provide scholarship funds for students at colleges such as Missouri Valley as youth leaders. He asked other Kansas Citians such as Cohen to join him in becoming founding members of the board of the new organization in raising an initial $100,000 to fund it. As Bartle wrote in the preamble of the founding articles of incorporation: "America's huge philanthropic effort in behalf of its youth faces a critical need for adequate executive leadership. The acute and growing shortage of self-trained youth agency administrators poses a serious threat to the effectiveness of our nation's private philanthropic effort. This shortage of professional leadership has been evident to those who interview and employ the executives for America's youth-helping agencies; great concern has been expressed by representatives of the Boy Scouts, Girl Scouts, YMCA, YWCA, Boys' Clubs, Campfire and many others. The American Humanics Foundation is a non-profit educational foundation providing college training for America's future youth group executives. Through its sponsorship of a special Humanics program at selected colleges, The Foundation will provide a vital source of trained professional manpower for youth agencies."

When the fall semester opened in 1949 at Missouri Valley College, American Humanics Foundation through Bartle and Cohen had 46 students enrolled in its program. The program has sponsored hundreds of students through the years since its founding and these hundreds have gone on to become youth leaders in a variety of fields. In addition, the program has spread to such colleges as High Point College in High Point, N.C.; Indiana Central College, Indianapolis, and Salem College, Salem, W. Va., as well as continuing at Missouri Valley. As a promotional brochure says of American Humanics in the intervening years: "In close cooperation with its host institutions, the American Humanics Foundation provides needed specialized resources — underwriting the cost of additional faculty, administration services, student counselling and guidance, special library collection, workshop and field trips, summer job placement and retreats. It aids in career placement upon graduation." Through all the years, Cohen has remained one of the hardest-working supporters of the Bartle brainchild. In 1965, when the foundation wanted to pay tribute to Bartle with a dinner in the Grand Ballroom of the Hotel Muehlebach after Bartle had served as mayor of the city, Cohen was the general coordinator for the dinner which succeeded in retiring $130,000 that was the foundation debt in tribute to Bartle. A galaxy of distinguished Americans spoke. When the event was over, there was no doubt that Cohen had made the event the success it was and saved it from what might have been a disaster. This was indicated in the letters Cohen received from those involved: Zenon C. R. Hansen, president of Mack Truck Co., the dinner master of ceremonies, "This is a belated thank you and compliment for the wonderful job you did in connection with the Bartle testimonial dinner. Many of us had misgivings of how this was going to work out and, from the distance that I viewed it, there were grave doubts as to the possibility of its success... Jerry it was a grand job in every respect." George F. Cahill, Boy Scout executive: "You are one great guy! All of those in America, who know within their heart that Roe Bartle is immensely deserving of a warm, honest and genuine testimonial, are deeply indebted to you for turning what could have been a catastrophe, into an excellent testimonial to a great guy." Thomas Stephens Haggai, national public speaker and longtime friend of Bartle: "There is no doubt that the reason that the dinner for Chief Bartle is the finest that any of us ever experienced was that it had your guiding hand behind it.

For a while, I was very concerned whether it would come off all right but when I found out that you had taken it in tow then I relaxed and knew we would have a good evening together."

In many respects in their lives, Cohen and Bartle had come from similar backgrounds. Cohen was the son of a deeply religious Jew while Bartle was the son of a Presbyterian church minister who put his faith first. Both of the fathers were immigrants, Cohen from ghettoes of Russia from what is now Lithuania and Bartle's father, the Rev. S. D. Bartle, came from Scotland. Both had had very little formal education when they arrived as young men and continued to help themselves through self-education. Both had mothers to whom they were devoted. Both were poor when they were growing up and vowed they would try to overcome their poverty in their adult lives. It was this kind of background between the two of them that caused Cohen to remain loyal to American Humanics long after Bartle had died. As late as 1994, The Kansas City Star carried a news story about the $1.4 million grant being donated by the W. K. Kellogg Foundation of Battle Creek, Mich, to American Humanics through the effort of Cohen. Accompanying the article is a photograph of Cohen with Robert F. Long, a longtime friend of Cohen and executive of the Kellogg Foundation along with Constantine Curris, president of the board of American Humanics and of the University of Northern Iowa, Cedar Falls; David Oliver, American Humanics board member and lawyer, and Kirk G. Alliman, American Humanics president. The caption on the photograph describes Cohen as "trustee of American Humanics and philanthropist." While Harry S. Truman, the man from Independence, was still president, Cohen, Bartle, and their long-time friend, Dad Land of DeMolay, came to the rescue of the president. Truman called to tell them that the light of his life, his daughter, Margaret Truman, was coming to Kansas City to present a singing concert. The President wanted them to use their influence to ensure a full and enthusiastic house in his hometown for Margaret, who had been receiving less-than-enthusiastic reviews from some critics, prompting at least one irate letter to one of the critics from the president. Thanks to the efforts of Cohen, Bartle, Land and the Oriental Band of Ararat Shrine, Margaret came on stage to a sold-out Music Hall audience. There is a great photograph of a smiling Cohen presenting a huge bouquet of flowers to Miss Truman after the concert while the others looked on appreciatively.

During those years immediately following World War II, there was a coterie of prominent Jews who were making major contributions to community life in Kansas City along with Cohen. These included Ike and Mike Katz, who had made the huge figure of a neon-lighted cat in striped pants and cutaway coat a sensation as the symbol of their Katz Drug Co. stores; Nat Milgram and his son, Les Milgram, with their Milgram Food Stores; Fred and George Goldman, of the Goldman Jewelry Stores, Charles Hipsh; Louis H. Ehrlich; Nathan Rieger; Sherman Dreisenzen; Irvin Fane and A. J. Granoff, lawyers; Hy Vile, a printing plant owner; Dr. Morton Helzberg; Herman Talge, of Rival and Dazy manufacturing company; Eddie Jacobson a haberdasher and longtime friend of Truman, and Rabbis Mayerberg and Gershon Hadas. Bartle was also a favorite of most of them long before he became mayor of Kansas City and he served on the boards of many of their businesses, Bond Stores, Milgram's Food Stores and Textile Distributors, Inc., among them. Bartle was fond of saying, as he did in one published news interview: "I enjoy my relationships with people of the Jewish faith. I serve on many of their boards and in most cases I'm the only non-Jew on them." Another centerpiece of the Jewish community activity was President Truman, to whom they felt they eternally owed a debt of gratitude for his quick action in recognizing Israel as a Jewish state shortly after it was formed in Palestine in 1948. In 1951, when Truman decided he had to establish wage and price controls during the Korean War, he called on Bartle to serve as head of the regional office of the newly created Office of Economic Stabilization with jurisdiction over several states under Charles Wilson, the General Motors executive who was later to become secretary of defense. Truman reached Bartle in Chicago where he was making a speech and told him on the phone, "I've told Charley Wilson that I don't care what kind of appointments he makes but I have only one recommendation for a regional office, the one in Kansas City to head up several states in the economic stabilization program. Chief, I've decided that responsibility is yours." Bartle, who had developed a reputation as a motivational speaker and was in demand, tried to decline because he thought he already had too many commitments. Truman bellowed back: "Now listen here, Chief! We have been friends a long time. You have given the best speeches on Americanism I've ever heard. They were the longest I ever heard and I sat through them. And they were the loudest I ever heard and I suffered through them. Now the hour has come for you to put your talent where your mouth has been for the past thirty years." Bartle meekly accepted.

From the time Truman recognized the state of Israel in 1948, Cohen became a strong supporter of the newly created Jewish state, both from the standpoint of time as well as of financial backing. Cohen continued the support all of his life, being one of the leading backers of the U. S. Bonds for Israel. He visited Israel and received numerous awards for his efforts for Israel. But the Jewish community in Kansas City was not always in agreement over the desire for a state of Israel in the Middle East during World War II and immediately preceding that. Even Eddie Jacobson, who had been a partner in the failed haberdashery business with Truman, was not an early member of the Zionist movement, which was pushing for the creation of Israel among the Jews. Jacobson joined other Kansas City Jews and many others across America in a neutral stance, fearing that the creation of Israel might hamper the freedom and prosperity of the U. S. Jewish community. Alex F. Sachs, a third generation member of Temple B'Nai Jehudah who was serving as Jackson County highway engineer after being appointed by Truman, then county judge, and later to be named postmaster of Kansas City by Truman in 1949, had written the president in 1945: "If Drew Pearson in his Merry-Go-Round is right — and he sometimes is — your views are in accord with a majority of liberal (i.e., Reform) Jews. Those to whom I have talked have only the highest commendation for you on your stand opposing a Jewish state — and for urging every assistance for the refugees to enter Palestine." Jacobson had reopened a haberdashery store on Westport Road in Kansas City and Truman, as president, visited the store on June 28, 1945, but Jacobson did not mention the Palestine question despite efforts from Zionists. On June 16, 1946, Jacobson did arrange an appointment with Truman at the White House for himself; Rabbi Arthur J. Lelyveld of New York, director of the Committee on Unity for Palestine, and Charles Kaplan, of New York, who was president of Shirtcraft Corp., from whom Jacobson bought merchandise for the haberdashery. The United Press reported the next day: "Jacobson said afterwards that Lelyveld 'wanted to clear up several things' with the President regarding Palestine. He looked at his two colleagues as he left the White House and wisecracked: 'Kaplan sells shirts, I sell furnishings and Rabbi sells nations.' " Six days later, Jewish leaders learned Truman would see that the U. S. would assume technical and financial responsibility for the transfer of 100,000 Jewish immigrants to Palestine. As late as 1947, Rabbi Mayerberg, himself not a Zionist, told the annual meeting of Temple B'Nai Jehudah: "Though many of us still hold the same opinion about the historic value of a Jewish state, we must all be agreed that it is the duty of every Jew to help to the utmost in the rehabilitation of Palestine... We must devoutly stand by our brothers in their heroic endeavor to build their homeland... (But) we will not permit any tradition or any practices that came to us from Palestine or elsewhere to becloud our American expression of Judaism or to interfere with its progressive unfoldment." Cohen shared the uneasiness of American Jews across the nation and directed his efforts to building his thriving business as Jacobson was doing during the interim as well.

Jacobson was not happy with the way Jewish Zionists in America were treating President Truman over the creation of the state of Israel. Elinor Bornstine, daughter of Jacobson, quoted her father as saying: "Truman had been up to his ears with highly emotional, distraught and somewhat illogical Zionists and his appointments secretary had received instruction to admit no more of them — but, most in particular, Abba Hillel Silver, who had more than once raged into the office of the President of the United States and pounded his fist on his desk and shouted at him." In 1947, the U. S. supported a resolution in the United Nations for the partition of Palestine to allow for the creation of an independent state of Israel and Jacobson congratulated Truman on the move. In early 1948, Chaim Weizmann, the beloved leader of the Israel concept, flew to the U.S. to sound out Truman on the proposed Jewish state. Weizmann could not get an appointment at the White House and Jewish leaders intervened with Jacobson to try to get Weizmann an appointment with Truman. Truman received a wire from Jacobson which read: "I have asked you for very little in the way of favors during all our years of friendship, but I am begging you to see Dr. Weizmann as soon as possible. I can assure you I would not plead to you for any other of our leaders." Truman rebuffed the effort. Several days later, Jacobson flew to Washington to see Truman personally. Truman agreed to see him but Truman still refused to see Weizmann and Jacobson said later: "My dear friend, the President of the United States was at that time as close to being an anti-Semite as a man could possibly be." Truman later wrote that Jacobson pointed out that Truman had a hero in Andrew Jackson, and that, he, Jacobson, had a hero in Weizmann. Jacobson, according to Truman, went on to say: "I am talking about Chaim Weizmann; he is a very sick man, almost broken in health, but he traveled thousands and thousands of miles to see you and plead the cause of my people. Now you refuse to see him just because you were insulted by some of our American Jewish leaders, even though you know Weizmann had absolutely nothing to do with these insults and would be the last man to be party to them. It doesn't sound like you, Harry, because I thought you could take the stuff they had been handing out to you." Truman remained silent for some time and then blurted out, "You win, you bald-headed son of a bitch. I'll see him." Weizmann rose from a sick bed in New York to meet with Jacobson following his White House meeting and to hear that Truman would now see him. Weizmann traveled immediately to Washington, met with Truman and, as Truman said later, in his memoirs, "I felt that he had reached a full understanding of my policy and I knew what it was he wanted." Truman apparently agreed secretly that day that the U.S. would recognize the state of Israel and the boundaries it set as soon as the British mandate in that era ended. That was March 18, 1948. Despite some momentary setbacks between then, Truman fulfilled his agreement on May 14, 1948, by immediately recognizing Israel. The decision brought great joy to two Kansas City friends, Jacobson and Cohen.

THE SOAP BOX DERBY BOOMS — *For 17 years following World War II, Jerry Cohen, in dark clothes with white sun helmet, ran the annual Swope Park Soap Box Derby races for the Ararat Shrine Temple. Under the chairmanship of Cohen, the races achieved phenomenal success with General Motors as the sponsor and drew thousands annually to the Kansas City park to watch.*

BARTLE AS A SOAP BOX DERBY RACER — *The Soap Box Derby races sponsored under the chairmanship of Jerry Cohen for 17 years drew all kinds of celebrities for the opening ceremonies. Even Mayor H. Roe Bartle, for whom Bartle Hall is named, participated one year in a specially-built car for his rotund girth in honor of his friend, Jerry Cohen.*

7

New Success Horizons

n the years from 1938 to 1960, the lowly bet of $300 Jerry Cohen had placed on the duplicating business when he started back in 1938 was paying off like a slot machine gone mad, pouring thousands of dollars into the coffers of his company, the Tempo Sales Co., in increased sales as the technology of copying business documents grew beyond his wildest dreams. The success of Cohen, however, was more than a gamble with luck. It was a tribute to his willingness to look at innovations in copying technology as they came along and the fact that he was a master salesman who could not only sell a product himself but who was able to convince his expanding force of employees as the business grew that they could sell as well. As for his willingness to take on new products, Cohen himself once said: "We've never been afraid to pioneer new products. From the time I was a little kid I was always very inquisitive about how things worked. I guess that has carried over because I've never been afraid to invest my time and money in trying something new. Investing a little time and money in a new product is an investment in tomorrow. In fact, 25 per cent of the products we sell today were not even on the market five years ago." It also never bothered him that in taking on new products he was faced with the dilemma of having to explain to a customer how a product worked and why he needed it. As Cohen described this aspect of it: "As a sales-man of anything, you've got to believe it's going to help the customer or you can't make the sale anyway. Besides, as a new business, we were having to create a market for ourselves and why not do it with a product that was new as well. I'd go in and try to sell a customer on buying a copier and he'd ask me why he needed a copier. I'd look him right in the eye, point to the telephone on his desk and say 'you didn't know how much that thing was going to mean to your business either did you until somebody invented it and sold it to you did you?' That generally stopped him and then he was willing to listen to what you had to say about your product."

Cohen had also been a firm believer in the concept that being in the sales of merchandise was a noble profession that required skill, understanding of the customer to whom the sale is being made and the ability to persuade him that the product would be of help to him. He summed up his sales philosophy in part in these remarks he made to a graduate marketing class at a Midwest university: "Selling seems to demand just a little effort, however, a little bit more stick-to-itiveness than other occupations. It is easy to see why. In most other fields of endeavor the work comes to the man, in selling the man goes to the work. It is no casual choice of words that describes sales people as live wires, as aggressive enthusiastic personalities. The work and effort of selling demands these dynamic qualities in the salesman — hard work, industriousness and good salesmanship are in a very real sense synonymous. It takes understanding.

"A clearly essential requirement of successful selling is the ability to comprehend what is happening on both sides of the sales interview. What you say is important but what the customer says is also of equal importance and in my opinion of greater importance. It's a two-way street. A truly competent sales person is finely attuned to everything of significance that's said or done in exchanges that take place during the interview. He or she is subconsciously busy with the answers to such questions as what tactful ways do I use to reduce the price objection, prejudice, bargaining, wheeling dealing tactics. What are my sales goals? What effect does what I say and do have on this customer? Without this understanding no intelligent selling can take place because there can be no real communication between the sales maker and the customer.

"Another important thing for a good sales person is it takes good health. The poorly conditioned athlete doesn't run a good race, doesn't play a good game, doesn't bat successfully, doesn't carry the ball against an opponent and so it is with the sales maker. It is the wise sales maker who doesn't overeat, doesn't take that extra cocktail, doesn't overtax his or her physical and mental well-being. If you let it happen, you just can't perform with any real effectiveness. That 'on the ball feeling' of enthusiasm and energy have their source in the simple medical fact of good mental and physical health. Good health is the key to success in just about every business but selling it is probably more so than in most other occupations. Now, of course, it takes persuasiveness and it is something more than pertinent argument logically and dramatically presented, something much more vital and complex than skill and rhetoric and education. As important as they may be at times, persuasion is the goal of every sales interviewer. No persuasion, no sale; it's as important as that. Persuasiveness is the sum of all the impressions made on the customer during the sales interview and includes all the elements of the sales makers' personalities: Their dependability, their sincerity, their understanding, judgment, courtesy and friendliness. As in most professions, the skill of persuasion can be acquired by steady exposure and application. Here again veteran sales makers, friends or competitors, are great teachers. Listen to them and watch them closely, analytically. Then practice what you have observed. Simple and obvious as this may seem, don't delude yourself into thinking it's an easy course to follow. It is worth the effort. Persuasion is at the very heart of the skill of learning how to sell most of the people most of the time."

What Cohen told the university class in his remarks was nothing more than what he practiced all his life in building his business enterprises into a multi-million-dollar operation and gave him a long and healthy life, carrying him well past the age of 80. As the 1950s dawned, however, Cohen was only 37 and many more years of following the regimen he outlined in that speech was necessary for him to achieve his goals. In 1950, all five Cohen brothers were operating together as a business at 1423 Grand Avenue where their father, Reuben Cohen, still had his small jewelry store. One of the reasons Jerry Cohen had purchased the building when it became available was so that they could keep an eye on their aging father who continued to live at the family home at 3716 Park Avenue where the boys had grown up even after his beloved wife and their mother died in 1944. He showed no sign of wanting to retire and the sons were not about to discourage their strong-willed father into giving up his business. An item in the December 20, 1950, edition of The Kansas City Star indicated why the sons wanted to be near their father. It described how a well-dressed man had entered the father's shop, Ruby's Jewelry and Pawn Shop, and told the elderly man, now 76, it was a holdup. The newspaper account described how the elderly Cohen had been unable to reach two floor alarms the sons had installed for just such an emergency and gave the man $4. When the man demanded more money, The Kansas City Star article goes on: "Cohen informed him there was a safe in the rear and was ordered to open it. He proceeded to the back of the store. He opened a door leading to the Tempo Duplicating Company, 1423 Grand, which adjoins the jewelry store, and shouted 'Holdup! Holdup!' "

The five brothers all happened to be in the business at the time and immediately started to the aid of their father. The newspaper item described how the five brothers chased the bandit north on Grand when he fled, how a pedestrian, hearing the shouts of the brothers, tripped the intruder and how the five brothers pounced on the would-be bandit, hauling him back to their father's shop. The older Cohen had called the police when the chase began and they arrived just as the brothers returned with the culprit. He was linked to similar robberies in the area.

The elder Cohen was still not convinced to give up his jewelry store but fate was to intervene in two ways. One involved Bernard Cohen, who had been the first of the brothers to join Jerry Cohen in his duplicating business in 1941 when Jerry bought out his original partner, Nathan Wedlin, for $4,000. Bernard Cohen, who had been working as an accountant as Jerry had done earlier, came into the business, now known as Tempo Sales Co., as a full partner, a relationship which continued between the two of them as the other three, brothers, Harry, Robert and Al, joined the firm. In 1952, however, tragedy struck when Bernard died unexpectedly at the comparatively young age of 44. Fortunately, however, Jerry and his brother had been smart enough to take out partnership insurance in the event of such a development. With the proceeds of this insurance agreement, Jerry Cohen was able to pay off Bernard's widow for her share of the business on the death of her husband. Cohen then incorporated the business, changing the name from Tempo Sales Co. to simply the Tempo Company. Under the new arrangement in the company, Jerry Cohen took over full direction of the firm with the title of president and chief executive officer. His two other brothers, Robert and Al, became vice presidents. After the estate settlement with Bernard's widow, the remaining brothers finally convinced their father to retire and close the jewelry store he had operated in the same location since 1911. In 1956, when Reuben Cohen had reached the age of 83, The Kansas City Star carried an item with the headline, Ends 45 Years on Grand, with a photograph of the elder Cohen. The article said in part: "Cohen established the shop there in 1911 when the area was much busier because of the old Kansas City Power & Light Co. building at 14th and Grand and the Public Service Company (the street car company) at Truman Road (then Fifteenth Street) and Grand." The elder Cohen was to live seven more years after his retirement until he died in 1963 at the age of 90.

Thanks to his willingness to use his company to try new experimental products in the burgeoning duplicating business, Jerry Cohen had positioned Tempo with what were to become giants in the new dry copying process, 3M Company, with whom he had developed a relationship in 1948 when it was first entering the copying field with an aluminum presensitized duplicating plate, the first such to be made of metal, and the British firm, the Gestetner Company, which was ready to enter the American market following the expiration of its cartel agreement with A. B. Dick Co. barring it for a time from the U. S. market, in 1949. Cohen had worked with 3M in the developing of a wet copy machine that was less involved than the one Eastman Kodak had developed but was not quite as good. This was to pay off in 1953 when 3M was ready to market a infrared dry copying process developed by one of its researchers, Carl Miller, in part for the U. S. intelligence agency, the Central Intelligence Agency, which had been established in 1947 under President Harry S. Truman. It was known as the 3M Thermofax Model 12. Within two years of its introduction to the public, 3M made another major breakthrough with the readying for market of a new much smaller desktop dry copier called the Thermofax Secretary. It was this that launched Cohen into his television career demonstrating the new small unit on the nightly newscasts of what was then known as KCMO-TV, Channel 5, now known as KCTV-5. The television promotion brought with it instant success for the Tempo Company. Within a year, Tempo under Cohen's direction had sold its first 1,000 of the new Thermofax copiers, causing the company to remodel its offices and building at 1423 Grand. With its success, 3M Company asked its dealers such as Cohen to separate out their 3M related operations into separate businesses from their other duplicating equipment lines. Cohen complied and formed a new company, Electronic Business Equipment, Inc., with offices at 1616 Grand, a couple of blocks from Tempo, which stayed at 1423 Grand.

Just how fast Cohen was pushing the Tempo company ahead was indicated by an advertisement he ran July 1, 1958, in a publication called The Kansas Citian. It featured photographs of the 1423 store and offices, the new Electronic Business Equipment, Inc., offices, and display rooms at 1616 Grand, and a photograph of Cohen on a television set together with a headline which read: "Tempo Company Again Expands! Since we put Thermofax Copying Machines on Television, KCMO-TV, Channel 5, a Year Ago, We have sold over 1,000 KC Business Offices Thermofax Copying Machines." It featured an open letter from him which read: "Yes, give the credit to television. Just a little over a year ago we remodeled our Tempo company sales office at 1423 Grand. About a thousand of our customers and friends attended the open house and wished us well. At that time we had sold about 500 Thermofax Copying Machines. Things looked pretty good for the future of this new division of our Tempo Company. So, we employed advertising people. They advised us to go on television and personally demonstrate Thermofax copying. The first show ran in February of 1957 on Channel 5, KCMO-TV. I wasn't too happy getting out there in front of the camera and doing the commercial myself. But Dave insisted. Boy! I really started something! Some friends patted me on the back and told me what a big ham I was… others told me I was off my rocker and shouldn't do the show personally… others were kind and said nothing. But, before the first year was over we had sold over 1,000 Thermofax copying machines! Of course, our splendid selling team did a great job. Then Minnesota Mining and Manufacturing Company, which makes Thermofax copying products, came along and said 'Jerry, it's time for you to set up a Thermofax copying products sales office.' It was about that time the 'recession' began to stir everybody up. Our business was good. But, I kinda wondered about opening another sales office… bigger than the one I had just remodeled. But you good folks kept on buying Thermofax copying machines and I had no choice. So here it is... a definite reality. I'm more amazed than anybody. Here I thought I had fixed up the Tempo sales office for life! And, now, less than a year later, I'm starting another one... twice the size. Well, I guess it's the American way. A fellow starts out with $300 borrowed capital, works twenty years and things begin to happen I am deeply grateful to all my wonderful friends; to all our loyal customers; to my great selling team and to my service and office associates. I'm grateful to Jeannette for putting off her promised new car another year; and I thank the good Lord that everything could work out so nice for (then came his scrawling signature) Jerry Cohen."

As the demand for greater copying ability grew in offices, Cohen and his businesses grew to meet the demand. Following on the heels of opening the new Electronic Business Equipment firm at 1616 Grand, Cohen proceeded to open two branches as the business demands grew. The first expansion occurred in 1959 when Cohen opened an EBE branch in Jefferson City to serve the needs of state government and 31 additional counties in central Missouri. A year after the Jefferson City office was opened, Cohen constructed his own building at 401 Madison Street there to house his operations only a step away from the state capitol building itself. In 1962, he opened the second branch office in St. Joseph, Missouri, with responsibility for sales of Electronic Business Equipment products in 15 counties in northwest Missouri, five counties in northeast Kansas and one in Nebraska. As the 3M dry copying success increased, the Kansas City office was increased to cover sales in 11 counties in western Missouri and seven counties in eastern Kansas along the Kansas-Missouri border. While he was separating out the 3M-related products into a separate business as 3M had demanded, Cohen had remained loyal in his other duplicating supply business to Sir Sigmund Gestetner, the British duplicating mogul who had befriended him and selected him as one of five Gestetner representatives in the U.S. in 1950 when its post-World War II agreement with A.B. Dick Co. had expired. Gestetner was the leader in stencil duplicating equipment worldwide with the founder of the firm, David Gestetner, having invented a duplicating machine for market in 1897 in England. For the first time in 1950, Tempo and Cohen had its own complete line of duplicating equipment and not just supplies, an outstanding stencil duplicating machine from the originator of the stencil duplicating system. Within a comparatively short span of years,

Cohen had placed over 6,000 of the duplicating machines from Gestetner in the trade territory he had been allotted consisting of all of the state of Kansas and the western half of Missouri. Having followed the progress of Cohen with the development of the 3M dry copying process, Sir Sigmund came to Cohen and asked him to help them enter the offset duplicating field. Cohen quickly agreed and within a comparatively short time Gestetner was in the field with its own offset machine incorporating many suggestions made by Cohen and his staff. Gestetner marketed the device in the United States and Canada as the Whitten Offset Press and in the rest of the world as the Gestalith Offset Press.

Gestetner had furnished the duplicating machine on which the staff of Gen. Dwight D. Eisenhower had cut the original order for the invasion of Normandy on June 6, 1944. When Eisenhower broke up his headquarters following the victory of Allied Forces in Europe, he returned the now-historic machine to Gestetner. When the Eisenhower Library was dedicated in Abilene, Kansas, Gestetner turned the duplicating machine over to Cohen to present to the library as a gift. Cohen continued to provide the paper and ink for the duplicating machine for years after it was installed in a display at the Eisenhower Museum so that thousands of school children and other visitors could have copies of the order churned out on the still operating machine. That historic order issued by Ike on June 6, 1944, and which Cohen saw was preserved in the hands of thousands of visitors reads as follows:

"Soldiers, Sailors and Airmen of the Allied Expeditionary Force! You are about to embark upon the Great Crusade, toward which we have striven these many months. The eyes of the world are upon you. The hopes and prayers of liberty-loving people everywhere march with you. In company with our brave allies and brothers-in-arms on other fronts you will bring about the destruction of the German war machine, the elimination of Nazi tyranny over oppressed peoples of Europe, and security for ourselves in a free world.

"Your task will not be an easy one. Your enemy is well-trained, well-equipped and battle-hardened. He will fight savagely.

"But this is the year 1944. Much has happened since the Nazi triumphs of 1940-41. The United Nations has inflicted upon the Germans great defeats, in open battle, man-to-man. Our air offensive has seriously reduced their strength in the air and their capacity to wage war on the ground. Our Home Fronts have given us an overwhelming superiority in weapons and munitions of war, and placed at our disposal great reserves of trained fighting men. The tide has turned! The free men of the world are marching together to Victory!

"I have full confidence in your courage, devotion to duty and skill in battle. We will accept nothing less than full victory!

"Good luck! And let us all beseech the blessing of Almighty God upon this great and noble undertaking."

Gestetner was impressed with the sales ability of Cohen and his staff from the beginning. When he reached the point of sales of his first 1,000 Gestetner machines, Cohen was honored by Gestetner himself with a full-size, operating Gestetner duplicating machine entirely plated in 21-carat gold. Although Cohen kept many momentoes with which he was honored for his sales and community work, this one overwhelmed him with its apparent value. He immediately presented it to one of his favorite charities, the Shrine Crippled Children's Hospitals, in ceremonies in which Walter Guy, the Imperial Potentate of the Shrine at the time, participated at the Shrine Imperial Convention in Chicago. The gold from the machine was used to provide funds for the hospitals.

THE D-DAY MIMEOGRAPH MACHINE — *In recognition of the outstanding sales work for his duplicating machines in the Kansas City area by Jerry Cohen, Sir Sigmund Gestetner, head of the British duplicating firm which manufactured such items decided to present the original duplicating machine used by Gen. Dwight D. Eisenhower in preparing the orders for the Allied invasion of Normandy, June 6, 1944, to the Eisenhower Library and Museum in Abilene. Earl J. Endacott, curator of the Ike Museum in Abilene at the time, accepts the machine from Ralph Barnett, a British Gestetner official representing Sir Sigmund, center, while Cohen, right, looks on.*

THE COMMERCIALS GO ELABORATE — *In the years television was making Jerry Cohen a household word in Kansas City in the 1950s, the commercials he was making to sell his duplicating equipment got more elaborate. This is one of the last ones designed by TV producers to stage commercials calling attention to the fact Bing Crosby was starring in an annual 3M golf tournament in Pebble Beach, California.*

8

His Friend, Bartle

I n the 1950s while the duplicating equipment and sales business was growing like a brush fire out of control for Jerry Cohen, Cohen was also being pushed center stage in community affairs by his longtime friend and mentor, H. Roe Bartle, the Kansas City Boy Scout executive. Cohen and the rotund, good-natured Bartle, who had a speaking ability that listeners said could charm the gold out of your teeth, had taken to each other like bread and honey from the time they had first met shortly after Cohen had graduated from Central High and joined a young men's youth group, the Order of DeMolay. They met through their mutual friend, Frank Land, the Kansas Citian who had founded the order and was a long-time friend of Bartle. Cohen had won the affection of Bartle for life when Cohen played an integral part in helping form the American Humanics Foundation in 1948. As the 1950s dawned, the Citizens Association, the city government reform movement started by The Kansas City Star and civic leaders such as Rabbi Samuel Mayerberg and Cohen himself, was suffering the pangs of success and starting to run out of steam after fighting the good fight for nearly 20 years. It had reached the acme of success in 1940 when it succeeded in wresting City Hall from the clutches of the then-corrupt political machine of Tom Pendergast. All during World War II, the city was presided over by Mayor John B. Gage, the son of a distinguished Kansas City lawyer who had served as city attorney for the city as far back as 1863. The elder Gage had come to Kansas City in 1859 and had taken an active role in politics from the beginning so it was only natural that John B. Gage would follow in his father's footsteps.

When the new city council and Mayor Gage took over in 1940, one of the smartest moves the reform city government made was to hire a new up-and-coming city manager from Saginaw, Michigan, L. Perry Cookingham, to be the city manager in Kansas City. Cookingham was able to make the city government one of the most efficient and best financed in the nation in the 20 years he served as city manager. When Cookingham and the reform government began digging into city matters in 1940 they found the city "virtually bankrupt and all kinds of kited funds and graft," as one writer described it. When he came to Kansas City to be interviewed for the job of city manager by the reform group, Cookingham showed his mettle and the way he was to approach the job when he said: "I know no one in Kansas City. I don't know the 'good' people from the 'bad' people. I don't know what sections of the city favored the change. But I want to tell you there is only one way I know to serve a city under this form of government and that is to treat everyone equally — regardless of race, color, or political affiliation. Everybody and every section of this city will be treated exactly alike. If Tom Pendergast himself should come to my office asking for service to which he is entitled he will receive it with the same courtesy and dispatch that I would give to Mayor Gage." Within the first year after the reform movement took over, Mayor Gage and Cookingham were able to report these improvements: Concrete and asphalt costs, to which Pendergast had had exclusive rights, reduced by 30 percent, 1,095 employees removed as incompetent; private use of city cars discontinued; free access to city supplies stopped; warehouse for central buying started; gone from a $20 million deficit to a surplus of $1.6 million; a new and modern budget and new accounting system; a format personnel program and merit system; and improved credit rating followed by the lowest interest rates on its bonds in city history; a new garbage contract saving $1 million over the next 10 years.

With the old Pendergast machine destroyed, the reform movement under the Citizens Association firmly established and the city entering a new period of economic boom following the end of World War II, Mayor Gage decided after being elected to three 2-year terms to step down in

1946. When the Citizens Association began looking around for a candidate for mayor to replace Gage in 1946, it was only natural that its leaders should turn to another lawyer who had not been afraid to fight the old Pendergast machine. They found one in William E. Kemp, who had come to Kansas City in 1919 and had become so incensed with Pendergast that he began openly opposing the machine when the reform movement began to pick up speed in the 1930s. His efforts so impressed Gov. Lloyd C. Stark that the governor had named Kemp to the Kansas City Court of Appeals in 1938. When the Citizens Association achieved success in 1940, Kemp resigned from the court and took the post as city counselor under the new city government. In that post, he had been successful in defeating some 90 percent of $10 million in lawsuits filed by machine leaders following their ousting. He also successfully prosecuted machine lieutenants for fraud in connection with funds they had allegedly taken illegally from the city. Thanks to Gage, the election of Kemp and the Citizen slate was almost a foregone conclusion in 1946. Mayor Kemp resided over the centennial celebration of the city in 1950, the high point of which was the construction of the outdoor amphitheater, Starlight Theater, an operation that was to be dear to the heart of Cohen for the rest of his life. Among the accomplishments under Mayor Kemp was the approval of a $41,560,000 bond issue and the annexation of 2.38 square miles to take the city south to 85th Street and Indiana Avenue. Other accomplishments under Mayor Kemp included the start of three federal housing projects; dedication of the new Paseo and Chouteau bridges across the Missouri River; organization of the first Community Service and Human Relations Commissions; creation of a city traffic department; paving of 80 streets; installation of voting machines and the first United Funds drive was organized.

Everything was not all sweetness and light for Kemp, however, during his nine years as mayor. Heavy snowstorms during five of those years increased snow removal costs and slowed city operations as street crews struggled manfully against the drifts; one of the worst building industry strikes in city history occurred and disaster struck on a major scale on July 13, 1951, when the Kaw and Missouri Rivers flooded the Central Industrial District with its Kansas City Stockyards, packing plants and the American Royal. Cookingham did an admirable job in organizing the city emergency effort but it took months for the city to fully recover from the unprecedented disaster.

By the time the 1955 city elections rolled around, the Citizens Association had been in power 15 years and dealt with a variety of problems and improvements. Major league baseball had come to Kansas City in the last months of the term of Mayor Kemp when the Philadelphia Athletics, under the all-time baseball legend, Connie Mack, announced they were moving from Philadelphia to become the Kansas City Athletics for the opening of the 1955 season. Kemp and the city council went all out to provide funds to transform the old Muehlebach Field at 22nd Street and Brooklyn Avenue into a double-tiered major league stadium known as Municipal Stadium in time for the A's to open there against the Detroit Tigers on April 6, 1955. Despite the auspicious events, there were signs of new stirrings of the remnants of the Pendergast machine brought on in part by a move in 1946 to annex 19 square miles of territory north of the Missouri River in Clay County. Harry Davis, who was a councilman from the First District on the north side still under machine influence, maintained the annexation was a move by the Citizens Association and The Kansas City Star to diffuse the Democratic majorities in the First District but said publicly the citizens of Clay County didn't want it and it would cost Kansas City more than it would provide in new revenue. The Star pointed out that Davis was opposed because he was afraid of losing the last Democrat council seat and said also that it would mean the end of the last Pendergast stronghold because the new Clay County Democrats would not be Pendergast Democrats. When the residents of Kansas City voted in November 1946, they voted 39,978 for the annexation to 37,920 against it. For some hours after the election, the city thought it had lost because of an old Missouri statute which required a three-fifths majority rather than a bare majority in such cases. It took Cohen's old employer, Jerome Joffee, former state senator who was now utilities and legislative counselor for the city, to straighten out the issue. Joffee agreed with Cookingham that the three-fifths rule was no longer in Missouri statute books and the issue had carried. Joffee discovered that the Missouri constitution had been amended in 1945 and the three-fifths rule enacted in such cases before the turn of the century had not been reenacted in the constitutional revision.

Davis, however, was reelected to the city council after the annexation and picked up an ally in his fight against the Citizens Association and Cookingham in Garrett Smalley, the editor of a fiery little Kansas City journal known as The Kansas City News-Press. Smalley had never liked the Citizens Association and Cookingham and resented their success in turning around the city. His voice was seldom heard until the annexation fight and the reelection of Davis with the resurgence of the northside machine under Alex Presta. Smalley always referred to Cookingham, who used the initials L.P. Cookingham as city manager, as Lousy Planning Cookingham and Moneybags. Asked later about the attacks by Smalley in the News-Press, Cookingham said: "Oh, they were just having a little fun at my expense, I guess. Actually, I got along fairly well with their publisher, Garrett Smalley, but he was always giving me hell in his paper about one thing or another. He was just fiercely opposed to non-partisan government and the council-manager plan for running a city. He was wedded to the old way, the partisan way. He wanted the city to be run by the Democratic party again and he just wasn't about to let up in his campaign to get rid of the so-called do-gooders — the members of the Citizens Association — who kicked Pendergast's boys out in 1940 and put the city back on its feet."

Still another factor was coming into play in the resurgence of the old Democratic party machine in that The Star and its morning edition, The Times, the principal newspaper in the city and a strong supporter of the Citizens Association, had its hands full with its indictment in late 1952 by the U.S. Department of Justice in the last stages of the administration of Harry S. Truman for anti-trust violations in connection with its newspaper, radio and television operations. As the 1955 city elections approached, The Star had seen its reputation tarnished in the eyes of many Kansas Citians by its subsequent trial and conviction on the charges in U.S. District Court and being forced to sell its radio and television interests and take other actions in connection with its circulation and advertising operations under federal mandate. The Citizens Association was still powerful with the leading citizens still at its helm but it was little wonder that Cohen's friend, Bartle, had misgivings about becoming its candidate for mayor. Cohen was trying to get Bartle to run as the Citizens Association candidate. Bartle had already decided that he was finally going to retire as the Kansas City district executive for the Boy Scouts of America in 1956 to spend full time on another project dear to his heart, the American Humanics Foundation. That alone was enough to make him not want to be a candidate for mayor, the current unrest in the local political situation notwithstanding.

How difficult the situation was at the time that Cohen and the others were trying to get him to run for mayor was indicated later by an article about Bartle published in 1956 in the prestigious publication of the time, The Saturday Evening Post. The article written by Hartzell Spence, a noted writer of the time, said in part:

"At the time, the political situation was critical. Since the overthrow of the Thomas J. Pendergast machine, Kansas City had been governed by the non-partisan Citizens Association. Bartle had been one of the founders in 1934 and for this impudence he had been punished by the Pendergast regime; his property tax had been quadrupled. The citizenry ousted the machine in 1940 and installed a city-manager government which has since become a national model. But the passage of time robs political reforms of their impetus. By January 1955, the Democrats, who can command a 20,000 plurality if they are united, appeared ready to reassert their power. Leaders of the Citizens Association were panicked. They asked one another: 'Who could translate the impersonal efficiency of city-manager government into dynamic human terms?' The committee of 200 which makes policy for the Citizens Association had an obvious answer — H. Roe Bartle, the portly Boy Scout. Since he was a Democrat, he could split the opposition. Thousands of former Boy Scouts, now voters, loved Bartle and called him 'Chief.' He was a Presbyterian elder who said grace before meals even in public restaurants, a trustee of the Catholic Youth Organization and a national-executive-board member of the Conference of Christians and Jews. He belonged to 57 organizations and clubs and was praised by labor leaders, some of whom were Scoutmasters. He was a combat veteran of World War I. Possessed of an adhesive memory, Bartle knew thousands of citizens by name, and had done sentimental favors for hundreds of them. He was loudly on the record in favor of every virtue known to man, against sin of every description. He could attract the electorate with his magnetic tongue. He was an organizer without peer in the city. For some reason not clearly understood, he was the choice of business and industry. As a clincher, it was pointed out that everybody loves a fat man. He couldn't miss."

The only problem was that Bartle was not convinced that he wanted to run for election as mayor. He continued to reject the overture from the

Citizens Association leaders. They took the unusual step of sending a delegation of 47 leading Kansas Citians to call on him to urge him to run. They were men who had achieved the Eagle Award, the highest rank in Scouting, under Bartle. Clinton W. Kanaga, a leading Kansas City insurance broker, was the spokesman for the group. He handed Bartle a copy of the Boy Scout manual with a section of the citizenship merit badge requirements underlined in red reading: "Adult citizens have not only the right but the duty to take part in the elections... The participating citizen volunteers for office if he believes himself capable... even at the sacrifice of his own time and pleasure." Kenaga put the clincher on the argument when he looked Bartle straight in the eye and said: "How can you ever pin a citizenship badge on any Scout if you refuse to do your own duty?" By then tears were streaming down Bartle's face. He expressed his gratitude to the men for coming to him with their message. He told them he would let them know of his decision within a short time. Only a short time before the men arrived, Roy Roberts, publisher of The Kansas City Star and a rotund stalwart like Bartle, had called Bartle and told him: "You've got to go. It's up to you to pull us through. And if you take it, I'll promise you The Star will never tell you what to do." Bartle was to say later: "Despite all of the rumors, neither Roy nor The Kansas City Star told me what to do. However, I asked The Star to support me on some things and they never let me down." After the call from Roberts and the departure of the Scouts, Bartle spent a lonely hour in meditation on what to do. He emerged to tell the Citizens Association he would run for mayor.

After Bartle decided to accept the invitation of the Citizens Association, Cohen, Roberts, and the others, the campaign made it apparent that all the pluses The Saturday Evening Post had listed subsequently as to why he would make a good candidate turned out to be true. His opponent with whom the old remnants of the Pendergast machine hoped to sweep back into offices at City Hall was another popular civic leader, Berl Berry, the top Ford Motor Co. dealer in the area who had made over four million dollars in 10 years since the end of World War II. Although they did not become as apparent as they were subsequently to become, some difficulties were encountered by the Citizens Association in trying to deal with Bartle as its candidate for mayor. As The Saturday Evening Post said in that 1956 article, "He was a difficult candidate. He refused to make any political deals or promises. 'I will take my honor, integrity and ability to City Hall and nothing else,' he reiterated at every speech. He would not malign his opponent, a motor car dealer named Berl Berry. Asked by the Citizens Association publicity men for some disparaging comment about Berry, Bartle produced this, 'Any man who would take unto himself and adopt four homeless orphans and endow them all with all the rights and privileges of a Godly home can't be such a bad fellow.' Told that such a statement was inadequate, Bartle tried again. 'Anybody,' he said, 'who has made four million dollars since 1945 without being indicted for income tax evasion is an extraordinarily honest man.' " The Post was right about how good a candidate Bartle would be, however, despite what some might consider shortcomings. He swept the Citizens Association back into office for another four years, swamping Berry with 56,958 votes for Bartle compared to only 28,474 for the old machine Democratic party candidate. In addition, the Citizens Association elected all its candidates for city council except the one spot help by the North End candidate. Reluctant or not at first, Bartle was now the mayor of Kansas City for four years.

Kansas City was on a roll already when Bartle was sworn in as mayor on April 11, 1955. The city was all agog over the arrival of major league baseball with the completion of the revamping of the old Muehlebach Field into a double-deck Municipal Stadium at 22nd and Brooklyn and the transfer of the old Philadelphia Athletics under Connie Mack to the new Kansas City Athletics. On the very day Bartle became Mayor Bartle, the A's and the Detroit Tigers were arriving in town for the major league opener the next day on April 12, 1955. Mayor Bartle was on hand for the opener when Harry S. Truman, having only just arrived home from the presidency in January 1953 threw out the symbolic first pitch before 32,884 screaming fans in the largest attendance at a sports event in Kansas City history up to that time. The pace never slackened for Mayor Bartle from that point on as he appointed two blue-ribbon commissions of top business leaders, one to study and make recommendations on overhauling the archaic city tax system and a second to work to attract new industries. He led an effort to create a bi-state authority for approval by Congress with an ability to issue bonds for badly needed sewer improvements and treatment facilities, parkways and boulevards, water treatments and distribution facilities and other capital improvements on a metropolitan-wide basis across state lines. With the help of Harry Darby, a Kansas City industrialist who lived in Kansas, civic leaders were able to get the bi-state compact through the Kansas Legislature where it was deemed the backers would have the greatest difficulty in selling it. Once through Kansas, the compact was pushed in the Missouri General Assembly by Bartle and other civic leaders. Clay County authorities, still smarting over annexation of large chunks of its territory by the city, joined Platte County leaders in putting together an amalgamation of rural legislators that blocked the plan in Missouri. One wonders how much different the growth of the bi-state metropolitan area would have been if the bi-state authority operated by members of both sides of the state line would have been created.

While Mayor Bartle was appointing the two special commissions and shepherding the far-seeing bi-state authority plan, Bartle was also trying to get Kansas Citians interested in improving their own city. As the 1956 article in The Saturday Evening Post said of his first seven months in office: "He has approached humble citizens on the street for their views on government, had cheered the baseball team and had visited every fire station, police precinct and social agency in town. In the evenings, he had met with two score neighborhood associations which had civic grievances. He distributed 122 keys to the city to visiting celebrities. His office had been open until 1 a.m. almost daily to all who wished to see him or telephone him." As he said in a speech to the Kansas City Advertising & Sales Executives Club to which Cohen belonged, his theme as mayor was: "It will take more than the Athletics to make Kansas City a big league city. We must become big league in every aspect of life and living... Our job is to sell the efficient, businesslike, low-tax, forward striving honesty of Kansas City to manufacturers all over the world, and at the same time make our town honest and pure, vitalized by a religious life in which the spirits of men are rekindled... We have thrown aside the swaddling clothes of civic infancy for the full mantle of manhood." In his first four-year term, Bartle was also able to preside over the construction of the famed Sixth Street Trafficway through the downtown municipal area as a part of the Interstate highway system undertaken by President Eisenhower and the construction of the famed Municipal Garage to provide badly needed parking for the Municipal Auditorium in the square-block area bounded by Twelfth, Thirteenth, Central and

Wyandotte Streets. What was to be the Achilles heel of his first four years as mayor for Bartle was to be the deterioration of his relations with the city manager, Cookingham, who had been city manager under the reform movement for 15 years when Bartle took office in 1955. Both strong-willed men, Bartle and Cookingham never had the working relationship the city manager had had with Mayors Gage and Kemp.

9

Here Comes Lamar Hunt

n his first term, Mayor Bartle made one of his smartest moves during his first term in office. He appointed his hard-working and longtime friend, Jerry Cohen, as a member of the Kansas City Board of Parks and Recreation. For the next seven years, until Bartle left office following the 1963 elections, Cohen gave his time and energy to making major improvements to the already renown Kansas City park system, including the operations of Starlight Theater and the Swope Park Zoo, and to help Bartle get through some rough spots during the remainder of his eight years in office. Cohen approached his assignment with the park board in the same way he approached the task of making his business so highly successful. Like everything else to which he was assigned through the years, Cohen vowed to leave the parks better than they were when he first came on board. As a member of the park board, Cohen showed his usual uncanny ability to recognize the members of the real power structure in the city and to use his influence to serve their needs when doing so was in the best interests of the city. When he left the park board in 1963 when Bartle was no longer mayor, Cohen could take pride in many of his accomplishments, including expansion of the zoo through construction projects and the acquisition of new wild animals; construction and dedication of two of the city's most spectacular fountains; actions to ensure the Kansas City Chiefs of the American Football Conference accepted the invitation to move here from Dallas, and the rededication of the Liberty Memorial on the 40th anniversary of the original groundbreaking ceremonies with Harry S. Truman and Dwight D. Eisenhower taking part in the celebration. As a park board member, Cohen also used his influence to get the first private support group established for the Swope Park Zoo, the Friends of the Zoo, an organization Cohen would continue to support strongly throughout the rest of his life. As a charter member of the Starlight Theater Association since its establishment in 1951, Cohen did not find it difficult to support whatever improvements were necessary in the physical plant of the outdoor summer theater during his seven years on the park board.

Of all the contributions Cohen made as a park board member, however, the one that would have the most far-reaching consequence for his beloved Kansas City was in helping Mayor Bartle clear legal hurdles to use city owned park land on East Sixty-third Street, adjacent to Swope Park, to construct office and training facilities together with a full practice field that finally persuaded Lamar Hunt to move his Dallas Texans to become the Kansas City Chiefs football club, opening here in the 1963 season. Make no mistake about it, Bartle more than anything else got the Chiefs to move here and at the same time focus the attention of Hunt, the millionaire son of the Texas billionaire, H. L. Hunt, founder of Hunt foods and oil magnate, on the Kansas City metropolitan area. As Joe McGuff, the sports editor of The Kansas City Star, wrote in a column some years later: "H. Roe Bartle will be remembered for many things, among them his philanthropy, his Scout work, his dramatic oratorial style and his long love affair with Kansas City. His interests were as expansive as his girth and his personality, spreading into every aspect of community activity. Bartle was a confirmed sports fan and of all his accomplishments perhaps none brought him more enjoyment than the role he played in bringing the Chiefs to Kansas City. Bartle did a remarkable selling job on Lamar Hunt and had it not been for his interest and his persuasiveness Hunt unquestionably would have taken his team elsewhere."

Mayor Bartle first heard of the fact that Hunt was interested in moving his team out of Dallas when Bartle was in Atlanta on a speaking engagement. Hunt was considering Atlanta as a possible location, in the strictest secrecy, but Bartle learned of his plan anyway. He called Hunt in Dallas and Hunt agreed to meet with him there. The meeting went well in Dallas and Bartle invited Hunt to come to Kansas City to look over the facilities at the Municipal Stadium. Hunt balked at coming to Kansas City, however, for fear that secrecy of the talks would be penetrated and he was not yet ready publicly to cut his ties with Dallas. Mayor Bartle persuaded him, however, with a James-Bond-like secrecy scenario. Hunt bought a coach airline ticket to Kansas City under an assumed name and checked in at the old Muehlebach under the same assumed name.

As McGuff described the cloak-and-dagger operation in his column in The Star: "A short time later, Hunt left the hotel through the 12th Street exit. A blue limousine pulled up. In the back seat was a big man smoking a cigar. Hunt entered the limousine and was taken directly to 22nd and Brooklyn. At this point only Bartle and his chauffeur, Carroll Dean Lassiter, were aware of Hunt's presence in Kansas City. Bartle and Hunt toured Municipal Stadium. When Bartle felt compelled to introduce Hunt to anyone he reverted to what he called an old Southern custom and referred to him by his first name, introducing Hunt as "Mr. Lamar." Cohen, who as a member of the Kansas City Parks and Recreation Board, played a major role in getting the Swope Park location for the Chiefs. As Cohen himself recalls the events: "One day, Roe called me and asked me to meet him at the Cask Room of the Hotel Muehlebach for lunch. I went to the luncheon at the Muehlebach and Roe introduced me to two men he identified only as 'Mr. Lamar' and 'Mr. Jack.' I said: 'Roe, I'm a big boy! Who are these people?' He told me one was Lamar Hunt, the owner of the Dallas Texans football team in the American Football League. Roe went on to say: 'They have two pro football franchises in Dallas and Mr. Hunt wants to move his. I want him to move it to Kansas City. He has a lot of money and I want him to invest some of it in Kansas City.' I said: 'Fine, Roe, but why am I here?' Roe said: 'I appointed you on the park board and I have never asked you to do anything for me. Now I am ordering you to go back to the park board and get the other two members to join you in building an office and a practice field for this new football team for Kansas City.' I said: 'Yes, sir, Roe!' At the next park board meeting, we voted to carry out Roe's wishes to build the facilities for the team in Swope Park.

"Two weeks later, I met Jack Steadman at Swope Park and he showed me where he would like to be in the park on East Sixty-third Street. When

I saw where it was, I told Jack we couldn't do it there because if we were to build commercial buildings on Swope Park property the land would revert back to the Swope heirs under the terms of the Swope will. I then showed Jack some land about two blocks east on Sixty-third Street which we had purchased from Mrs. James A. Reed — Nelly Don — and which was not under the will provisions. He said that would be fine and we spent about $100,000 to build the facilities. Right off the bat, the city got some of the Hunt money. We had a $43 million bond issue to build both Arrowhead and Royals Stadiums but it didn't look like it was going to be enough. Roe got Lamar Hunt to put up an additional $10 million for luxury suites to be leased at Arrowhead. When Hunt agreed, Roe got Ewing Kauffman, the new Royals owner, to do the same thing for the baseball field. Bartle was right about getting Hunt to invest in Kansas City. After he brought the Chiefs here he built Worlds of Fun, Oceans of Fun and an underground warehouse facility that is one of the largest in the world."

The whole operation with Hunt continued to be conducted in the utmost secrecy. Reynolds D. (Pete) Rodgers, an assistant to Bartle at City Hall, acted as the intermediary in the negotiations. Mail from Hunt about the proposal was addressed to Reynolds at his home address, as Reynolds Rodgers, U.S. Army Reserve. Mail from Bartle to Hunt in connection with the talks was taken from City Hall and mailed elsewhere. Finally, on February 9, 1963, Hunt was ready to announce that the Dallas Texans were moving to Kansas City to open the 1963 season at Municipal Stadium. As Hunt was to say later: "I was impressed with Mayor Bartle. He spoke highly of Kansas City and I felt he believed what he said even though he said it in a flashy way. We were looking for a home where we would be welcome and he just made me feel we could do well in Kansas City." When it came time for Hunt to name the Kansas City football team he chose the name "Chiefs" out of deference to Bartle, who was known to hundreds of area Boy Scouts as "Chief." McGuff quoted Steadman in one of his columns as saying about the team name: "When we had our name-the-team contest we had a lot of entries and one that turned up frequently was Chiefs. Roe was known as 'The Chief' and finally I told Lamar, 'There's just no other name we can select.' " In that same column McGuff also quoted Steadman as saying that the action Bartle took in getting Cohen and the park board to approve dedicating park land for use for office and training facilities for the Chiefs was also a factor: "Bartle was totally instrumental in the decision to move here. He wanted the team very badly. He said it could be accomplished and he set about accomplishing it. Without his influence we never could have put things together. He worked out so many problems for us. For example, when we were trying to locate our practice field in Swope Park there was some question that this might void the Swope will. He remembered that the city had purchased additional property in Swope Park. We found out where it was and that's the reason we selected the location we did for our office and practice field."

How much the work by Bartle and Cohen to lure Lamar Hunt to Kansas City would mean to the metropolitan area would be obvious to all concerned as the years unfolded following the 1963 debut of the Kansas City Chiefs. In three years after the debut, the Chiefs won the American Football League championship in December 1966, by defeating the Buffalo Bills 31 to 7 in Buffalo under Len Dawson as quarterback and Hank Stram as coach. The league championship really focused the national television spotlight on Kansas City because it also gave the Chiefs the right to compete against the champions of the National Football League, the Green Bay Packers, under the immortal Vince Lombardi, on January 15, 1967, in the first-ever professional football Superbowl. Hunt and his fellow AFL owners had finally been able to negotiate an agreement with its longtime rival league for the postseason championship game, a bonanza of wealth for all the football owners with the lucrative television contracts for the event. The fact that the Chiefs lost the first Superbowl 35 to 10 to the invincible Lombardi team of the time failed to dim the luster of the fact the Kansas City Chiefs had been in the first-ever postseason football championship.

Within three years, however, Stram, Dawson and the other Chiefs were able to redeem themselves on behalf of Hunt and Kansas City for the first Superbowl game. On January 12, 1970, The Kansas City Times, the now-defunct morning edition of The Star, was able to carry an 8-column banner headline of one-and-half-inch black boldface type declaring "Chiefs Champs of the World" with another 8-column headline underneath in slightly smaller type reading "Sing 'We're No. 1' in Celebrations." The Chiefs had defeated the Minnesota Vikings 23 to 7 before millions of televiewers in Superbowl IV. In addition to the Chiefs,

Hunt contributed millions of dollars more in development through the years. First he built Worlds of Fun, a sprawling, multi-acre theme park of exotic rides and shows that annually draws millions of visitors throughout the Midwest. Then came the development of an international trade zone featuring the world's largest developed underground storage facilities at controlled temperatures and humidity for perishable goods and equipment under the supervision of Hunt Midwest Enterprises, Inc. Another theme park was opened adjacent to Worlds of Fun with acres of water slides, streams, beaches and a giant pool with sandy beach featuring artificially made ocean waves and known as Oceans of Fun, which also drew thousands of visitors. Bartle and Cohen had seen their willingness to take a gamble with Hunt initially pay off handsomely in development, jobs and millions of dollars in revenue.

Another of the major developments by the Kansas City park board under the leadership of Cohen was the construction of the St. Martin of Tours statuary fountain designed and constructed by the noted Swedish artist, Carl Milles, and donated to the memory of William Volker, noted Kansas City philanthropist who left millions of dollars to Kansas City civic beneficiaries through his will. The famous fountain which was dedicated in 1958, was a major work by Milles who finished the main sculpture figures before he died in 1955 with only a few minor details left to be completed in connection with the installation of the operating fountain by his assistant, Berthold Schiwetz, who had worked with him from the beginning. St. Martin of Tours was a patron saint of France who had been a tribune in the Roman army who was converted to Christianity while he was quartered with his Roman legion in Amiens, France. According to the legend, St. Martin was passing through the gate of Amiens one night in 332 A.D. when he encountered a beggar shivering in the cold. According to the legend, St. Martin drew his sword, clashed his cloak in half and gave half to the beggar to protect him from the cold. That night Jesus appeared in his dreams wearing the cloak given to the beggar. The noted Swedish sculptor said St. Martin was an appropriate figure to memorialize Volker since both had "profound respect for the dignity of every man."

The Milles statuary in the fountain is larger than life measuring 28 feet in height, 200 feet long and 60 feet wide, featuring St. Martin on horseback rending the cape in half with his sword above a figure of the beggar below. An angel playing a flute watches from above; there is also a startled fawn and a seated angel who is wearing a wristwatch. When asked about the angel with the wristwatch, Milles was quoted saying: "What I try to do is combine the serious with a touch of humor. This forms a bridge between the people and the artist." In connection with the placing of the fountain, the park board under Cohen had undertaken the construction of a sweeping landscaped mall leading from the famed Midwest Research Institute facing Volker Boulevard on one side to the magnificent William Rockhill Nelson Gallery of Art on the other. To accomplish this, the board had to condemn and purchase a series of houses built by Nelson, after whom the gallery was named, creating some opposition. In creating the mall, Cohen and the board were following the suggestion of Dr. Charles Kimball, president of Midwest Research who was the son-in-law of the late Frank Theis, who had served as president of the park board before he died shortly after Bartle had appointed Cohen to the board. By the time the Volker fountain was dedicated in 1958, the new park in which it was located had been completed and was named Frank Theis Park. The park created the sweeping mall Kimball had envisioned.

Another of the magnificent fountains created while Cohen was serving on the park board was the J.C. Nichols Fountain located on park land on the north side of Forty-seventh Street between J.C. Nichols Parkway and Main Street. As one publication said: "After these two fountains were installed, interest in fountains gained momentum." Nichols, the developer of the famed Country Club Plaza, had been a principal force in developing statuary and fountains on the Plaza and through the adjacent residential areas, including his Meyer Circle seahorse fountain at Ward Parkway and Meyer Boulevard, so it was fitting that his principal Kansas City memorial be a fountain. The fountain consists of four larger-than-life Indian figures on horseback representing the major waterways of the United States. The figures were originally created in bronze by a noted French sculptor, Henry L. Greber, in 1910 for the Long Island estate of Clarence Mackey, who was president of Postal Telegraph at the time. In 1952, Miller Nichols obtained the statuary pieces through the efforts of a friend, Mitchell Samuels, president of French and Company in New York. Herman Frederick Simon, a Kansas City sculptor who did the bronze doors of the City Hall and of the Jackson County Courthouse, was employed to provide the missing parts of the fountain as designed by Edwin Tanner, Kansas City architect. The park board agreed to put up $20,000 of the fountain cost with an additional $125,000 coming from private donations, including gifts from Kansas City school children. The fountains are located with the statuary in an 80-foot circular pool. Lawrence Sickman, director of the Nelson gallery, said of the fountain dedicated in May 1960 while Cohen was serving on the park board: "The horse has been a key figure in mankind's eternal struggle as civilization forges ahead. Here, the sculptor has given a dramatic interpretation of the terrible fear, the wild ferocity and the tremendous action of the powerful stallion as it carries its rider to the attack. A study in sheer realism. Kansas Citians are most fortunate to have this beautiful memorial to one who himself gave so much beauty to our city, Mr. J.C. Nichols."

With the burst of major fountain construction while Cohen was on the park board, James M. Kemper, Sr., president of Commerce Bank, decided to add a major new fountain to the downtown area when he began construction of the new 29-story Commerce Tower building at 911 Main Street. He conceived the fountain in tribute to his son, the late David Woods Kemper, who was killed in World War II, and commissioned a New York sculptor, Wheeler Williams, to create a fountain representing the spirit of the Missouri River. The park board agreed to a site on Main Street between Eighth and Ninth Streets. A statue of a beautiful bronze goddess, the Muse of the Missouri, was created by Williams as the center piece of the fountain. The goddess is holding a net from which bronze fish are spilling. Two hundred bursts of water form pools in three basins at the foot of the fountain, which was dedicated in ceremonies conducted by the park board in 1963.

Another of the high points of the tenure of Cohen on the park board while Frank Theis was still president was the ceremonies in connection with the rededication of the Liberty Memorial November 10-12, 1961, on the 40th anniversary of the groundbreaking ceremonies for the famed monument to veterans of World War I during the third annual national convention of the American Legion on November 1, 1921. Calvin Coolidge had come as vicepresident for the groundbreaking ceremonies for the magnificent monument and then had returned four years later as president to formally dedicate the artistic structure. At the 1921 groundbreaking ceremonies, there had been a historic meeting of the heroes of the victorious Allied forces with the attendance of Gen. John J. Pershing, commander of American forces in Europe; Marshal Ferdinand Foch of France, General Issimo of the Allied forces; Admiral Lord Beatty of Great Britain; Gen. Armand Diaz of Italy, and Lt. Gen. Baron Jacques of Belgium.

It was fitting that the two heroes of World War II, Dwight D. Eisenhower and Harry S. Truman, two former presidents of the United States as well, would return for the rededication ceremonies in 1961 since both came from this area. Eisenhower, who had been commander of the Allied forces in Europe in World War II as well as the 34th president of the United States, was the principal speaker on November 10 while Truman, the man from Independence who had presided as the 33rd U.S. President over the successful conclusion of World War II, was the principal speaker on November 11, Veterans Day. There was a huge parade through downtown streets to the Liberty Memorial as well on November 11 with Truman riding in the same open Locomobile in which General Pershing had ridden at the 1921 groundbreaking and which was still in operating condition. The 1961 event also featured the largest foreign gathering in the United States with the exception of Washington, New York and San Francisco in 1945 when the charter of the United Nations was signed. Ambassadors and representatives of 64 nations were flown here from Washington aboard a chartered jet to take part in the three days of ceremonies. Joyce C. Hall, chairman and founder of Hallmark Cards who had helped Eisenhower found an international relations group known as People-to People, which still has its world headquarters in Kansas City, was named general chairman of the celebration and worked with a committee that included Mayor Bartle, Theis, William N. Deramus, Armand Glenn, James A. Hazlett, Lem T. Jones, Morton T. Jones, James M. Kemper, Jr., Dr. Charles N. Kimball, Arthur Mag, Louis B. McGee, Judge Albert A. Ridge, Charles S. Stevenson, the Rev. Maurice Van Ackeren, Dr. W. Clarke Wescoe and A. B. Weyer. Gov. John Anderson, Jr., of Kansas and Gov. John M. Dalton of Missouri were honorary co-chairmen. The general tone of the 1961 celebration was set by Hall in a statement on the event: "Forty years ago this architectural masterpiece was erected by the citizens of this community as a tribute to those who gave their lives in World War I, the 'war to end all wars.' So that their cause will not have been in vain, the people of the world must work together to build mutual respect and understanding. It will only be after hatreds, fears and prejudices are destroyed and true understanding takes their place that the struggle to end all wars will succeed. It is our earnest desire that this memorial, located in the heart of America, will become a rallying point for the peoples of the world who would work together to achieve the understanding so urgently needed in the world today."

As a part of the ceremonies, Charles Bacon, a noted Kansas Citian, who had just been elected as the new national commander of the American Legion, was honored the evening of Nov. 11, 1961, at the Hotel Muehlebach at which a famed American Navy officer, Adm. Arleigh Burke, was the speaker. In many ways, the three-day ceremonies were one of the few bright spots of the time for Mayor Bartle for who troubles were deepening at City Hall. For Cohen, whose park board had the responsibility for maintaining the 173 acres of park land which surround the Liberty Memorial and contributing to the upkeep of the monument, the ceremonies were one more quiet way he was serving his beloved city.

10

Pendergast Ghost Arises

As the 1959 election rolled around, the Citizens Association, the reform movement that had ousted the Tom Pendergast Democratic machine in 1940, had been in power for nearly 20 years. More importantly, L. P. Cookingham had been the outstanding city manager since the reform movement had taken over and had a brook-no-nonsense approach to the operations of city government, allowing for no cronyism in city contractors or favoritism in city employment. The remnants of the Democratic party machine still remembered the good old days when they could get patronage jobs for friends and relatives and you could get lucrative contracts if you knew the right people. Jerry Cohen's good friend, Mayor Bartle, had proved a popular and hard-working mayor who was bound to be renominated in 1959 as the Citizens Association candidate. There were signs of trouble on the horizon, however. For the first 15 years of the reform movement, the city had been able to finance its operations through the elimination of graft and corruption, annexing additional territory to broaden the tax base and taking advantage of the postwar economic boom. When Bartle became mayor in 1955, however, the rapidly-expanding city was faced with a need for additional tax revenues to meet the increased demands for sewers, water distribution and traffic congestion of a growing city. Having not had a tax increase in 15 years, the reform council under Mayor Bartle and

Cookingham had decided to ask voters to approve an earnings tax to be collected by employers on all earnings of employees. The voters, however, voted overwhelmingly to reject the earnings tax proposal by a four-to-one majority. The city then turned to a series of what were termed nuisance taxes voted by the council to provide needed revenues. Even so, the city needed more taxes to meet the growing demand for revenue. As Cookingham himself said: "We deferred maintenance on all our facilities and reduced programs to the very minimum consistent with health and safety standards. We cut back on city planning. We quit installing streetlights and accumulated a backlog of work that will take years to overcome."

The Citizens Association, the city and Cookingham might have survived all that in the 1959 elections if one of the Citizens Association members of the city council under Bartle over the previous four years, Charles C. Shafer, Jr., had remained loyal. For whatever reason, Shafer called a press conference in January 1959 to denounce the Citizens Association as kingmakers and demand the resignation of Cookingham as city manager. Shafer had apparently heard that some of the leaders of the Citizens Association had been less than enchanted with Shafer as a councilman during his first four years in office under Bartle, during which one observer put it, he "had displayed erratic tendencies, which had forced several of his colleagues in the association to call his qualifications for continuation in office into serious question." The question of whether the reform group would have gone ahead and endorsed him for a second term in the final analysis will never be known for the press conference Shafer held only enhanced these allegations that he would not be on the team in 1959. On March 31, 1959, the board of governors of the Citizens Association met to consider its slate of candidates for the upcoming election. Shafer had the gall to ask for the endorsement of the reform movement but he had already sunk his ship with the earlier blast and the board voted overwhelmingly, 106 to 3, to reject him and endorsed another candidate for his seat, Clem Fairchild, another civic leader. Shafer immediately announced his candidacy for reelection as an independent candidate and began blasting Cookingham and demanding his resignation, the editorial writers of The Kansas City Star, the Citizens Association and an unidentified group of civic leader whom he called "kingmakers."

Two political bosses who still controlled large areas of Democratic workers, Alex Presta, a leader of the remnant of the old Italian North End, and Henry McKissick, a ward Democratic leader, saw an opportunity to use the unrest to seek to regain City Hall. They put together a shrewd political maneuver by forming a Democratic coalition that fielded a slate of five candidates, including Shafer, in council races against those endorsed by the Citizens Association but discreetly left Mayor Bartle and three other council candidates from the Citizens group unchallenged. What followed was the most brutal and jarring city political race since the 1940 election when the reform movement finally wrested control from the Pendergast machine, threw out the spoils system and brought in Cookingham as city manager. Going into the 1959 elections, the Citizens Association knew it had the political fight of its life and mounted an aggressive campaign to make Kansas City voters aware of what was at stake. Cohen worked hard in support of the reform efforts and his friend, Mayor Bartle. His rabbi, the veteran Rabbi Mayerberg, who had been a spark in the 1940 success, came out swinging and in one speech reminded Kansas Citians what the city had been like under the Pendergast political machine recalling how "through machine guns and fear he forced people to follow him. John Lazia, a mobster, made a deal with Pendergast... to control the police department." John B. Gage and William Kemp, the first two reform mayors, warned the voters that apathy could lose the city all strides of progress it had made since 1940. The Kansas City Star blasted away through its columns against the efforts to return Democratic machine control even though Roy Roberts, the publisher, was ill and the newspaper was still suffering in the eyes of the public from its federal anti-trust prosecution and conviction. Its principal thrust was the danger of the return of mafia influence if the Citizens Association was defeated. In one editorial just before the election, it pinpointed this by saying one of the new faction leaders, Presta, was "a boss who can't vote because he never received the necessary pardon for two federal prison sentences. The other is led by Henry McKissick, former partner of the late Charles Binaggio, who was front man for the political underworld. Binaggio died before the gunfire in 1950 but his underworld is very much alive in factional politics today. At best, the factions depend for their existence on spoils politics which is now largely confined to the Jackson County courthouse. Between these two—the Citizens Association and the factions — there can be no compromise. They are the opposites of city government. Such is the deep issue of this election."

On election day in April 1959, a series of events were to effect the outcome. The Democratic coalition leaders were able to turn out six per-cent more of their ranks than they had done four years earlier in the last city election. The Citizens Association turnout dropped by one percent. A severe thunderstorm with high winds and torrential rains struck the city at 6 p.m. and continued almost unabated until the closing of the polls at 7 p.m., the time when many Kansas Citians and Citizens Asso-ciation supporters normally would have voted. When the votes had been tallied, the worst fears of the reform movement had been realized. All five races in which the machine remnants had filed challenges were swept by the Democrats, giving them control for the first time since 1940. On election night, a crowing Shafer in a photograph with the other four anti-reform candidate winners was demanding the immediate resignation of Cookingham. After a secret meeting of the new council members, Tom Gavin, a friend of Harry Truman and one of the holdover council mem-bers who were endorsed by the Citizens and the new Democratic coali-tion, told Cookingham the new majority would not fire the city manager because of the respect he had had from the public and his reputation but, he added, "They'll make it so rough on you they'll make you want to resign." As Time Magazine said of the election in its edition of April 13, 1959: "The real enemy was L. Perry Cookingham… City Manager Cookingham cleaned up the town, got going on new roads, schools, sew-ers, etc., created an environment that brought new industry and new, if less spectacular, vitality to the city. In so doing, Cookingham also made a nationwide name for himself, three men who had served under him went out to become city managers in other cities… With Shafer leading the coalition bush-beating, the Citizens Association lost five of its eight mem-bers on the council, and the city was assured of a new kind of rule. Also assured: the eventual resignation of City Manager L. P. Cookingham, the man who gave Kansas City that clean look."

On April 16, 1959, Cookingham announced his resignation, effec-tive June 30, the 20th anniversary of his appointment in 1940, before a crowd of civic leaders that came to show support for him, including U.S. Senator Stuart Symington. Later that same day, Cookingham accepted an offer to become city manager of Ft. Worth. As Bill Gilbert, a former member of the staff of the Washington Post, wrote of Cookingham: "He had been manager longer than any other manager of any other major American city, a remarkable achievement made even more astounding by the condition of the city at the time of his arrival." Consternation was everywhere in the city after the city election. As Al Mauro, friend of Cohen and an aide to Cookingham at City Hall at the time, said: "I think the most traumatic part was after the elections came in. I don't think anybody really expected there would be that big a change. I think that most people thought there would be some shifts but not a total change. When that happened there was really a shock for everyone." One of the big fears was that the Democrats would try to make the Citizens Association look bad in retaliation for their defeat 20 years before that. The result was that while Cookingham was still in office he an Mauro went through all the city files. As Mauro recalled: "We made sure that we made copies of all the files that would be relevant in case someone came in with the new administration and tried to change the facts. We spent a lot of time going through the files, picking out policy issues and matters where you could interpret the facts any way you wished if you didn't have the historical documents to contradict any allegation." There were all kinds of testimonial luncheons and dinners given for Cookingham. Henry Talge, a Jewish businessman who became known for his annual birthday luncheons for Truman, held one such luncheon for Cookingham and some 50 other business leaders at the Hotel Muehlebach to honor Cookingham. All of them signed a Bible which was presented to Cookingham by Rabbi Mayerberg, another of the city manager's strongest supporters. Rabbi Mayerberg told Cookingham then: "You have given to the people you work with a sense of honor, of pride and of courage. You have put us on the way. We will not forget."

One of the principal disasters for Kansas City growing out of the victory of the Democratic factions in 1959, of course, was the loss of Cookingham but beyond that was the division between the Citizens Association holdover members of the council, including Bartle, and the old machine remnant council member majority which made it impossible to hire a permanent replacement for Cookingham as city manager for the next four years. When Cookingham left office on June 30, 1959, Reed McKinley, who had been director of public works under Cookingham, was named acting city manager and Cookingham was hopeful that McKinley would be able to continue the policies that had been in effect from the time the reform movement had ousted the Pendergast machine in 1940. Such was not to be the case however. As Mauro, the aide to Cookingham, said later: "It soon became clear the McKinley was going to do what the leadership of the council told him to do. He didn't really have any choice. It was a great disappointment to me." McKinley had the acting position less than a year before he had all the council wrangling he could stand and resigned in mid-1960.

The divided council then decided on a man who had been a longtime friend of Cohen and a lawyer, Ben F. Powers, who had been a member of the Citizens Association and who had served as assistant city counsellor and city counsellor from the time the reform movement took over in 1940. Powers also had the distinction of serving for a time in the city government from 1915 through 1923 when the Pendergast machine was just beginning to gain ground. He lasted only a matter of weeks when he found there was no hope of resolving the disputes. The divided council then turned to Harry M. Fleming, a former Jackson County court judge who had been elected to county judge in 1951 and served until 1955, to fill in as city manager. Fleming served from July 1, 1960, until ill health forced him to step down shortly before he died of cancer on August 7, 1961. For the remainder of 1961, the post was filled by three men, Reynolds D. (Pete) Rodgers, aide to Mayor Bartle, who had acted as an intermediary for the mayor in getting the Chiefs here in late 1962; John P. Ryan, and Powers, who had come back for a brief stint. In late 1961, the Democrat majority had decided to hire Robert P. Weatherford, former mayor of Independence and longtime friend of Harry Truman. Weatherford lasted about a year until he gave up in disgust.

By now, civic leaders were in an uproar over the chaos in professional management of the city and with the help of Mayor Bartle forced the city council to appoint a distinguished holdover from the Cookingham era, Rollin F. Agard, city auditor, to serve as acting manager while they searched the nation for a qualified city manager. By now Shafer; his top colleague against the Citizens Association, William C. Royster; Joseph M. Welsh, another Democrat councilman; and Sal A. Capra, young lawyer and ally of Alex Presta who had been elected in the 1959 upset, had failed to produce and were feeling the wrath of The Kansas City Star and civic leaders generally.

During his second four-year term, Mayor Bartle had remained a bright spot for the city, continuing to make speeches; keeping a watchful eye on the Democratic factions and creating his crowning achievement of his eight years in conducting the secret negotiations that convinced Lamar Hunt, the owner of the Dallas Texans American Football League franchise, to move the team here to open the 1963 season. Bartle had a magnetism about him that overcame the image of chaos in his final four years in office as mayor. As one writer said of him: "Large of body and soul, Bartle had a dynamic manner of speech. It reflects, in a rich flow of words, his own dedication to the ideas that have made America great. He has been called 'that fluent speaker for American democracy.' " Bartle had thought for a time after the 1959 upset victory by the Democratic factions that by keeping his word and following his long-practiced concepts of virtue he could bring the factions together in the city but as one observer said, "His message of brotherhood was severely battered by machine politicians." The machine remnants in control were perfectly happy to let Bartle "cut ribbons, spade up earth at dedications, welcome conventions, greet dignitaries, bestow keys to the city — all of which Bartle did with a vigor and a virtuosity, but they would not follow his efforts at compromise for the good of the city."

As The Kansas City Star said later: "It was then that he came face to face with a political fact of life. His tried and true formula of brotherly love and conquering all obstacles was not working. Nor did it in the months ahead. But it must be said that his very presence at City Hall — after he had expressed himself on one major occasion — had the effect of putting a break on the factions. There would have been greater damage to the charter form of government and to the city's image throughout the country if Bartle had not been the occupant of the mayor's chair in that period. It is highly unlikely that any man accomplished much more in that political situation."

By the time the 1963 elections rolled around, the Citizens Association was up in arms about what had been happening at City Hall. The actions by Bartle in trying to work out a compromise in the early months after the machine remnants again took control of City Hall had soured some of the powerful elements of the reform movement, some of whom blamed the mayor for not supporting Cookingham more strongly when the city manager came under attack from Shafer. As Robert J. Saunders, associate dean of administration at the University of Missouri-Kansas

City, said: "Mayor Bartle contributed heavily to Perry's resignation... Perry 'threatened' political leaders because he, too, had a power base. Although built very differently from that of the elected leadership, it was as potent or more so since it was built on demonstrated competence. Bartle, who was an imposing figure but not a leader in the sense of the other two mayors, Gage and Kemp, neither wanted to lead nor let the manager lead. The council had several members of similar persuasion. All of this might have been of little consequence if there had not been issues of serious consequence to be dealt with such as the city's financial base."

Bartle stayed in the race, however, while he tried to get the Citizens group to endorse his 1959 manager, Clinton W. Kanaga, but the reform movement voted instead to endorse Ilus W. Davis, a former city councilman. Cohen remained loyal to Bartle in his first split with the Citizens Association since Bartle had filed for another term when he announced. He has in his files a letterhead prepared for the 1963 campaign with a large picture of Bartle and issued in the name of Bartle Boosters, Inc. Officers listed were Frank B. Jackson, president; Angus McCallum, Rev. John S. Williams, vice presidents; Mrs. George H. Charno, Jr., secretary, and Alex J. Barket, treasurer. Listed as members of the board of governors in addition to Cohen were some 75 prominent Kansas Citians such as Rabbi Mayerberg, George Goldman, Hy Vile, Herman A. Johnson, Frank Spink, Sam Montague, Rollie Hall, Dr. D. M. Nigro, Frank Vandergrift, Sam Eddy, Tony DiPardo, Tudie Patti, Vincent Dasta, Jerome Walsh, Abe Yeddes, Francis J. Tallman, Joseph H. Scanlon and many others. As Cohen said, however: "The Chief called us off. He said he was tired and didn't want to campaign and did not want us to work for him. What could we do but go along?" As Bartle said of the 1963 campaign, "I stayed on the ballot but I asked people who knew me not to vote for me. Take your pick between two fine candidates: Davis and Brookfield, I said. Vote either way but not for Bartle." He was talking about Davis who had served on the city council from 1948 to 1955 for the Citizens Association, and Dutton Brookfield, a young industrialist and Republican who was running for mayor. When the smoke cleared and the ballots were counted in that 1963 election, Kansas City had had enough of faction politics. The Citizens Association had swept City Hall as they had done in 1940, electing Davis as mayor and unseating Royster,

Shafer and all the other renegades. The machine was forever gone.

Bartle was not bitter and left office with his head high. As he said later in an interview: "I gave nothing to the factions and especially nothing to Bill Royster. Alex Presta never asked nor was given anything by me. For two years while I was mayor, Councilman Royster was a thorn in my flesh. Finally, on the day Ilus Davis was inaugurated and I went out of office, Royster followed me down in the elevator and caught up with me, 'For years I've been trying to get you to call me a S.O.B.,' he said, 'and you still haven't.' I told him that I just don't operate that way and I've never turned down a man in an act of friendship. When I left office, I did it with a clear conscience. When a person keeps his honor, he doesn't have to apologize to a soul. And nobody can accuse him of wrongdoing if he has used his best judgment and kept a deep and abiding faith in his community." Bartle continued to belong to the Citizens Association for the rest of his life but he had some suggestions for them. "The biggest mistake the Citizens Association makes is forgetting its candidates after the election. The members work hard to elect a slate of individuals, usually a cross-section from every facet of the community. But then when the election is over, the association lets the office holders sink or swim — offering neither help, suggestions or bodies to help run the city. Personally, I think people who get so excited at election time should continue to have a deep and abiding interest in the corporate city. These same people who work like trojans to elect a mayor never once appeared at a councilmanic session when there were hearings on major issues of vital concern."

With the Citizens Association candidates back in office, Cohen offered his resignation as a member of the parks and recreation board after eight years of service, and Davis accepted it. Both Bartle and Cohen could take pride in the strides that had been made in the parks and recreation area during those years, even under the trauma of the machine faction-dominated years for the last part of the park board tenure of Cohen. Like Bartle, Cohen continued his membership in the Citizens Association for the rest of his life.

COHEN HELPS LAND LAMAR HUNT — *As a member of the Kansas City Parks and Recreation Board appointed by Mayor H. Roe Bartle, Jerry Cohen led Park Department actions to help Bartle bring Lamar Hunt and the Kansas City Chiefs here from Dallas to open the 1963 season. Cohen got the Park Department to approve constructing an office building, gymnasium and practice field for the Chiefs on land which was a part of Swope Park on 63rd Street.*

FRIENDS OF H. ROE BARTLE CELEBRATE — *Longtime friends of H. Roe Bartle got together to celebrate the election of their friend as mayor here under the Citizens Association reform ticket in 1955. In the back row, left to right, are Ira B. McCarty, longtime political writer for The Kansas City Star and The Times; Jerry Cohen; Francis J. Tallman and Clint Kanaga, businessmen who encouraged Bartle, a Scout executive, to run. Seated at the table with Bartle are the Hipsh brothers, Charles and Lou.*

11

A Jewish Santa Claus

f there ever was anything Jerry Cohen could not be accused of being during his life, it was of being a quitter, a person who picked up his marbles and quietly strode away when the game did not go his own way. If anything proved that, it was his reaction after the voters and the Citizens Association had turned their backs on his close friend of years, H. Roe Bartle, in 1963. As he did so often during his life when he suffered setbacks, he kept on swimming harder then ever. Several things had happened during his eight years of service under Bartle as mayor when he served as a member of the board of parks and recreation that kept him loyal to the Citizens Association and his beloved city of Kansas City for 40 years after Bartle left office. One of these was his being asked by Bartle in 1955 to head the annual holiday charity drive known as the Mayor's Christmas Tree Fund; a second was his love of animals which he had learned in the Kansas City public schools and led him to form a support group for the Swope Park Zoo known as Friends of the Zoo in his first year on the park board, and a third was the fact that he was a charter member of the Starlight Theater Association, the support group for the magnificent outdoor summer theater operated as a non-profit group under the auspices of the city since its inception in 1951. Perhaps the most important of these was serving as the chairman of the Mayor's Christmas Tree Fund during the eight years Bartle was mayor.

Nobody knows for sure why the first such holiday effort to help the needy was started, but city records seem to indicate that the first was undertaken in December 1884, when the mayor at the time, Mayor L. J. Talbot, directed that a city Christmas tree be erected and decorated in the old City Market, to serve as a rallying point from which city charities of the time could distribute food and clothing to needy families. The effort seems to have sputtered out after a couple of years and lay dormant through the turn of the century until it was revived in 1908 by the mayor at the time, T. T. Crittenden, Jr. It had continued annually from that time on until Bartle asked Cohen to take on the task in 1955.

Mayor Bartle, who had worked with the children all of his post-college life, mostly in the Kansas City area, did not like the way the holiday effort was being handled. It had developed into a event that was attracting thousands of city youths from kindergarten through high school to the Municipal Auditorium annually on a Saturday during the holiday season. They were treated to a live stage show of music and variety acts and then handed Christmas packages of candy, fruit and toys as they left the auditorium. Over the past several years before Bartle had become mayor, there had been several instances in which a portion of the crowd had become unruly when the time had come to hand out gifts and had stampeded toward the distribution points. Fortunately, no one had been seriously injured but the possibility was there. When Bartle asked Cohen to take over the direction of the event, he told him he wanted to change the format of what was being done. Cohen remembered the mayor telling him: "Jerry, we've got to change the way this thing is being handled. The crowd's too big anymore and we can't control it. We're lucky we've not got somebody badly hurt or even killed when they made a run to those presents." He also wanted to expand the base of who was being helped. He wanted to include the elderly, whole needy families, mental hospital patients and those in jails as well as children. Cohen, who always relished challenges, agreed to work with others to see how the changes could be brought about. One of the first moves was to break the Municipal Auditorium party into smaller, more manageable units. It was decided to hold the parties on neighborhood bases centered on the city community centers. City officials were asked to certify lists of elderly persons and families who were in need to be presented baskets of food and gift certificates. A party of entertainers, music and small gifts was organized for inmates of the Municipal Farm, for patients at the Western Missouri Mental Health

Center and at the Children's Mercy Hospital.

The effort had undergone a thorough reorganization during the eight years Cohen had directed it on a volunteer basis under Bartle. When Ilus W. Davis became mayor in 1963, Cohen offered to step down as chairman of the Mayor's Christmas Tree Fund. Instead of accepting the offer and naming a replacement as he had done on the board of parks and recreation with Cohen, Mayor Davis enthusiastically urged Cohen to continue to head the Mayor's Christmas Tree Fund for the way in which he had led the effort to reorganize the holiday charity effort on a more sound basis. Cohen accepted, being the kind of a good citizen he was, and the result was that he continued to head the effort under each successive mayor, Ike Davis, for eight years; Mayor Charles B. Wheeler, for eight years; Mayor Richard Berkley, for 12 years; and Mayor Emanuel Cleaver II. In the nearly 40 years he has been heading up the annual holiday charity effort for the city, Cohen has raised over $10 million in cash and services and has provided Christmas cheer to more than 1 million needy persons, according to estimates. In 1993, for instance, the records of the Mayor's Christmas Tree Fund showed the effort by Cohen provided food and toys for 752 needy families made up of 2,675 persons not cared for by any other agency; provided $100 gift certificates to 6,645 needy senior citizens, conducted 28 neighborhood children's Christmas parties for over 15,400 underprivileged children; conducted a party and distributed clothing at Children's Mercy Hospital; distributed 3,130 Christmas packages to 29 municipal charity institutions and provided holiday assistance to patients at the Truman Medical Center and the Western Missouri Mental Health Center. In addition, the fund assisted the park department in establishing Santa's Workshop holiday displays for all metropolitan area children from Thanksgiving through New Year's Day at 41st and Gillham Road and Vivion and Norton in Kansas City North.

As the years go by, increasing numbers of Kansas Citians have come to realize how much Cohen has contributed through the years in his effort to make the yuletide holidays a little cheerier for the needy. For instance, the city council of Kansas City said of the effort in a resolution adopted and presented to him by Mayor Berkley on the 25th anniversary of his heading the Mayor's Christmas Tree Fund: "Mr. Jerome Cohen has served his fellow men with distinction and dedication for the past quarter century as an officer of the Mayor's Christmas Tree Association, a benevolent organization which has raised and distributed funds over the past 70 years to provide Christmas cheer in the form of toys, food, clothing, toilet and personal articles, and entertainment to those needy persons whose holiday would otherwise be bleak and dreary, including children, welfare recipients, persons in various public institutions and the ill and elderly in nursing and convalescent homes. His superb leadership and selfless devotion of his time, his unique talents and his boundless energy on behalf of his less fortunate neighbors have over a quarter of a century, touched the lives of succeeding generations of Kansas Citians by spreading holiday cheer among the needy and by assuring contributors that their gifts for the worthy purposes of the association would be faithfully applied in such a manner as to provide the maximum benefits to the ultimate recipients with the minimum of administrative costs."

There were frequent references on a good-humored basis to the fact that the principal mover in the Christmas effort was Jewish. Kansas City, a slick-paper magazine, in a December issue carries a color photograph of an adult and a child looking at the colorful Mayor's Christmas Tree at Crown Center with the headline "Santa's Top Aid is Jewish." The magazine article began: "Jerry Cohen's cherub features might easily qualify him for a role as Santa Claus. That quick smile, unfailing humor and accommodating manner would need only an ermine trimmed suit of red velvet, snowy beard and perhaps the 80 pounds back Cohen shed from his frame by dieting over the last two years. Thus amended, the perennial chairman of the Mayor's Christmas Tree Fund might even pass in person for what he had traditionally embodied in spirit — despite the ironic contrast of his own Jewish convictions." On a recent Christmas, The Kansas City Star carried an eight-column banner across one of its inside pages which read: " 'Jewish Santa' Serves Customers, Those in Need." As James J. Fisher, one of the best columnists in the history of The Star, wrote in the accompanying article after citing figures about how the duplicating equipment business sales were still going strong in the face of a national economy softening at the time: "If the figures are an anomaly, then Cohen is even more so. As chairman of the Christmas fund, he is a Jewish Santa Claus."

Despite some of the good-natured ribbing on the point from his friends, Cohen thinks the Christmas operation he carried out is in line with the terms of his Jewish faith he had practiced all his life. As he said: "It's not really so out of context for me to be active in work devoted to the Christmas holiday. Part of our Jewish religion teaches us to think about others and look out for their welfare. I consider that the fact that this work centers around Christmas to be rather inconsequential." Certainly civic leaders recognized the meaning of his Christmas effort to the community. A friend had sent him a copy of the magazine article with the following written in a bold hand beneath his photograph accompanying the article "Kansas City's #1 'pickpocket' for the less fortunate." Jerry Smith, a heavy supporter of philanthropic efforts in his own right, wrote: "We're all extremely pleased that some long overdue recognition of your continuing efforts have surfaced. These good people didn't dig very deep or they would have had to do a much longer article. You are a very special guy and I'm so glad to have you for my friend." Alex George, a nationally known sports figure and civic leader, wrote: "Congratulations on your well-deserved article in KC magazine. I don't know of another program that brings more joy to people than the Mayor's Christmas Tree Fund. Jerry, I'm awfully proud to call you a dear friend. We have known each other since childhood and any person who brings happiness to young children, as you do, certainly holds a high place in my heart. God bless you for making so many happy." Thomas F. Eagleton, a former Missouri attorney general who was a U.S. senator at the time, wrote: "Dear Santa Jerry: I very much enjoyed the Kansas City magazine article detailing your holiday activities as chairman of the Mayor's Christmas Tree Association. I can well understand the satisfaction you feel from this involvement, and I was so pleased to see you receive the recognition you deserve in connection with your work on behalf of the area's disadvantaged citizens. I send you every good wish for continued success and for a happy holiday season." It was signed simply "Tom."

One of the things that has made Cohen so successful in running the annual holiday fund-raising effort has been a lack of reluctance to ask others to help him in the effort and then seeing that those who do help get the maximum publicity value out of their efforts. He has also learned that people generally are a little more willing to be helpful when they are under the spell of the Christmas glow that gives them the warm, fuzzy feeling. Elements of the U.S. Marine Corps, both active and reserve members, have been active in collecting thousands of toys for needy children at Christmas time. Off-duty firemen lend their efforts in sorting and wrapping gifts for fund recipients. Ararat Shrine Temple, which Jerry serves as a member, provides an annual bowling tournament which has raised thousands of dollars for the effort over the years. The Heart of America Quilters Guild annually has its members work on an artistic quilt which is auctioned at the close of its annual show in September with the funds from the auction going exclusively to the Mayor's Christmas Tree Fund. Perhaps the biggest single boost Cohen got in his efforts came from his recruiting Hallmark Cards and its Crown Center Square to assist the effort. Williamette Industries, an Oregon-based company, selects a giant fir tree from its Oregon timbering areas and brings it to Kansas City by truck to become the focal point of the kickoff for the annual drive when Cohen, in all his glory, directs the ceremonies lighting the tree on the Friday night following Thanksgiving. The tree is taller than either the famed Rockefeller Center tree in New York City or the White House Christmas tree on the lawn in Washington. Following its holiday season run, the tree is cut up into small slices which are used by Hallmark to make an annual Mayor's Christmas Tree ornament which is sold at Crown Center throughout the holiday season with the proceeds going to the annual holiday effort headed by Cohen. The list of those who help changes annually with the exception of these mainstays.

Another benefit coming to Kansas City as a result of the relationship between Bartle and Cohen similar to the Mayor's Christmas Tree Fund was the fact that Cohen was able to bring the 64th annual conference of the American Institute of Park Executives, Inc., to Kansas City. Like everything else he touched during his lifetime, Cohen had made an impact on the national park organization during the years he served as a member of the Kansas City Board of Parks and Recreation after being named by Mayor Bartle as a member of the board in late 1955. Under the tutelage of Frank Vaydik, who was to serve as superintendent of parks for Kansas City, Cohen immediately joined the American Institute of Park Executives. Always a hard-working member of any group he joined, Cohen approached the national chairman of the organization. It was also an opportunity for Cohen and his charming wife, Jeannette, to show off a special project on which they had been working since shortly after Cohen was appointed to the park board by Bartle, one of the finest Japanese gardens in the U.S.

Shortly after being named to the park board in late 1955, the Cohens sold the house they had occupied since early in the 1940s at 6940 Brooklyn Avenue to move into a new address in one of the prestigious areas of Kansas City, a modern brick residence at 6616 Ward Parkway, a residence they continued to use into the 1990s. Cohen and his wife had always been interested in Oriental furnishings and artifacts so it was only natural that they would want to try to create a Japanese garden as the focal point of their new home. Cohen persuaded a leading Kansas City landscape designer, John P. Baumgardt, who was also serving as director of the Loose Park Garden Center, to design the garden which took over four years to build. The distinguished delegates and their spouses who toured the garden and the residence were serving on the board of the American Institute of Park Executives, Inc., under Cohen. They included Andre T. Fontes, chairman of Oakland, California, Board of Park Commissions, vice chairman of the institute; William M. Gosdin, superintendent of grounds and an instructor of Texas Technology College, Lubbock, secretary; and George Martin, Niagara Park Commission at Niagara Falls; Mrs. John E. Crimmins, Minnesota Board of Park Commissioners; the Rev. Charles S. Hubbard, North Carolina Recreation Commission; Elmo W. Curtis, London, Ontario, Commissioner of Parks; John J. Ligda, Gary, Indiana, Park Commission, and Cohen's fellow Kansas City board member, Frank Theis, all members of the national board.

The garden was such a sensation that The Kansas City Star sent one of its top writers, Bill Moore, to write a two-column article describing it. The article also included a two-column photograph showing some of the Japanese garden wonders. The article said in part:

"There are at least 50 varieties of Japanese flora... Dwarf Mungo trees, a Japanese maple which turns bright red in the spring and green in the fall, Japanese weeping cherry trees... In the way of flowering bushes and shrubs there are such items as Bonsai evergreens, Japanese holly, weeping crabs and some with even more unfamiliar names, pachandra, cotoneaster apculata and eunonymus. In the corner of the garden is a Japanese tea house. Wind chimes made out of bamboo, glass, metal and wood are all over the place. A durama wash basin, carved from granite and sculptured with the face of a one-time Japanese god, sits on the side of one pool. It is fitted with a bamboo spout called kakehi. Walls are hung with large copper plaques which the Japanese say denote happiness and joy. Actually, they appear to be outsize replicas of Japanese coins.

"One of the pools is, of course, bridged by a stone arch in traditional Japanese style. Some of the rocks which line the pools weigh hundreds of pounds and required a crew of men and a derrick to place them in. The gates in the bamboo fence are faithful copies from Japanese gardens, decorated with iron and hand-carved granite lanterns from Japan. Walkways, and a sort of patio, are of bluestone brought from New York."

Large numbers of goldfish inhabit the waterways in the garden. As Moore described the scene in the September 20, 1962, edition of The Star: "We find Jerry Cohen, an early riser, feeding the fish in one of the pools... breaking slices of bread into chunks and casting them into the water. There's hundreds of goldfish in there, 22 of them king-sized, weighing maybe half a pound. Some of the fish slither up and eat out of Jerry's hand."

The gardens and his Oriental-decorated house also brought Cohen a two-page feature in a Masonic magazine, Scottish Rite Herald, in its May 1970 issue. The feature was entitled "Jerome Cohen, 32nd Degree, KCCH, A Kosher Santa Pours Sake" and featured large photographs of Cohen and his Japanese garden. The article began: "Sipping warm sake poured in from an azure porcelain whistling sake pot amidst a panoply of Japanese and Oriental treasures is not included in this reporter's usual Sunday routine. But the host and the merry monarch of this gallery of bamboobrush landscape art, gorgeous silk, jade, ceramic and ivories is no ordinary acquaintance! Santa Claus, Dean of the Soap Box Derby, Park Board Commissioner, television's 'Jerry, the Tempo Man' and Scottish Rite membership chairman are but a few of the appellations answered to by civic titan and native son, Jerome Cohen. Cohen himself strikes a mirthful resemblance to Hotei, the Japanese god of wealth and wisdom reproduced in decanter form and squatting atop an elaborately-appointed bar, a focal point in his rattan driftwood embellished recreation room. Even the most casual observer of the Japanese influence had smiled at a commercial replica of this balding, jolly looking statue saint with his arms stretched above an enormous stomach clay counterpart. Jerry claims no special attainment of the wisdom of Buddhism though much of his philosophy as well as his lifestyle is threaded with the simple profundities of the Eastern mystics... Through his bamboo gates into a 'sepulcher bridged by a bluestone archway,' you pause while Jerry stops to tickle the water banquet summoning hundreds of goldfish expecting a dole of bread crumbs and you inhale the earthly paradise, realizing the impact of the contact with the elements — the sympathy with the seasons as they rise and roll, gleaning why the ancient Japanese gardens were among the foremost creations of oriental art. To walk in the garden is to befriend benevolence in the presence of a man who conceives of life as a summons...and responds to the call with eloquence."

The garden of Jeannette and Jerry Cohen had become so famous with Kansas Citians over the next several years that it was included with seven other well-known area gardens for the prestigious 40th annual Wellesley Garden Tour, sponsored by the exclusive Kansas City Wellesley Club, an organization of women graduates of the internationally known women's college, Wellesley University, as a fund-raising effort for needy women for scholarships at the school. The other gardens opened for the noted anniversary were those of Mrs. J. Noland Franz, Mrs. Walter L. Murphy, Jr., Dr. and Mrs. Samuel A. Montello, Mr. and Mrs. Jerry Gaines, Mr. and Mrs. Forest P. Gill, Mr. and Mrs. James Patrick Quinn, and Mr. and Mrs. Irwin Adel. The anniversary handbook contains descriptions of the gardens on the tour and gave this description of the Cohen garden in part: "Hidden behind the bamboo fence in this Ward Parkway home is an Oriental garden, a quiet refuge for meditation and peace. There is a tea house, large goldfish pond and waterfalls as well as unusual plant specimens effectively lighted at night. The Oriental theme used throughout the landscaping and house came from a stained glass room divider made by Arthur Kraft, depicting a Japanese woman... The free-form pool is filled with goldfish who come to the edge of the pool every morning to be fed bread crumbs. In winter, a piece of heated wood wound with a heating coil keeps small hole open in the ice so the fish can live here all year round. Three Austrian birch grow by the bridge, and flagstone paths with moss wind through the garden. Notice the use of river pebbles by the pool and raked sand by the tea house... The night lighting of this garden is most effective. Lights are in the pool and under each weeping tree; at night the garden appears to have lighted lampshades. The granite lanterns along the pool and candles are used for lighting, too. There are lights in the tea house and in the euponymous espaliered on the wall of the house..."

A PROUD FATHER AND GRANDFATHER — *Reuben Cohen, the father of Jerry Cohen, celebrates with his son, his daughter-in-law and his two granddaughters a family occasion. In the back row, left to right, are Jerry Cohen's daughter, Rosalyn Cohen, Jerry and Mrs. Jeannette Baier Cohen. In the front row with Grandpa is the second daughter of Jerry, Elaine. Reuben Cohen was always grateful for his American business success after coming to the U.S. in the 1890s as a Jewish immigrant from Eastern Europe.*

JERRY COHEN LEADS BARTLE TRIBUTE — *Jerry Cohen, standing right, is shown leading a tribute to H. Roe Bartle for his eight years as mayor and for his other years of service at a testimonial dinner Cohen headed at the Hotel Muehlebach. Bartle, after whom Cohen was successful in getting the city to name its convention center, sits with arms folded at right, while Mrs. Margaret (Maggie to her friends) Bartle accepts an accolade from Cohen.*

12

Stage Shows to Gorillas

Two things that were life-long interests of Jerry Cohen fit right in like a glove with the eight years he served as a member of the Kansas City Board of Parks and Recreation from 1955 into 1963 under Mayor H. Roe Bartle. One was his interest in animals which prompted his interest in the Swope Park Zoo; the other was an interest in theater which caused him to join with the Starlight Theater from its inception in 1951. Cohen was to say his interest in animals stemmed from a dedicated teacher in elementary school in Kansas City who got him interested in joining the school Audubon Club with its interests in wildlife. His Jewish background with its followers long support of theater through the ages was the source of his theater interest.

Cohen began to take a really strong interest in the Swope Park Zoo as a successful businessman following World War II when the veteran animal man, William T. A. Cully, befriended him after Cully came here as zoo director. Cully's efforts in interesting Cohen in the zoo was not difficult since in reality Cohen had enjoyed the zoo and the animals since he was a small boy making treks there with his family. The 1,334 acres of Swope Park had been given to the city in 1895 by Col. Thomas H. Swope, an early-day Kansas City real estate dealer who migrated to the city from Kentucky. A zoological society had been formed as soon as the park was accepted by the city and the fledgling organization got the city to set aside a 60-acre tract of the total parcel to be used for a zoo. It was finally established with the menagerie from a circus which folded in its quarters the previous winter in Kansas City. A building was built to house several rhesus monkeys, two tigers, a lion, a bear and an elephant taken over from the circus. Norman "Tex" Clark was named to head the zoo and continued to run it until he died in 1942.

Clark had greatly expanded the zoo during his years as director so the city launched a nationwide search for his successor after his death in 1942. The search committee chose a member of the staff of the Bronx Zoo in New York City, Cully, to succeed and he accepted. Through his friendship with Cully after his arrival in Kansas City, Cohen had become concerned about the future of the zoo even before Bartle named him to the Kansas City parks and recreation board. Cohen had learned the zoo budgets were tight and did not provide funds for adding animals of the more exotic species that would attract visitors to the zoo or to obtain replacements for animals which were dying off because of old age or other infirmities. Cully had conceived the idea of trying to get wealthy Kansas Citians and businessmen to make substantial gifts to purchases for the zoo just as they gave funds to support other cultural arts organizations. This made sense to Cohen, and he offered to try to help Cully get the idea going. In this light, Cohen and his wife, Jeannette, provided funds, some $500, to purchase a pair of patas monkeys Cully thought would make a worthwhile contribution in attracting visitors to the zoo. This gift marked the beginning of a long personal relationship of Cohen in making the zoo grow through financial contributions for the purchase of animals the zoo was seeking. He tried to interest others in following his lead in giving such funds and it was probably this that provided the genesis in his mind for establishing a support group for the zoo similar to those which existed for other cultural arts groups in town. Through the years of trying to establish a concept by example, Mr. and Mrs. Cohen made private contributions of a pair of double-humped or Asian camels. One contest was held to name the baby giraffe and one of Cohen's friends entered the name Jeannerry, a combination of the first names of the Cohens, Jeannette and Jerry. Zoo officials thought the name appropriate in the light of the animal gifts given so generously by the couple so the Swope Park Zoo had a waddling young giraffe named Jeannerry that drew hundreds of visitors to their rounds to view it, thanks to the publicity given the birth by The Kansas City Star. Cohen was not able to attract the many other civic leaders to form the support organization he envisioned for the zoo, however, until Bartle named him as a member of the parks and recreation board.

From the time Cohen became a member of the parks and recreation board, the supervision of the Swope Park Zoo became a hands-on operation for the board members in meetings with Cully. Frank Theis, who was the president of the park board when Cohen was appointed; Wade D. Rubick, another member, and Cohen would meet weekly with Cully, generally on Sunday, to make a tour of the facility. They were concerned about the lack of money available at the time for zoo operations from city revenues. During those years, the Swope Park Zoo was operating on an average annual budget of only about $155,000 with an average of only about $5,700 of that amount available annually for animal purchases. It was then that Cohen really began to push for the establishment of a volunteer financial support organization for the zoo and which he proposed calling Friends of the Zoo. The original Kansas City Zoological Society, which had been formed when Swope had given the park to the city in 1895 and had continued to operate since that time, had faded away during the dark days after the entry of United States into World War I. From that time until Cohen came on the board, no new society had been created to fill this need. Finally, on October 29, 1959, shortly after Bartle had been elected to a second four-year term as mayor, Cohen arranged a meeting of community leaders with Cully and Bartle to discuss plans for the growth of the zoo. Friends of the Zoo, a not-for-profit support group for the zoo, was formed to assist in providing funds for new construction and purchase of animals at the zoo. R. Hugh (Pat) Uhlmann, a friend of Cohen and a fellow member of Temple B'nai Jehudah, was elected president with John A. Moore as vice president. On November 23, 1959, the Jackson County Circuit Court, acting under a Missouri statute in effect at the time, established Friends of the Zoo as a not-for-profit organization by formal decree. The first meeting of the group under the charter was held at a luncheon at the Hotel Muehlebach with Uhlmann presiding. Fifty civic leaders attended the luncheon with 20 agreeing to become charter members by pledging to contribute $1,500 each to the support of the Swope Park Zoo. All Kansas Citians were invited to become members during the first year with annual dues at $15 per person.

From that humble beginning, the Friends of the Zoo, a longtime goal of Cohen, was off and running and through its efforts the Kansas City Zoo since then has managed to become one of the leading metropolitan zoos in the nation. Within the first 10 years, by 1970, Friends of the Zoo had contributed over $46,000 to purchase a variety of animals such as Indian and African elephants, giraffes, gorillas and other large animals as well as $35,000 for construction projects such as a marina for otters, a pool for polar bears and other exhibits. During the 1960s, the organization also published the first guidebook in the history of the Swope Park Zoo. More meaningful, however, was the work in recruiting civic leaders to active support of the zoo as well as attracting rank-and-file Kansas Citians to participate in zoo activities by becoming members of Friends of the Zoo, a membership which gave them special zoo privileges as well. Not the least of these were the annual zoo picnics which the organization started its first year and of which Cohen served as chairman for more than 20 years. Members and their families got fried chicken and barbecue with all the trimmings at the zoo, free rides on the zoo train, free elephant, camel and pony rides and a variety of other novelties such as free balloons and free cotton candy for the youngsters. As the organization grew, private support for the zoo grew. In five years from 1970 through 1974, another $54,600 was provided through private contributions for the purchase of such animals as lesser pandas, musk oxen, kangaroos and more than $47,000 in such contributions went for construction of an island exhibit for gibbon apes, improvements in the habitat for tropical animals and a revision of the zoo guidebook to make it one of the finest in the nation. By 1983, private contributions for animal acquisition since Friends of the Zoo was first organized in 1960 under Cohen's leadership had exceeded $200,000 with an additional $56,000 from 1975-82 going for acquiring kulan, a type of wild donkey, additional gorilla, giraffe, two-humped or bactrian camel and others. By 1983, private contributions for new buildings and facilities exceeded $750,000 including $250,000 for an animal nursery where zoo attendants could care for newly born animals and their mothers, gorilla habitat improvements of $20,000; $67,000 going to polar bear exhibit development; $45,000 for giraffe house improvements; $20,000 for habitat improvement for orangutans and $267,119 for improvements in elephant exhibits. Friends of the Zoo in the early 1980s also provided funds to hire a consultant, Marvin Jones, under a contract to help the zoo develop a more efficient record-keeping system. This kind of attention also had been largely responsible for the fact that the zoo budget had grown from $155,000 annually when Cohen went on the park board to a whopping $2,142,497 budget for the 1982-83 fiscal year.

Ten years after he left the park board in 1963 when Mayor Bartle gave up on his bid for a third term and was succeeded by Mayor Ilus W. Davis, Cohen agreed to become president of Friends of the Zoo and served during the period from 1972 through 1974. After Uhlmann had served as the first president of the support organization, Cohen had been instrumental in persuading more distinguished Kansas Citians to head the group. They included John A. Moore, Harry Ellsworth, Col. S. D. Slaughter, Jr., John Latshaw and Jeffery P. Hillelson, former member of Congress and Kansas City postmaster, just before Cohen took the helm. Although he had a background role in the officer ranks of the organization before he agreed to take the presidency, Cohen did not take a back seat in his efforts to make the support group a success. He had made the annual zoo picnics a delight for the rank-and-file members of Friends of the Zoo and their families as chairman shortly after the organization was founded. In the September 1965 issue of 3M Roundtable, the highly-readable house organ for duplicating equipment dealers of 3M, the Minnesota Mining and Manufacturing Company, whose efforts had contributed so much to the success of the Cohen duplicating business, Cohen succeeded in getting national recognition for the Swope Park Zoo. Sandwiched in among articles about the National Governors Conference held in Minneapolis that July with a photograph of Vice President Hubert Humphrey and Gov. Karl Rolvaag speaking to the governors and one about how 3M duplicating equipment helped speed news of the Gemini 4 space mission to the world was a full page of photographs under the headline "Who's Zoo' in Kansas City!" Cohen had arranged a picnic as a promotion for his employees at the zoo and there was one photograph of him in a railroad's engineer's cap at the driver's seat of the zoo train with his employees on board, one of him holding the trunk of an elephant in the air while one of his employees rides on its back and a third of him holding two young orangutans in his arms while his employees look on admiringly along with two others, one of the employees on the zoo jungle train and other with employees listening to a zoo puppet, the latter two dealing with a 3M Company promotion called: "On Our Way to

Monterrey."

One of the greatest attention-attracting efforts for the zoo that occurred while Cohen was serving on the park board and while he was trying to get Friends of the Zoo underway resulted from a friendship he had developed with a Kansas City area veterinarian, Dr. Deets Pickett. As a veterinarian, Dr. Pickett shared an interest in animals with Cohen and had begun making safaris to Africa in the 1950s to see the untamed wildlife still roaming free there. Dr. Pickett began his African safaris hunting elephant, lion and water buffalo but the thing that really caught his attention were the mountain gorillas he got a chance to see in the wilds in a safari to the Cameroons in the mid 1950s. On the way back from the wild gorilla habitat, Dr. Pickett and his party came across a group of natives who had a baby gorilla in their possession. They said the mother had been killed with the infant in her arms but the baby had been saved. Dr. Pickett negotiated with the natives and managed to purchase the baby gorilla from them. With treating the baby as a human infant with love and affection, Dr. Pickett learned the gorillas could be made to survive. Thus began the career of Dr. Pickett and his wife in importing the gorillas to their home in Leawood. Within three years, Dr. Pickett through agents he employed in West Africa was able to secure 10 of the infants and bring them back to the U.S. to be sold to zoos. Dr. Pickett explained his gorilla importing operations by pointing out the natives hunt the adult gorillas for food but are uninterested in the youngsters they capture with their slain mothers. Pickett got his agents to search these out and buy them.

The gorillas were a sensation in Kansas City and The Kansas City Star featured many articles and photographs on the gorillas being cared for as human babies by the Picketts at their home. Pickett gave his first gorilla, named Big Man, to the Swope Park Zoo where it was an instant success, drawing thousands of visitors. In all, the Picketts placed some five gorillas with the zoo in Kansas City, always increasing the focus on the zoo. They were still a rarity in U.S. zoos, having grown from a total of around 10 in zoos across the nation in the beginning of World War II to some 40 in 1960, many having been saved by the efforts of Dr. Pickett and his new expertise with the animals. The Picket gorillas helped the zoo get another rare animal, a black rhino. The Swope Park Zoo had no funds for such a purchase. Because of his friendship with Cohen, Dr.

Pickett donated two of his gorillas to be traded to another zoo for the black rhino. Through the efforts of Cohen, Mayor Bartle made leaders in the French Cameroons, where Pickett collected most of his gorillas, honorary citizens of Kansas City, complete with framed, artistically emblazoned certificates. Pickett gave the action by Bartle credit for helping him with his animal operations in the French Cameroons "tremendously."

With his efforts in expanding the zoo and increasing the number of visitors, Cohen was also lending his efforts to watching the fledgling outdoor amphitheater in Swope Park grow from its humble beginnings in 1951 to a summer attraction drawing thousands of visitors to Kansas City annually. The theater had been constructed for the Kansas City centennial in 1950 to be used as the setting for a specially written musical pageant on Kansas City history that proved to be a popular theatrical experience for hundreds who attended the outdoor spectacle during its summer-long run. Civic leaders under Mayor William E. Kemp were organized to keep the outdoor theater running as a setting for Broadway musicals during the summer similar to those staged by the St. Louis Municipal Opera which had started in the rival Missouri city some years before that. Cohen was one of the group that formed the Starlight Theater Association on a not-for-profit basis to begin the summer musicals in 1951. One of the principal decisions that led to the successful early years of Starlight was the decision to hire a young Broadway and Hollywood producer named Richard H. Berger to stage the annual productions. Berger had a knack that was essential to the success of the Kansas City venture, a knack for spectacle that would enable him to put the musical productions on a giant outdoor stage to satisfy the desires of some 7,700 spectators each performance rather then feeling that the show had to be staged exactly as it had been on a smaller indoor stage before a smaller audience. Berger also had the good sense to chose a staff of young theatrical professionals who fitted exactly into his scheme. They included Roland Fiore as musical director; G. Phillipe de Rosier as scenic designer and Anthony Ferrara as stage manager, among others. The summer of 1951 did not prove to be the most auspicious year to begin the venture in an outdoor theater since it was a period of incessant rain that culminated in the disastrous 1951 flood which inundated much of the city on July 13. The sun came out on June 15, 1951, to the delight of the 7,700 residents who showed up for the opening performance of the famed musical Desert Song, written by the noted composer, Sigmund Romberg, whom Berger had inveigled to come to the Kansas City grand opening.

As The Kansas City Star said in its front page feature of the opening: "The Starlight Theater opened last night under auspicious circumstances, if that can be taken to mean that it offered a vista of dramatic color and beauty. The sky was cloudless, a fine breeze blew out of the south and the proceeding on and off the stage moved with precision and flourish. Under this magnificent canopy of heaven, as Mayor William E. Kemp commented with fine phrasing in his dedicatory speech, the 1.5-million-dollar bowl was set in a spot of outdoor loveliness. Swope Park was at its lush and verdant best, a touch of daylight touching the area as the crowd assembled, and finally the night coming on with a brilliance overhead." It was Romberg who entranced the opening night crowd, however. As The Star said in its story of the opening: "This was Sigmund Romberg's show, 'The Desert Song,' and Mr. Romberg was the star performer of the preliminary proceedings. He appeared in front of the orchestra, blinded by the spotlight, and told his audience he had been given a speech to read, that he had lost it and that, moreover, he didn't need it."

It was halcyon days for Kansas City to open its outdoor version of Broadway with a procession of top name stars in leading productions since television was only just beginning in Kansas City and had not yet produced the big demands for high payments for star appearances or to keep residents in their homes with their eyes glued to the black-and-white screens. With the help of Cohen and other civic leaders, the outdoor theater got off to such a successful start in 1951 that its momentum was to carry it through at least the next 40 years through good times and bad. In addition to the ability of Berger to attract top name stars for the opening season, the civic leaders had seen fit to hire a topflight Kansas City business manager, William M. Symon, who kept a close eye on expenditures and receipts from ticket sales so that the outdoor theater would remain financially sound.

By the time the sixth season had ended, there was no question about the success of the operation and its ability to attract thousands of visitors from Kansas, Missouri, Nebraska, Arkansas, Iowa and Oklahoma. By the end of the sixth season, Starlight had drawn a remarkable 1,990,638 customers. Berger was still going strong, having staged 52 different operettas and Broadway musicals in a total of 462 performances during the summer seasons. Seven of his productions had been so successful with patrons they had been staged twice as a part of the 60 productions: The Desert Song, The Chocolate Soldier, Brigadoon, Bittersweet, Babes in Toyland, Naughty Marietta and Annie, Get Your Gun. Liberace, the popular piano virtuoso noted for his dazzling costume changes during a performance and the candelabra on his grand piano while playing, had the opening production in 1957 and showed up at a seventh anniversary celebration for the outdoor theater on June 16 given on a Sunday afternoon backstage by the Women's Committee headed by Martha Franklin, chairman; Margaret Falke, Mrs. John R. Keach and Jean Mullane, vice chairman, and Adalain Lee Taylor, secretary. Berger brought along Liberace's brother, George Liberace, and Jean Fenn, a Metropolitan Opera and Broadway musical soprano who had graduated from Stephens College in Columbia, Missouri, and who was appearing in the opening production with Liberace. During the week-long Liberace production, the Starlight Theater reached another milestone when the two millionth visitor went through the ticket gate on June 19, 1957. The startled patron, Loretta Lickteig, of Greeley, Kansas, was pulled gently from the crowd by John Doohan, Starlight house manager before television cameras whose crews had been alerted for this historic approaching moment. She was taken backstage by Doohan where she was introduced onstage and received a hug and a kiss from Liberace.

By the time the 1957 Starlight season rolled around, Cohen, who had been a member of the Starlight board of directors since its inception in 1951, had now moved into a position to be of more help, the Kansas City board of parks and recreation. Now a member of the Starlight executive committee as well. Cohen was featured in a photograph with the other two park board members at the time, Frank Theis, who was president, and George Fuller Green, in the program distributed to thousands of spectators during the week long run of the musical, By the Beautiful Sea, starring Lillian Roth and Webb Tilton. With the photograph of the three commissioners with park staff the page carried the legend: "Residents of the Greater Kansas City area have the board of park commissioners to thank for the beauty of its boulevards and parkways. And Starlight Theater patrons can be greatful to this municipal group for the well-kept surroundings of the theater and Swope Park. Many hours of imaginative planning go into the maintenance of the park areas of the city, and in the tradition of the city, and in the tradition of the past, the job continues to be well done." In a second program for the 1957 season, that for the production of Silk Stockings, starring Julie Wilson and Tony Bennett, there is another full page with a photograph of Cohen and Theis and other members of what is called the Theater Plant and Concessions Department of the outdoor theater. That page carries the following legend which said in part: "The Theater Plant and Concessions Department of the Starlight Theater Association has the responsibility of seeing that the plant and grounds are in top shape for the busy summer theater schedule. They also make recommendations to the executive committee regarding the concessions at the theater. Several committee members are prominent in construction and engineering firms in the area and several double in duty as members of the park board." Cohen was eventually to become vice president in charge of the department during his more than 40 years of service on the board.

In the successful 1957 season, William E. Kemp, former mayor who was succeeded in the office by Bartle in 1955, had become president of Starlight. It was a blue ribbon list of officers with R. Crosby Kemper, Sr., and Cliff C. Jones, Jr. as vice presidents; Paul E. Connor, treasurer, and Kenneth G. Gillespie as secretary. Another Cohen was also sharing the spotlight in the Starlight Theater programs, Elaine Cohen, the 10-year-old daughter of Jerry and Jeannette Cohen. Elaine got her picture taken in one of the summer programs at Starlight with Julie Wilson, the noted Broadway star and singer, who was playing the leading role in the hit musical, Panama Hattie. Young Miss Cohen, following in her father's footsteps in interest in the theater, had made her first appearance at Starlight three years earlier in 1954 in the musical, Sweethearts, and had come back in 1955 in Babes in Toyland. It was in 1956 that she got a major role when she played one of Annie's sisters in Annie, Get Your Gun. She had two other featured roles in 1956, one as a royal daughter in The King and I and the second in Plain and Fancy, in which the 1957 article said: "She made a great hit with the theatergoers with her rendition of Vegetable Song, rattling off the names of vegetables from A to Z." The program distributed to thousands of theatergoers during the week-long run of Panama Hattie also said in part of Elaine: "Ten-year-old Elaine is the daughter of Mr. and Mrs. Jerome Cohen of 6940 Brooklyn, and will be in the fifth grade at the Border Star School this fall. She has studied singing and dancing for seven of her ten years and is now a pupil of Virginia Loncar of Kansas City... As a matter of fact, Elaine is not alone in her family in participating in Starlight theater activities. Her father is a member of the Theater Plant and Concessions Committee and, as a Park Board Commissioner, has a great deal to do with the pleasant surroundings of the theater. Mrs. Cohen, needless to say, is involved in keeping both her husband and daughter in good shape for their varied activities."

ALMOST TOO MUCH TO HANDLE — *Jerry Cohen, always a lover of animals, almost found himself with too much to handle in trying to hold two young gorillas in his arms at the Swope Park Zoo. Cohen, as a member of the Kansas City Parks and Recreation Board, was instrumental in helping a Kansas City veterinarian, Dr. Deets Pickett, in his efforts to preserve West African gorillas. Dr. Pickett imported several homeless young gorillas to Swope Park.*

A MORE DOCILE YOUNG GORILLA — *Jan Armstrong, an associate director at the Swope Park Zoo for several years and still active in civic affairs here, has an easier time of it with a younger of the Pickett gorillas. The gorilla looks at Jerry Cohen adoringly in hopes of getting the grape Cohen is holding.*

13

Business Brings Celebrities

While he was getting much greater exposure in civic life through his nearly eight years as a member of the Kansas City Parks and Recreation Board, there was no slow down in the business operations for Cohen and his companies, the Tempo Company and Electronic Business Equipment, Inc. Cohen had to thank his lucky stars repeatedly that he had the business acumen to get into the duplicating field at a time when no one could have dreamed, in their wildest imagination, how the demand for paper copies was going to mushroom in business, industry and government. As William Ecenbarger wrote in early 1990 in an essay, Copy Cat, published in an internationally circulated magazine: "The photocopier has altered the course of history and changed forever the nature of bureaucratic and white-collar life by revolutionizing the production, flow and distribution of information. It has replaced the water cooler as the social nexus of the modern office and put carbon paper, once the office workhorse, out to pasture. It is estimated that 600 billion photocopies were made worldwide last year (1989), but how can anyone know for sure? Probably the number is too low. The human urge to reproduce anything and everything seems insatiable. Like human reproduction, the copying mania seems to satisfy a primal need." The article said that foreign governments had come to fear the new ease of making information available and that totalitarian systems had set up stringent regulations on ownership of the duplicating machines to try to restrict the flow of the information from copying machines. It said that in Russia under the old communist regime "Photocopiers are controlled like nuclear warheads. Only approved individuals, usually responsible to the KGB, are allowed to use photocopiers." The 1990 article went on to say in part: "In less than three decades, the photocopier has revolutionized office practices worldwide. In addition to carbon paper, it destroyed the old 'buck slip' — the memo with various names on it to be initialed and passed on to the next name; the memo could take weeks to get through a large office. Now everyone gets a copy of the memo at the same time. Not surprisingly, the photocopier has caused a proliferation of paper work, challenging the forests of the world to keep up with its demands. A 1986 study by Accountemps, a New York City research firm, found that of the estimated 350 billion copies made by U.S. businesses each year, about 130 billion — or 37 percent wind up in the trash can."

As the copying business continued to expand and grow, the physical facilities required by Cohen had to grow to meet the burgeoning business demand. When 3M Company suggested that he had to separate the part of the copying business devoted to the equipment and supplies, he had established Electric Business Equipment, Inc., and moved its operations to 1616 Grand Avenue, just two blocks from where his business had operated since later in World War II in the building in which his father had had his jewelry store for 46 years at 1423 Grand Avenue. The Tempo Company continued to grow and prosper at the old location, while EBE, Inc., opened branches in Jefferson City and St. Joseph to meet its increasing sales of duplicating equipment and supplies. Cohen thought his business buildings in Kansas City were set for a time but by the late 1950s fate took a hand when Kansas City and the state decided to build a new interstate highway as a part of the system started by President Dwight D. Eisenhower from the west side of the downtown area east along Fifteenth Street now known as Truman Road in honor of Harry S. Truman. The new six-lane superhighway with the divided medial strip running to the east edge of the downtown area would run right through the old jewelry store of Reuben Cohen and the larger space of Tempo Company of his son, Jerry.

Fortunately, while he was taking part in the non-partisan city reform movement of the Citizens Association, Jerry Cohen had kept an active hand in the Democratic party in Missouri, serving as treasurer and ticket chairman for fund-raising efforts for such leading figures as John Dalton, James T. Blair, state governors; Hilary Bush, lieutenant governor; Stuart Symington, United States Senator who was an unsuccessful candidate for the Democratic nomination for President in 1960; and Senator Thomas Eagleton, former Missouri attorney general. This gave him innumerable contacts to help him get through the condemnation proceedings and the acquisition of his business headquarters for the new superhighway. Still, there was stress for Cohen and his brothers who were associated with him in the businesses from the time they heard of the pending development until it was successfully concluded over a period of more than three years. When Cohen acquired the building for EBE at 1616 Grand and remodeled his quarters at 1423 Grand they thought they were set for the foreseeable future until the highway development. After some negotiations, Cohen was able to obtain a suitable site running along Grand Avenue at 1500 Grand Avenue for his new business home. He also acquired a site across the alley running to Walnut Street along Fifteenth Street, or Truman Road, to be used for a parking lot for employees at the new headquarters.

Even when he acquired the new site and was ready to start building his new operations at Truman and Grand it was not a smooth road but Cohen showed the determination which had always stood him in good stead in all ways while moving his life ahead. Just as everything else in his life, Cohen thought it was worth doing well if you were going to do it. When he originally bought the site at Truman and Grand, he had planned for it to be used for the Tempo Company and leaving EBE at 1616 Grand. He hired Sam Price, an architect, to design the new building and employed the Estrin Construction Company to carry out the building. It was designed to feature a two-story glass front with what a press release called "a highly decorative aluminum and gold solar screen." Beige and dark brown brick were to be blended with marble for the balance of the building. In the brightly-lighted two-story entrance which faced directly on the busy corner of Truman and Grand, Cohen got the architect to design what The Kansas City Star called "a spiral staircase of unusual proportions, including steel, terrazzo and marble in its components." The stairway led to the second floor of the building and an automatic elevator was also installed linking the basement, first and second floors. In all, the new structure included 15,000 square feet of air conditioned space. As usual, however there were delays in the construction and Cohen had to vacate the longtime home at 1423 Grand for demolition for the new superhighway before the new building was ready to occupy. For a time, he moved Tempo from the old location into leased space at 1506-08 Main Street while the new building was being completed. Cohen, however, was so entranced with the new structure that he decided to move his biggest moneymaker, EBE, into the new building and send Tempo to the building at 1616 Grand which had been remodeled into 6,000 square feet of office space on the first floor and parking for 16 cars in the basement area. The Star described the change in plans under a headline "Two Cohen Firms in Space Switches." The lead on the newspaper story read: "The dual enterprises of Jerome Cohen assume new addresses this weekend. His Electronic Business Equipment, Inc., moves into a new building at the southwest corner of Truman Road and Grand Avenue from space at 1616 Grand. And Cohen's Tempo Company, in operation in temporary quarters at 1506 Main, occupies the old 1616 Grand location."

But Jerry Cohen was always one to overcome difficulty and move on to something else as quickly as he could. His idea that all persons were created equal, he said frequently throughout his life, meant that God gave each of them 24 hours a day. How they used the 24 hours was what made the difference. As he frequently told his sales force: "I have a little sign I keep in front of me constantly. It says: 'Let's thank God for today. This is the beginning of a new day; I can waste it or I can use it for good. What I do today is important because I am exchanging a day of my life for it and when tomorrow comes this day will be gone forever, leaving in its place something I've traded for. Now, I want it to be gained, not lost. Good not evil, success not failure; this is in order that I shall not regret the price that I have paid for today.' Another little axiom that we use is: 'Do you believe in minimum necessity or maximum opportunities?' You can accomplish the task if you believe this basic: You CAN move on to greater accomplishments. Now the reason most people accomplish so little in life is because by nature most of us accomplish what we must just to get by. Perhaps you have just been getting by and now you find yourself in sales where the opportunity is unlimited you discover how much you must sell each week to get by. Then you make the mistake of adjusting your goals downward to minimum necessity rather than upward to maximum opportunity. Once you are aware that what you accomplish is due to your state of mind you can do something about setting goals of greater accomplishment. People who are destined to be great set their goals on what is possible rather than what is necessary."

While he was going through the process of changing locations and expanding his business, Cohen continued to use every avenue at his disposal to promote publicity for himself and thereby his business operations. In the December 1958 issue of Heart of America Purchaser, the official publication of the Purchasing Agents of Kansas City, for instance, there was a photograph of a smiling Cohen representing his friend, Mayor H. Roe Bartle, in presenting a key to the city to Gordon Afflect of Salt Lake City, the president of the National Association of Purchasing Agents and purchasing agent for the Mormon Church. With Cohen and Afflect in the photograph were A. W. Smallfield, of Rival Manufacturing Company, president of the Kansas City Association at the time, and Kenneth A. Cruise, of Bendix Aviation Corp., first vice president of the group. In a speech to the Kansas City Association of Purchasing Agents at the Hotel President, Afflect gave some advice which sounded as though it had come right out of one of Cohen's lectures: "After 18 years in purchasing, I have found these fundamentals to be true. First, there are no real substitutes for brains. Brain power is still the most important factor in effective purchasing. Nothing can replace it and common sense in personal negotiations and evaluations of economic factors that affect purchasing. You are never through learning in purchasing. Your restlessness will make you find new ways of doing things better. Second, there is no legal substitute for personal contacts. Third, there is no substitute for the art of negotiating. We should not use gouging, begging or the tactics of 50 years ago. And fourth, there is no real substitute for personal interpretations of economic factors which pertain to our field."

How well Cohen was doing in making his businesses grow could be garnered from an award conferred on him for the first time in 1960 by the 3M Company. It was its prestigious outstanding sales award which had just been created by the company for such recognition annually, membership in something called the Turtle Club. On December 15, 1959, Cohen was notified by E. F. Boverman, general sales manager for the graphic products division of 3M, that he was one of the 15 dealers selected across the nation. Boverman said in the letter the award would become annual, "much like an Oscar Award in the movie industry or like the pennant displayed by the Los Angeles Dodgers for having shown to one and all that for the year 1959 they are the leaders, they are the best. The Dodgers can be champions again next year but they have to earn the title again—there will be nothing automatic about it." Boverman went on to say in the letter: "In early December our area representatives submitted to their field managers their nominees for the 1960 Turtle Club and it was gratifying to see the high regard our area representatives had for so many dealers because we did have a large number of nominations. Our instructions to our area representatives pointed out that they were to nominate those who were recognized as leaders in our program because of their aggressiveness, attitude, cooperation, desire, flexibility, foresight, sales leadership and understanding... Remember the slogan: 'Behold the Turtle... he makes progress only when his neck is out.'" Boverman then congratulated Cohen on being one of the 15 winners along with Bob Ball, Indianapolis; Jim Woodhull, Dayton; Charles Gallant, Washington, D.C.; Bob McCarthy, Evansville; Don Hershey, Chicago; Pete Marinovich, San Diego; Bob Black, Oklahoma City; Jim Turnock, Detroit; Bob France, St. Louis; Norm Kramer, Los Angeles; Walt Griffith, Akron; Don Mulvey, Houston; Charlie Biggs, Shreveport; and Francis Webster, Atlanta. How well the business was doing was indicated in a congratulatory letter Cohen received from one 3M executive, J. F. Higgins, after the Turtle Awards were announced: "Let me add my congratulations on your selection as a 'Turtle' and even more important, on the fine management job that you have accomplished in the 1st year. This management job is the real basis for 'Turtle' selection and it's your leadership here that should show the way to the dealerships. If we had 180 organizations like Electronic Business Equipment, Inc., in Kansas City, and 180 dealer managers like you, Jerry, our job here would be much easier and our rewards much greater."

Cohen continued to receive the Turtle Club nominations from 3M executives through the years as he continued to drive his sales operations higher for all his companies. Excerpts from papers prepared by a 3M executive nominating Cohen for the 1962 Turtle Award said "Jerry has unselfishly devoted all his time to our products and to his equally important civic duties that have helped promote our products in his area of service responsibility. Jerry has used his ability, experience and suggestions from 3M to build the finest organization in the Middle West." The 3M executive, William W. Wagner, Jr., went on to say in part nominating Jerry that year: "As all of you know that have been in the Kansas City dealership, it is an outstanding example of leadership in the area of design and location. Jerry's place of business is one of the best in the country. I have not heard one complaint on the service in the Kansas City, Jefferson City or St. Joseph areas. They are very prompt on emergency calls… It goes without saying that this man, Jerry Cohen, is probably the most active man we have in the program in civic activities. I have never known a more aggressive or progressive individual in the past six years of my association with a number of dealers, of whom some were Turtles. Jerry is never satisfied with second best. Even though the list of civic activities is long, Jerry still devotes almost all his time to our products and our efforts." Wagner then listed 28 Kansas City civic activities. He went on to say: "It is rather difficult to show in a written description the drive that Jerry Cohen has that results in a successful business. He is probably the busiest man I have ever been around and it all starts at 7 a.m. in his office almost every day except when he is out of town." Needless to say, Cohen was elected for the third straight year along with five others who had made each year since 1960.

As time went by, 3M company decided the Turtle Club no longer had the proper aura of dignity and in 1968 established what the company called the Business Products Council Association to promote the same kind of goals, getting dealers to achieve even higher sales figures and interest the dealers in taking on more products as they developed … Ray Herzog, a top 3M executive and longtime friend of Cohen, made sure the Kansas City dealer was on hand when the first meeting was held of the newly formed group. A. H. Pembroke was chosen as the first president of the newly formed association. Cohen, however, was elected president of the group when the third annual meeting was held October 24-26, 1970, at the New York Hotel in New York City. Other dealers from across the nation who were elected at the meeting to serve with Cohen for the year were Toby Martin, vice president; Josiah Heal, treasurer, and George Hanna, secretary. Members of the board of directors who served that year in addition to Cohen and the other officers were Charles Biggs, Earl Carroll, Robert McCarthy, William Reed, Robert Rahm and

Al Taylor. Many of the officers and board members had been Turtle Club members with Cohen from time to time. When the 10th annual conference was held October 29–November 2, 1978, at LaCosta Hotel and Spa in Rancho LaCosta, California, Cohen was once again serving as general chairman of the conference.

An interesting sidelight to the Association meetings at first was the effort being put into a sound system 3M had developed for providing background music for elevators and public areas of buildings. Cohen tried selling the background music systems successfully through a separate division of his companies in the Kansas City area but he never felt it had the profit-making potential of other 3M duplicating lines he was selling. It had disappeared, as well, from the meeting agenda of the 10th annual meeting of BPCA at LaCosta, California, at which Cohen presided.

During 1966, the 3M Company sponsored a sales contest promotion for the dealers and their salesmen with the title "Those Magnificent Men and Their Copying Machines." Cohen was not to be outdone among dealers conducting contests with the title that year and the August 1966 edition of Round Table, the 3M magazine, devoted more space to the Kansas City version of the concept than those of any other dealer, a full page of 10 photographs of the Kansas City event with accompanying text under the heading "Those Magnificent Kick-Off Meetings — Kansas City." The Cohen sense of theater showed in his ability to get the magazine editors' attention — he donned a complete Batman outfit of his shirt, cape and mask for the occasion and landed at the picnic site in a helicopter named the "The Batcopter." There are at least four photographs of the rotund Cohen as Batman with the helicopter. One photograph showed the sales force and their wives starting the evening at a local funeral home where they "buried the competition." Then there is a photograph of them lined up on the street in their cars with a motorcycle police escort to convoy them from the funeral home to the picnic grounds of the Howard Benjamin stables in suburban Kansas City. One photograph shows Cohen beside the helicopter with the caption: "Kansas City's Jerry Cohen — 3M's answer to Batman — arrives on the scene in his special 'Batcopter' carrying the rules of the Magnificent Men Contest." Benjamin pulled a covered wagon driven by live oxen alongside the helicopter for another photograph with the caption: "Jerry and the group exchange views on old and new modes of transportation." There are other photographs showing the group eating, drinking, being entertained by country singers on a hayride and one of the sales force and their wives lined up talking to Batman Cohen while they wait their turn for individual rides on the helicopter.

Cohen was not limiting his efforts to the 3M Company, however, in getting publicity worldwide for his companies efforts in the sales of duplicating equipment in the Kansas City Metropolitan area. In those days, Mobil Gas, a leading American gasoline company was holding a cross-country race called the Mobil Gas Economy Run with the finish line at the Muehlebach Hotel in Kansas City. Cohen made arrangements to have the press releases from the race headquarters at the Muehlebach in 1959 duplicated on the duplicator his company sold from the Gestetner company, a worldwide British company based in London. With his flare for showmanship which he demonstrated continuously throughout his history, Cohen invited one of the principals in the company, Mrs. Esme Pape, the daughter of one of the Gestetner founders, David Goldstein, to fly to Kansas City for the Mobil races. The result was a full-page article in the October 1959 edition of a Gestetner publication, Gestetner in the Picture. Across the tip of the page is a photograph of a late model car crossing the finish line in Kansas City while a flagman leaps in the air with a finish flag to signal the end of the race to the driver. Guess who is plainly visible in the action photo standing petitely on the curb with a crowd of Mobil officials? Mrs. Pape, who else? There is also a photograph of the crowded press room at the Hotel Muehlebach along with one of Mrs. Pape smilingly operating the Gestetner duplicator. There is a fourth photograph of Al Cohen, Jerry's brother, demonstrating the Gestetner to two Catholic nuns who were members of the Catholic Teachers Association convention meeting in Kansas City as the same time along with another Tempo executive working for Cohen, Len Pape. In the July 1961 issue of Gestetner Photo News there is a large photograph of Jerry Cohen speaking before a large audience to demonstrate Gestetner duplicating equipment. It carried the caption, Mimeo Doctor, with a cutline reading: "Mr. Jerry Cohen at a session of the customer clinic in the Hotel President in Kansas City, USA." The photograph ran above another on the same page of Mrs. Sigmund Gestetner, the wife of one of the company founders, London, looking over a model of a new building at Vitry in Paris. The issue also includes photographs of Belgian Gestetner dealers at a dinner in London; a Gestetner dealer in Lagos; Prince Wan Waithayakorn at a Gestetner display in Jaiphur; and Major General A. Rahm Khan at a similar display in Pakistan. It was heady company and worldwide recognition for a man who started life as a poor Jewish boy in Kansas City.

It was also during this period in his company life that Cohen began making annual trips in January to Pebble Beach to visit with a man who was to become an acquaintance of many years standing, Bing Crosby. His office at the headquarters of Electronic Business Equipment, Inc., has numerous momentos from the annual Bing Crosby golf tournament in Pebble Beach hanging on the walls, signed by Crosby himself. That relationship stemmed from the decision by the 3M company to sponsor the annual golf classics starring PGA golfers and celebrities from motion pictures and television hosted by Crosby at Pebble Beach until his death. The telecasts were launched in 1962 under 3M sponsorship with special direct mail literature, television, radio and newspaper announcements, all kinds of publicity releases and wall posters to help with sales of local dealers such as Cohen. For a showman such as Cohen, it was an opportunity which he utilized to the full potential through the years and enjoyed the comradeship of other dealers and 3M executives at Pebble Beach during the years with Crosby. As 3M executives said when they announced they were joining Crosby in the telecasts: "The millions who view the telecast will see demonstration after demonstration on the versatility of Thermofax copying products with plenty of emphasis on the latest uses and new models. Der Bingle himself will sing the praises of the easy-to-use Thermofax Copying Machine in two commercials, one each day of the tournament." As a salesman and a longtime admirer of Crosby, Cohen had no trouble in seeing the value in that for sales for his company.

14

America and Freemasonry

From the time he joined DeMolay, shortly after he had graduated from Central High School, Cohen had remained loyal to the units of the Ancient and Accepted Order of Freemasonry. From DeMolay, he continued to be active in a variety of Masonic organizations, first taking the third degree in Masonry to become a Master Mason in Heroine Lodge No. 104, then receiving the 32nd degree as a member of the Scottish Rite Body of the Valley of Kansas City and then as a member of the Shrine in Ararat Shrine Temple. Jews in the United States were proud of their acceptance in the orders of Freemasonry because it was one of the major places in the life of the nation where they were freely admitted from the time of the Revolution when an American Jew, Benjamin Rush, was one of the signers of the Declaration of Independence and a member of the convention committee. From the beginning, Freemasonry treated the Jews with respect in America and the Jews reciprocated. In his book, The Land That I Show You, Three Centuries of Jewish Life in America, Stanley Feldstein wrote of this feeling in 1776 at the start of the American Revolution: "Perhaps these remarks explain why the vast majority of the three thousand Jews threw caution to the wind and joined the patriot cause. One must look, however, beyond the principles of The Enlightenment to the practical considerations that encouraged Jewish 'radicalism.' The Declaration of Independence promised equality before the laws — and

Jews were highly conscious that the promise included themselves. Jews were Americans and wished to remain citizens of the new nation even if still hampered by discriminatory statutes."

Jews in Freemasonry and elsewhere joined in celebrating the adoption of the U.S. Constitution in 1789 at the conclusion of the Revolution against the British. As Feldstein also wrote in his book: "American Jewry was fully aware of the political importance of the new federal constitution and joined with Christian neighbors to celebrate. In Philadelphia, the parade was led by government officials and the clergy of various Christian denominations and a rabbi marching arm in arm. Naphtali Phillips, a young observer, describes: '....In an open carriage drawn by elegant horses sat Chief Justice McKane with other judges from the Supreme Court, holding in his hand the new United States Constitution in a frame. This was received by the populace with great rejoicing... The procession then proceeded from about Third Street near Spruce, northward toward Callowhill Street, then wheeled towards Bush Hill, where a number of long tables filled with all kinds of provisions, with a separate table for the Jews, who could not partake of the meal from the other tables; but they had a full supply of soused — pickled — salmon, bread and crackers, almonds, raisins, etc. This table was under the charge of an old cobbler, named Isaac Moses, well-known Philadelphian at that time. Benjamin Rush (the Jew who signed the Declaration of Independence) also commented on the ecumenical character of the celebration: 'Pains were taken to connect ministers of the most dissimilar religious principles together; thereby to show the influence of a free government in promoting Christian charity. The Rabbi of the Jews locked in the arms of two ministers of the gospel was a most delightful sight. There could not have been a more happy emblem contrived of that section of the new constitution, which opens all powers and offices alike, not only to every sect of the Christians, but to worthy men of every religion.'"

When another Freemason, George Washington, was inaugurated as the first president, congregations of synagogues in the new nation sent him messages of congratulations for his stands in his inaugural address. In his reply to a Jewish synagogue in Savannah, Georgia, Washington responded: "The citizens of the United States have a right to applaud themselves for having given to mankind examples of an enlarged and liberal policy; a policy worthy of imitation. All alike possess alike liberty

of conscience and immunities of citizenship. It is now no more that tol-
eration is spoken of, as it was by the indulgence of one class of people,
that another enjoyed the exercise of their inherent natural rights. For
happily the government of the United States, which gives to bigotry no
sanction, to persecution no assistance, requires only that they who live
under its protection should demean themselves as good citizens, in giving it on all occasions, their effectual support."

It was these long-standing traditions which attracted Cohen to
progress in the ranks of Freemasonry. He expressed these sentiments in
the Scottish Rite Herald of Kansas City for October 1962: "In Philadelphia on July 4, 1776, the Continental Congress adopted the final form of
the Declaration of Independence. The following Freemasons helped con-
ceive and signed this important document creating the United States of
America and insuring freedom for its citizens: Samuel Adams, Josiah
Bartlett, William Ellery, Benjamin Franklin, Ellbridge Gerry, Lyman Hall,
John Hancock, Joseph Hawes, William Hooper, Sam Huntington, Thomas Jefferson, Francis L. Lee, Richard H. Lee, Francis Lewis, Phillip
Livingston, Thomas McKean, Robert Morris, Thomas Nelson, Jr., Robert Paine, John Penn, George Read, Benjamin Rush, Roger Sherman,
Richard Stockton, George Taylor, Watt Thornton, George Walton, William Whipple, John Witherspoon, Oliver Wolcott, George Wythe. Today communism menaces the freedom that these and many other, great
Masonic Founding Fathers, helped preserve for you. It now becomes
your duty to join with our illustrious Masonic forebears and keep freedom alive in America. J. Edgar Hoover, 33rd degree, tells us the nation is
face to face with the greatest danger ever to confront it. The menace of
communism is no simple, forthright threat. It is a sinister and deadly
conspiracy which can be conquered by an alert, dedicated citizenry to
the preservation of the principles on which America was founded. We,
as Scottish Rite Masons, are doing our patriotic duty when we ask a man
to join Scottish Rite. Our fundamental beliefs and teachings are what
makes America great and insures freedom. The more men we can indoc-
trinate with the Scottish Rite teachings the better Americans we will have
and the better chance freedom will have to survive."

Cohen was also quick to point out the basic tenets adopted by the
Supreme Council of the Scottish Rite Masonic bodies reflected the kinds
of things embodied in American concepts that had made America great

over 200 years. He frequently cited them to his readers: "The American public schools, non-partisan, non-sectarian, efficient, democratic, for all of the children for all of the people, the inoculation of patriotism, respect for law and order, and undying loyalty to the constitution of the United States of America; the compulsory use of English as the language of instruction in the grammar grades of our public schools; adequate provision in the American public schools for the education of the alien population in the principles of American institutions and ideals of citizenship; the entire separation of church and state and opposition to every attempt to appropriate public moneys — federal, state or local — directly or indirectly for the support of sectarian or private institutions."

On November 6, 7, 8, and 9, 1962, Cohen presided over the 160th reunion of the Kansas City Scottish Rite and designated the class as the Freedom Class, dedicated to preserving freedom in the United States. In a letter to the members making the designation, Cohen said in part: "In 1776 our Masonic forefathers gave their heroic minds, hearts and lives to the birth of a new nation dedicated under God to the principles of a free government. Throughout our constitutional history the tenets, creeds and influence of Masonry are most evident. The immortal document, the Declaration of Independence, was conceived and signed by thirty patriotic Masons who were interested in winning and preserving freedom for the United States of America. When free men are threatened with a challenge they respond with action, rising to the occasion with honor. We are now being surrounded by an almost-world-encircling scourge of Communism. Apparently we have been lulled into a belief that 'it can't happen here,' but it is happening, growing, gnawing at our vital freedoms every day. We Scottish Rite Masons in this consistory feel it is our duty to take positive action against Communism to bring about the reawakening of the spirit of Americanism and appreciation for the freedom we enjoy. We can take positive action in this direction by bringing in recruits newly-dedicated and inspired with the teachings, principles, and tenets of our fraternity."

Cohen continued to hit at the theme as he continued as Scottish Rite membership chairman. After the Kansas City Chiefs won the Super Bowl on January 17, 1970, by defeating the Minnesota Vikings by a score of 23 to 7, Cohen designated the 1970 Scottish Rite class of inductees the World Championship Reunion Class. He got Bruce Rice, a noted sportscaster at the time at KCMO-TV, Channel 5, to serve as master of ceremonies at the dinner held in connection with the completion of the degrees by the new class and got two members of the World Champion Chiefs who were 32nd degree Scottish Rite Masons, Johnny Robinson and Jerrell Wilson, to be speakers at the dinner. The other Blue Lodge Masons on the team, Jan Stenerud and Mike Livingston, also showed up at Cohen's bequest.

In a special extra edition of the Scottish Rite Herald put out to recruit candidates for the class, Cohen again hit at his theme of the relationship between Freemasons and American patriotism. In the extra edition, he wrote: "Arnold Toynbee, the prominent world historian, hits us where we live when he points out that 19 of the 21 world civilizations died — not from outside enemy but from internal decay. In six years our country will be 200 years old! Each of these cultures have descended into their defeat in a patterned sequence moving from bondage to spiritual faith to great courage; from courage to liberty; from liberty to abundance; from abundance to selfishness; from selfishness to complacency; from complacency to apathy; from apathy to dependence; submerging back, at last, into bondage.' The cycle depends on you, him, we, them, together in Masonry. Our purpose of attempting to acquaint more men of good will with the principle of Masonry to best equip a man to do the job he must do comes at a time when we must gird ourselves most for Armageddon. This country of ours is in a difficult position. Never before has confusion been so rampant in peoples' minds. We have anti-business and anti-religious attitudes being promoted vigorously, and there is a question in the minds of many as to the effect this will have on the direction which this country will go as a nation. We say that if the change is not made between now and 1976 in moving back into the principles of Masonry, we doubt seriously that we will have further opportunity to do so."

For a devoted member of Freemasonry and a patriot who loved his nation with a passion, Cohen could dream of nothing finer than the fact that 80,000 Shriners from North America would be coming to Kansas City to open its international convention on July 4, 1976, the 200th anniversary of American independence. Making the whole thing even sweeter was the fact that his longtime friend and associate who had worked closely with him in staging the Soap Box Derbies in Kansas City for the Shrine,

W.W. (Woody) Bennett, who had been Potentate of Ararat Shrine Temple in Kansas City, would be presiding over the convention as the Imperial Potentate of the Shrine, the first Kansas Citian to hold the post since Dad Land was installed in Atlantic City in 1954. In addition to Land and Bennett, two other members of Ararat had served as Imperial Potentates of the order up until that time. The first was Ethelbert P. Allen, a Kansas City businessman who became the first Potentate of Ararat Shrine when it was formed in January 1, 1898. The other was James F. Chandler, who served as Imperial Potentate in 1924, just 30 years before Land held the title in 1954. Bennett named Cohen as the convention public relations chairman for the 1976 Shrine convention and Cohen established the public relations office on the mezzanine floor of the Hotel Muehlebach with all the duplicating equipment his users would ever need through his Kansas City companies. In one of his first press releases, Cohen pointed out that two previous imperial council sessions of the Shrine had been held in Kansas City, the first June 11, 1901, and the second on June 3, 1924. That press release also said in part: "The Shrine had thrived under the mantle of pageantry, ritual and ceremony. Its rituals are carefully and colorfully staged. Its members wear ornate oriental robes, gowns and medals in their ceremonies. They participate in any number of uniformed units within a temple such as the Oriental Bands, Marching Bands, Dixie Land Bands, Dance Bands, Foot Patrols, Horse Patrols, Clown Units, Scottish Bag Pipes and any number of mechanized units ranging from the largest motorcycles to various models of miniature cars and motorcycles. They parade, they clown and they engage in hi-jinks that are directed at themselves."

The official program for the 1976 Shrine Imperial Council meeting in Kansas City had a full length, colored painting of President George Washington clad in all his Masonic regalia standing at a podium in a Masonic grand lodge in tribute to the bicentennial of America being held that same year. Under a headline, "Bicentennial Session in America's Heartland," a press release came out of the press room presided over by Cohen with the following opening paragraph: "Red-fezzed Shriners from all over North America will begin arriving in Kansas City the first weekend in July to celebrate the nation's 200th birthday and to stage the 102nd Imperial Council Session, which is the annual convention for 180 Shrine Temples and nearly one million Shriners." What a celebration it was, too, with two of the largest parades in national history in recognition of the U.S. bicentennial. Beginning at 9 a.m. July 5th, a parade lasting more than seven hours began snaking its way through downtown Kansas City before thousands of spectators. Because of the bicentennial, the ranks of thousands of Shriners were further swollen by uniformed bands from the Army, Air Force, Marines and the Navy along with military units and equipment. A second giant parade, this one devoted more to the fun aspect of American life, drew thousands more spectators for another six-hour parade in honor of the occasion, winding its way through the same area beginning at 7 p.m. July 8th, replete with a magnificent fireworks display overhead in honor of the 200 years of American Independence. Issued during the convention over the Cohen imprint as public relations chairman in honor of the bicentennial was a list of prominent Americans who had been Shriners, including four modern day U.S. presidents, Warren G. Harding, Franklin Delano Roosevelt, Harry S. Truman and Gerald Ford, senators such as Barry Goldwater, Strom Thurmond, Harry Byrd, Stuart Symington, Henry Jackson and Leverett Saltonstal, and motion picture actors such as Harold Lloyd, who even served as Imperial Potentate; John Wayne, Red Skelton, Will Rogers, Ernest Borgnine, Tony Martin, Joe E. Brown and Clark Gable.

The most moving bicentennial tribute given at the convention perhaps was a statement by a friend of Cohen, Dr. D.M. Graham Clark, a member of Ararat Shrine and president of the School of Chaplains at the time. At a convention religious service conducted at the Community Christian Church, 45th and Main Streets, on July 4th for the Shrine officers and guests, Dr. Clark said: "When the Bicentennial Imperial Council goes into session on Independence Day, there will be many significant items on the agenda. One subject for discussion that should offer a special challenge to every delegate concerns the opportunity for our brotherhood to reaffirm its commitment to our patriotic heritage. As a basis for thinking through the justification of the democratic principle under which we live, let us consider an excerpt from a famous inaugural address. When our brother Mason George Washington was inaugurated in 1789 as the first president of the United States, he prayed this prayer: 'Almighty God, we make our earnest prayer that Thou wilt keep the United States in Thy holy protection; that Thou will incline the hearts of the citizens to cultivate a spirit of subordination and obedience to government; to entertain a brotherly affection and love for one another and for their fellow citizens of the United States at large.' It seems to me that the God to whom President Washington prayed has answered the prayer for our country's protection for these 200 years. Yet the response of citizens in whose name the prayer was given has not always been the response which President Washington might have expected from a people so blessed under this democracy. Our nation is plagued by indifference, non-involvement, on the part of its people. We have developed complacent followers, not obedient leaders. The challenge to every Shriner, it seems to me, is the inclining of our hearts toward obedience and brotherly affection, I believe our first president would have liked such positive action for it was this same George Washington who as a schoolboy, wrote in his copybook; 'Labor to keep alive in your breast that little spark of celestial fire—conscience.' A citizen of good conscience surely would be a citizen cooperative with and obedient to his government and one who strove to live in brotherly affection and love for his fellow citizen. In her novel, Let Love Come Last, Taylor Caldwell writes: '... all the evil that ever came to any man, to the whole world, comes when men say to themselves: 'I, but not my brother.' That old Canian question, 'Am I my brother's keeper?' somehow persists. The guilt of indifference to our brothers, which we often hide in group non-responsibility, somehow doesn't leave us alone. Our greatest sense may be the many sins of omission. Yes, currently, ideas of individual and corporate responsibility in morality and ethics in some instances are slowly permeating the thinking man's mind and troubling the waters of conscience. Long ago Shriners developed conscientiousness of good group responsibility; they became aware of the joy of fulfilling another's needs. And today we have the opportunity to share in an act of charitable love though support of hospitals for crippled children. This is an affirmation that we are in fact our brother's keeper. Isaiah wrote: 'If you pour out yourself for the hungry and satisfy the desire of the afflicted then shall your light rise in the darkness and your gloom be as the noonday.' Our Shriner's light shines through the heart of a child."

There was one other aspect of the 1976 Shrine Imperial Council meeting in Kansas City that was dear to the heart of Jerry Cohen. That was the fact that the Shrine Imperial Divan, led by Imperial Potentate Woody Bennett of Kansas City, were able to take part in ceremonies paying tribute to his longtime friend and mentor, who was also a Shriner, the late H. Roe Bartle. Musical organizations and honor guards from the Shrine were drawn up in array to take part in the ceremonies marking the dedication of the new multi-million-dollar Kansas City convention center, Bartle Hall, named for the former mayor, at 8:45 a.m. July 5. Cohen had helped Bartle form the American Humanics Foundation to provide assistance to college students who were studying for careers as paid leaders in national youth organizations. Bartle, when he became mayor, named Cohen as a member of the Kansas City Board of Parks and Recreation. One of the last acts in which Bartle took part before he died in 1974 was the ground-breaking ceremonies which were part of a multi-million-dollar city bond package that included Royals Baseball Stadium, Arrowhead Football Stadium and the Kemper Arena for basketball and ice hockey. On March 1, 1974, shortly after Bartle died, Mayor Charles B. Wheeler had introduced a resolution in the City Council to name the hall after Bartle. The resolution pointed out that Bartle had served as a supersalesman for Kansas City for more than 50 years in speaking engagements across the nation and had contributed to the city in many other ways, including eight years as mayor. The council adopted the resolution unanimously after it was introduced by Mayor Wheeler. The International Shrine convention was to be the first big convention to make use of the newly finished structure.

HUBERT HUMPHREY CHATS WITH COHEN — *Vice President Hubert Humphrey, who made an unsuccessful bid for the presidency in 1968, chats with Jerry Cohen, right, at a meeting in Washington with 3M officials.*

A U.S. SENATOR COMES TO CUT RIBBON — *When Jerry Cohen, standing at right beside a television newscaster, opened a new business location in the 1600 block on Grand, Sen. Edward Long, Missouri member of the U.S. Senate, third from the left, came to cut the ribbon in opening ceremonies. Mayor H. Roe Bartle, standing next to Mrs. Jeannette Cohen, left was on hand also. Visible looking up behind Cohen is L.P. Cookingham, longtime city manager of Kansas City.*

15

A Last-Minute Bailout

There is an old folk saying that goes something to the effect that for the want of a nail a shoe was lost, for want of a shoe a horse was lost, for want of a horse a battle was lost and for want of a battle a kingdom was lost. Something like that might have happened to the Kansas City Sports Complex and Convention Center when it was unveiled in 1966 if it had not been for Jerry Cohen. In its edition of February 23, 1966, The Kansas City Star devoted the bottom half of its first page to an 8-column artist's rendering of a new domed stadium for baseball and football and a smaller arena for basketball and ice hockey under a headline 8-column in width reading: "A plan for Giant Kansas City Sports and Convention Center." From the top of the page in that edition there was also a news story set in black type reading: "Unveil Sports Complex." The story began: "A comprehensive report on the proposed sports, entertainment and convention complex for Jackson County — and its anticipated impact on the community — was presented to the county court today. The 165-page report, prepared as a combined, 6-month effort of three major engineering firms, examines nearly every conceivable aspect of the proposal from construction designs and costs of the covered stadium, field house and exhibition hall to the inevitable loss of economic and competitive advantage if the facilities are not built." A little later in the news story The Star carried on the project it said: "Robert Drange, an engineer for Howard Needles, Tammen & Bergendoff engineering consultants and a coordinator for the three firms during the study, made the presentation. The other participating companies were Black & Veatch and Burns & McDonnell.... Engineers have said privately the report may be the most comprehensive of its kind ever assembled."

What the story did not say was that the project might not have met the almost universal acceptance it did if Cohen had not stepped in at the last minute to ensure that sufficient copies of the report were available at the scheduled press conference and public unveiling of the plan when it took place. Members of the county court learned to their dismay that the engineering firms had only a handful of copies available just hours before the press conference and gathering of civic leaders they had planned at the Hotel Continental. They turned to Cohen and his duplicating equipment business in desperation. Cohen was never one to say no to a civic project he felt was worthwhile if there was an emergency. He recruited his employees and the equipment in their sales rooms to try to meet the task and have copies available. The result was more than 75 copies of the massive report were ready by the scheduled time. Neatly typed, however, at the bottom of the covers of the report was this legend: "For release at 9:30 a.m., Wednesday, February 23, 1966. Press copies printed courtesy of Jerry Cohen, Tempo Co." There was never a question in the minds of the power structure of Kansas City about the contribution Cohen had made on an emergency basis. A letter from Dan Fennell, public relations man who was in charge of the press conference, said in a letter to Cohen later: "Now the many details connected with announcing the Engineers' Report on the Sports Complex have been completed, I want to take this opportunity to thank you, both personally and in behalf of the County Court, the Sports Commission and Bob Drange, for your most outstanding contribution to our efforts. Without your help, it would never have been possible for us to provide the more than 60 principal press, radio and TV outlets with most attractive bound copies of the 176-page report. At the time we received the original text of the report, barely 36 hours in advance of our press conference, it would have been actually impossible for us to have found a printing or other duplicating source. However, thanks to your most substantial contribution in manpower, materials, equipment and those wonderful 3M duplicating and printing machines, we were able to inform the press of details sufficiently in advance to permit the extensive coverage that came the following week. It was one of the most outstanding services, both financially and mechanically, that has been performed since my association with the commission. Again, the most heartfelt thanks from many who appreciated your efforts." The letter showed copies were also sent by Fennell to the members of the Greater Kansas City Sports Commission, Ernie Mehl, the chairman and longtime sports editor of The Star; Irvin Fane, a longtime friend of Jerry and secretary; John P. Miller, treasurer, and Dutton Brookfield, Ray Evans, Cliff C. Jones and Earl Smith, vice presidents; and the three judges of the Jackson County Court, Charles E. Curry, Morris Dubiner and Floyd Snyder.

Cohen continued to play an active role in the effort to get voter approval of the bonds for the massive expansion project unveiled in the 1966 engineering survey of a domed stadium for football and baseball, an expanded convention center and a field house for basketball and hockey. Several things helped throw cold water on the plans for a time after the press conference which Cohen helped bring to a successful conclusion with his last-minute effort. One was that the much-vaunted report did not choose between sites mentioned as possibilities for the stadium and field house, the so-called Leeds site located in the vicinity of the Fisher Body plant of General Motors in Eastern Kansas City and the Central Business District southwest of the downtown Kansas City loop. The report also mentioned a third possibility, the construction of the stadium at the Leeds site and the field house for hockey and basketball near the American Royal Livestock and Horse Show in the Central Industrial District. Another was the fact that Arnold Johnson, the original president of the Kansas City Athletics major league baseball franchise, had died and Charles O. Finley, a Chicago insurance executive, had acquired the team. He had a falling out with the sports department of The Kansas City Star and was already making noises about moving the franchise out of Kansas City to a new location in Oakland, California.

A third factor was the violence which occurred in the black ghettoes of Kansas City following the assassination of Martin Luther King, Jr., the noted black civil rights leader, in Memphis in April 1968. The Kansas City violence left seven persons dead, including six blacks and a police officer; a fire department member critically wounded and several others hurt from flying glass and random gunfire and millions of dollars in damage from fire bombings and lootings. Cohen and other business leaders in the downtown area adjoining the scene of the black rioting were visibly shaken by the development even though the incident was short-lived thanks to the efforts of the Kansas City officials with help from the Missouri National Guard. In 1967, the cantankerous Charley Finley got permission from the American League to move the A's to Oakland but not before Kansas City got the league to guarantee the city an expansion franchise in 1969. In a way, it was fortunate that Kansas City did not have major league baseball in 1968 when the rioting occurred since the old stadium at which the A's would have been playing was in the center of the riot area at 22nd and Brooklyn Avenue. Ewing Kauffman, an entrepreneur who had built a multi-million dollar pharmaceutical firm, Marion Laboratories, from a humble beginning manufacturing a calcium supplement for pregnant women from crushed egg shells, stepped forward to finance the new major league baseball franchise, the Kansas City Royals, who opened their first season in the spring of 1969.

When the smoke finally cleared, however, Jackson County voters approved a multi-million dollar bond issue to build a 40,000-seat baseball stadium and a 76,000-seat football stadium at the Leeds site and the basketball-hockey field house at the American Royal site with a seating capacity of 18,000. The expanded convention center was constructed adjacent to the Municipal Auditorium and the downtown area. Cohen was in the forefront with Mayor Ilus Davis and his friends on the Jackson County Court, Charles Curry, Floyd Snyder and Morris Dubiner, in the move to obtain successful passage of the bonds. The Kansas City Royals opened in the new Royals Stadium as a part of the Harry S. Truman Sports Complex at the Leeds site in the spring of 1973, while the Kansas City Chiefs began playing in the new Arrowhead Football Stadium in the fall of 1972. For a time in the 1970s after the Kemper was completed at the American Royal site in the Central Industrial District, Kansas City was home to four major league franchises. The National Basketball Association agreed to allow the Cincinnati Royals franchise to be moved to Kemper as the Kansas City Kings while the National Hockey League granted an expansion franchise, the Kansas City Scouts. The 18,000-seat sports and entertainment field house had been completed with a private gift from R. Crosby Kemper, Jr., in honor of his longtime Kansas

City banking family but the movable roof on the baseball and football stadium never materialized because of the shortage of bond moneys by the time construction was completed, thanks to inflation.

While he was making a major effort on behalf of the bond issue for the sports and convention center, Cohen continued to maintain his interest in the Swope Park Zoo and its support organization which he helped found, the Friends of the Zoo. He continued to serve as chairman of the Friends of the Zoo picnics at the park right up into the 1990s. In 1972, he finally became president of Friends of the Zoo. During his presidency, Cohen was able to raise enough money to enable the city to establish a new exhibition and housing area for the big cats of the zoo, lions, tiger, leopards and cheetahs, in the Great Cat Walk. The cat exhibit was dedicated in June 1972, with Mayor Charles B. Wheeler accepting the project on behalf of the city. William T. A. Cully, who had been superintendent of the zoo since 1942, finally retired in mid-1962 to be succeeded by Donald Dietlein, who came here from the National Zoo in Washington. Cully, who had been a major force in keeping the zoo alive during difficult times for zoos, thanks to his friendship with Cohen, died in October 1968. Dietlein was not enamored with the Swope Park Zoo and accepted another zoo post within two years. He was succeeded by Jack Armstrong, whose wife, Jan Armstrong, was to prove a longtime asset to the zoo and its animals. The Kansas City Star had been sold by its former employee owners in 1977 to a New York conglomerate, Capital Cities Communication, Inc., and almost immediately civic leaders such as Cohen realized the new owners were not the civic boosters the local owners had been. Armstrong was elevated to the post of zoo director after serving as an assistant under Dietlein just in time to feel the lash of the new investigative reporting style of the owners of The Star. In 1978, The Star got the U.S. Humane Society and the Department of Agriculture to join its reporters into an investigation of conditions at the zoo. As the newspaper reported, the study "found substandard animal care conditions and serious personnel problems, starting in the director's office. High animal mortality rates, low animal birth rates and rodent-infested cages and food storage areas." The damage might have been much worse if Cohen had not involved so many civic leaders in the operation of the Friends of the Zoo.

Needless to say, Armstrong was removed and a nationwide search was instigated for a successor. His wife, Jan, remained active in the zoo and in Friends of the Zoo with Cohen. Ernest Hagler, the assistant director of the Oklahoma City zoo who was highly regarded for his zoo abilities, was hired to fill the post vacated by Armstrong. Cohen, never one to let momentary adversity get him down, came out swinging in support of the zoo. In addition to a new zoo director, the city also had a new Citizens Association mayor, Richard L. Berkley, a longtime friend of Cohen. Berkley was interested in the parks and had three aggressive park board members who shared his views, Carl Di Capo, Anita Gorman and Ollie W. Gates. Cohen also persuaded Mayor Berkley's attractive and articulate wife, Sandy Berkley, to take an interest in the zoo, eventually making her president of Friends of the Zoo. Taking advantage of the shock that the adverse report by The Star on the zoo had had on the community, Mayor Berkley, the park board, Cohen, Mrs. Berkley and civic leaders joined forces to launch a program to improve the zoo.

The city under Mayor Berkley sought a top zoo planning firm to study the Swope Park Zoo and develop a massive plan for its improvement. The city settled on Jones & Jones, a nationally recognized zoo planning firm based in Seattle. While the study was going on, a copy of the Friends of the Zoo newsletter in early 1981 showed a large photograph of Jerry and Jeannette Cohen and a story about them giving the zoo the money to buy a pair of two-humped Asian bactrian camels to help the zoo on its way into its new era. The article also contained a photograph of the two Cohen grandchildren, Sherri and Richard Jacobson, the children of his daughter, Rosalyn and her husband, Howard Jacobson, saying the Cohens wanted the new pair of camel named after Richard and Sherri. In its study, the firm of Jones & Jones recommended a massive revamping of the zoo over 20 years at a cost in excess of $70 million. By early 1986, the city had moved to start the rebuilding program and Mayor Berkley named Jerry Cohen to head a committee of civic leaders to support a bond and revenue program on the August 1986 primary election ballot.

At a press conference on July 2, 1986, Mayor Berkley opened the session by saying that there were six issues on the ballot that need approval by the voters on August 5, if Swope Park and the other parts of the city parks and recreation system were to be improved. He then introduced Cohen as the overall campaign chairman by saying: "Jerry Cohen, chairman of the Friends of Parks and Recreation Committee, former Parks and Recreation Commissioner, who is probably best known for his perennial work with the Mayor's Christmas Tree Fund, is here this morning along with Park Commissioners Anita Gorman, Carl Di Capo and Ollie Gates to provide us with additional information on the August 5 election."

In a short speech, Cohen outlined the importance of the election to the zoo and other parts of the park system by saying: "We are all here today because we realize what a unique and valuable asset our parks and boulevards are to Kansas City, but we are also here today because we are aware that the future of Kansas City's 176 parks and 126 miles of boulevards are at stake. Inflation and cost increases have eaten away at the park and recreation department's ability to do essential maintenance services on these assets, so our parks and boulevards are not receiving essential maintenance services that make us proud to show off our nationally renowned park system. Some of the fees and assessments for the maintenance of our parks and boulevards have not been increased since they were implemented. Some are so long ago as 1925, over 60 years ago. If parks and recreation do not receive an increase in funding, our parks and boulevards will continue to deteriorate and Kansas City will lose one of its great assets. Voters can help save our parks and boulevards by voting 'Yes' for parks and recreation's new propositions on Tuesday, August 5. Your 'Yes' vote will improve the maintenance, appearance and upkeep of Kansas City's most unique assets — its parks and boulevards. Our park system is at a critical crossroads. It is up to the voters to improve the quality of life in Kansas City."

The word around Kansas City had always been that if you want a civic job done right give it to Jerry Cohen and Mayor Berkley chose well in giving Cohen the ball to run with on the zoo and other park and boulevard improvement programs. From the time of the press conference on July 2 until the vote on August 5, Cohen left no stone unturned. He got the Greater Kansas City Chamber of Commerce to endorse the issue. He lined up Freedom, Inc., and Committee for County Progress, two top area political organizations, to endorse the issues and held press conferences with their respective presidents, Archie Welch and Jack Holland, to announce the fact with Anita Gorman, president of Parks and Recreation, on hand as well. A steering committee to support the issues had some of Kansas City's leading citizens among many others: Art Asel,

Chuck Battey, Bill Berkley, Art Brookfield, Sal Capra, Bill Clarkson, Chris Clouser, Judge Lewis Clymer, L. P. Cookingham, Bill Deramus, Jay Dillingham, David Jackson, Henry Johnson, John and Marian Kreamer, Bob MacGregor, Henry Poindexter, Buck O'Neal, Joe Serviss, Don Stubbs, Victor Swyden, Don Watkins, Mike White, Sen. Harry Wiggins. Members of the Ethnic Enrichment Commission showed up in costume, there was a Polynesian floor show by the Cohen family and other events for a press conference Sunday, August 3, on stage at Starlight Theater to promote the park issues. The Star covered a specially staged event by Cohen with a photograph showing park workers cleaning and clearing in three parks to show what would be done if the issues passed. The Marching Cobras led a spirited parade from City Hall along Eleventh Street to Baltimore and south on Baltimore to the Barney Allis Plaza with Mayor Berkley and members of the City Council for a final press conference at noon August 4.

Thanks to all the efforts mustered by Cohen taking a leading interest, the park bond issues carried overwhelmingly. As Ernest Hegler, who had been zoo director for eight years, wrote Cohen on February 25, 1987: "When I first came to the Kansas City Zoo you were a member of the Friends of the Zoo board. I learned from others that you were one of the 'movers and shakers' — not only as far as the Kansas City Zoo was concerned, but also the Parks and Recreation Department, and, indeed, Kansas City itself. Not only was that true, I also discovered that you were a straight shooter... I can remember calling you on any number of times asking for donations to buy camels, interpretative graphics, equipment, or whatever we needed. You always said yes because you believed in the cause — to have the best zoo possible for Kansas City...You've always stood up for Kansas City, the Parks and Recreation Department and the Kansas City Zoo, particularly. We know 'one of our own.' I wish there was some way I could repay you for your kindness, courtesies and friendship that you've extended to me over the past eight years."

While Cohen was remaining loyal to the Swope Park Zoo through the years, he was also remaining loyal to his other love in Swope Park, the Starlight Theater. His daughter, Elaine, who had been so active as a child actress in Starlight Theater productions, was long gone by now, having gone on to a strong theater department at Northwestern University and living in Chicago. Richard H. Berger, the Broadway and motion picture figure who had agreed to come to produce the outdoor summer musicals at Starlight, had continued to shepherd top stars into top productions in Swope Park for years but had gone on to bigger things as the 30th anniversary neared in 1979, but Cohen had continued to provide the strong support he had shown to Starlight from the beginning. In the 1979 programs handed out to the thousands of theatergoers who were still coming, Cohen was listed as a vice president of the Starlight Theater Association and chairman of the Production Department. Many civic leaders who had been on the original executive committee with Cohen had gone on to other things but Cohen was still going strong in the operation. Other officers that year were Jim Britt, a noted Kansas City lawyer and lover of theater who was president; Aaron J. Levitt, Henry J. Massman III, John F. Pritchard, Jr., W. C. Theis and Robert K. Zimmerman, vice presidents; Carl E. Bolte, Jr., secretary; Clair Schroeder, treasurer; and Cathy Pfeiff, chairman of the Women's Division; A. G. (Tony) Ferrara, who had been active in the Starlight from the beginning in staging the summer musicals as an assistant to Berger, had now become the chief operating officer as executive vice president and general manager. The outdoor theater had undergone some shakey days for a couple of years following the rioting in the late spring of 1968 after the assassination of Martin Luther King, Jr., the beloved black civil rights leader. Theatergoers from Johnson County and the Country Club districts in Kansas City had to pass close by some of the affected areas and nationally televised newscasts of rioting in major metropolitan areas across the nation as well as Kansas City area had struck fear in the hearts of many urban dwellers.

Berger and Ferrara had worked hard in 1968 and 1969 to see that musical comedies that would be top box office hits with top stars were staged. In 1968, the summer season at Starlight had been Annie, Get Your Gun, Call Me Madam, Carousel, Music Man, Pajama Game, Show Boat, South Pacific and Sweet Charity. A similar blockbuster season in 1969 included Can-Can, Damn Yankees, George M! (about George M. Cohan), Mame, A Merry Widow, Nashville Sound, Peter Pan and State Fair. One of the reasons that Starlight could attract the kind of stars it was able to get was because the backers for the theater, including Cohen, had been able to put together a circuit of outdoor theaters that gave the stars extended runs. In addition to Starlight, the theaters included Starlight musicals in Indianapolis, the Dallas Summer Theater, the Theater of the Stars in Atlanta and the Municipal Opera in St. Louis. In 1979, for instance, the parade of stars and shows at Starlight included David Birney, Anita Gillette, Milo O'Shea and Murray Matheson in My Fair Lady; Abe Vigoda, Hugh O'Brian and Kathryn Crosby in Guys and Dolls; Farley Granger, John McCook and Victoria Mallory in Brigadoon; the Blackstone Magic Show; Arte Johnson, Avery Scheiber, Hans Conreid, John Carradine and Benny Baker in A Funny Thing Happened on the Way to the Forum; Robert Morse, Ken Berry and Donald O'Conner in Sugar; Ann Blyth and Richard Frederick in The Desert Storm; Howard Keel and Carol Lawrence in I Do! I Do!; Janis Tucker and Forrest Tucker in Ballroom and the black musical comedy of The Wizard of Oz, The Wiz.

When the Starlight celebrated its 30th anniversary in 1980, it was still going strong and so was Cohen in his support as a member of the executive committee. The line-up of shows and performers was more star studded than ever in the celebration of 30 years of successful outdoor summer theater operations. The shows and stars of that year included Cab Calloway in Bubbling Brown Sugar; Ginger Rogers and Sid Caesar in Anything Goes; Florence Henderson and Giorgio Tozzi in South Pacific; Gabriel Kaplan and Vicki Carr in Concert; An Evening with Joel Gray and Peter Nero; Bert Convy in Bye, Bye Birdie; Larry Kert in Al Jolson Tonight; Rose Marie, Rose Mary Clooney, Helen O'Connell and Margaret Whiting in 4 Girls 4; Joe Namath in Lil Abner; and Jack Jones and Marvin Hamlisch in Concert. By the time the 40th anniversary season had rolled around in 1990, both the Starlight and Cohen were still going strong together but in a somewhat revised format to meet the rising costs of stars and production. By the 1990s, the outdoor summer season was down to four major productions running 10 days each interspersed with single night musical concerts of stars.

16

Jerry Goes International

There has always been a restlessness and a desire to see what the world God gave them was really like for themselves on the part of Jews. For over 5,000 years since the stories of the book of Genesis were written, the Jews have been on a curious journey to learn and experience all they can during their lifetimes. The wanderlust that brought his mother and father half way around the world from Lithuania and Hungary to Kansas City was born into Jerry Cohen. During his lifetime, Cohen and his wife were always on the go, visiting Europe, Latin America, Asia and the South Pacific as well as the Middle East. It seemed only natural then that Cohen should wind up as one of the early travelers to mainland China after President Richard Nixon reopened relations with the China of Mao Tse Tung and Chou En Lai in 1972. By the time Jimmy Carter became president in 1976, a new strong man was emerging in China to succeed the ailing Mao, a short, determined Chinese, Deng Tsao Ping, who knew his nation had to have greater relations with the West, particularly with the United States, if it was to survive. The result was that President Carter was urging a flow of American visitors into the massive nation that had been off limits to most Americans since Generalissimo Chiang Kai Shek fled to Taiwan from China in 1949. As a longtime friend of a prominent Chinese American couple of Kansas City, Dr. William Wu and his wife, Francie Wu, who still maintained family ties in China, and a member of the U.S.-China Friendship Association, Cohen was invited to be a member of one of the first of these delegations to visit China and was there November 5-25, 1977, before President Carter finally announced full normalization of relations with China in December 1979. The American delegation Cohen accompanied was a cross-section of Americans pulled from all across the United States and with a wide variety of interests.

During the 20-day visit, the delegation visited Peking, Nanking, Yangschou, Wuxi, Soochow, Shanghai, the Ming Tombs and the Great Wall. They interviewed Chinese communist officials, were entertained with musical, acrobatic and folk dance performances and got an inside view of Chinese agriculture, industry, fishing and handicraft manufacturing. It was the time when the so-called Gang of Four, consisting of the widow of Mao and three of his top ministers, had just fallen from power and Mao had just died. At one of the first meetings with Chinese officials in Peking, the American visitors, including Cohen, heard an unusually frank discussion of the situation from Wan Ping Nan, the Chinese president of the U.S.–China Friendship Association, of the current conditions. He is quoted in a report by Cohen and his associates as saying. "There was a major occurrence last year. The Gang of Four was exposed and put down. The Chinese people did not know what was happening. Much was occurring in the party at high levels. Mao had tried to settle the problems of the Gang of Four before he died, to stop their attempt to seize the power of the party. In the history of the party, the premier would become chairman when the chairman died. When Chou En Lai died, Chairman Mao appointed Hua as first vice chairman, the first time we had this office. The Gang of Four had tried to oppose Chairman Mao, Chou En Lai and Hua. On October 6 last year, the Gang of Four was smashed by Hua with far-reaching significance for China. It is understandable that some foreign friends expressed concern about what was happening in China. Now it has been established that the Gang of Four were using their power they had usurped to disrupt the party, the army, our production and confuse the people. Then they could seize power through the disorder. They are actually anti-party and counter-revolutionary — not reactionary. Those leading the country now, including Hua, are carrying out the teachings of Chairman Mao. The Gang of Four developed the wrong idea that production must be reduced. It can be seen that what the Gang of Four did was contrary to Mao. Production must continue to grow. Production is essential. This revolutionary line of Chairman Mao must continue. Progress has been made in industry and in agriculture in spite of the weather. The whole party and the Chinese people are confident that progress will continue to be made."

Cohen brought out of China a 106-page document single-spaced on legal size sheets so loaded with statistics and quotations that it sounded as though it had been drafted by agents for the Central Intelligence Agency. The group laughed about it but did feel one of their members was an agent for the CIA. As a matter of fact, at a good-natured awards ceremony held the final night, one of the members was cited as such by Wayne Leaver, who was master of ceremonies. This award as Leaver made it: "Jody Gibbs receives our next award as 'The Most Likely to Be a CIA Agent.' Inspiration for this came from Virginia Roeder. We are all out of trench coats and hats, but we do have a secret decoder ring from a certain cereal box." Some examples of the kind of statistics in the report included these: One Cotton Mill No. 2 in Peking: "Built in 1954, began production in 1955; 115,000 spindles; 2,400 looms. Daily output — Before cultural revolution, 60,000 kilograms yarn, 220,000 meters cloth. Total number of workers: 6,400, 70 percent women." On a farm commune: "160 square kilometers in commune, 85,000 people in 129 brigades in living quarters; wheat and rice are chief crops; 7,000 kilos per hectare in average production; wheat is sown in winter and harvested in June; immediately after harvest rice is planted; two crops per year are thus produced; orchards with apples, peaches, pears and grapes are grown; last year 8,500 hogs were raised; nine dairy herds with 3,400 milk cows produced 12 million kilos of milk last year; 250,000 Peking ducks are raised per year; 170,000 kilos of fresh fish produced last year; 153 tractors, 90 tractors for agricultural use; 400 water sump tractors; tilling of soil is mostly mechanized; gathering of crops by manpower, threshing by machine." The Horai commune in the suburbs of Wisu: "Our first stop was to see the fish ponds where they raise bream, black carp and silver carp. The fish live together in the same pond. Upper water fish eat plankton, middle level fish eat aquatic plants, lower level fish eat snails. Small fish are raised in a hot house. Small fish are put in the ponds in January and in June they begin catching the fish with nets, keeping the large fish and putting back the small ones. November is the main fish harvest... The commune covers 12 square kilometers, has eight production brigades and 80 production teams. Teams are formed on the basis of natural villages. Brigades are formed on the basis of advanced cooperatives that existed before the commune. The commune has a population of 15,000, 4,500 households and 7,000 able-bodied men and women. Women make up 55.2 percent of the work force. They have 3,500 mews land in growing grain, 3,100 in vegetation, 800 in mulberry bushes, 2,000 in fishing areas, 7,000 in forestry, orchards and tea plants. They run seven factories, one construction team, two dairies, four chicken farms, 80 pig farms and they breed fresh water pearls and fish."

The comprehensive report also contains one item about a visit by Cohen and two other members of the group, Angelo Figueroa and Omowale Babalawo, to the Peking zoo to see the pandas there. Because of his interest in pandas and animals and his interest in the Kansas City zoo and as a member of the Parks and Recreation Board, Cohen did not want to pass up a chance to see the famous zoo. The report contains this reference: "They reported it was very interesting because Jerry was very well informed on the animals and their maintenance which added a lot to the visit. At one point, Jerry put his hand through a fence to pat a sitting camel. Omowale shouted: 'No! Stop! it would make terrible headlines: 'Foreigner's hand bitten off by camel.' Jerry went right ahead any way and turned out to be right. It didn't bite." His interest in Oriental art as demonstrated by the Oriental garden he and his wife had developed at their home back in Kansas City created a frenzy of buying carved jade, paintings and other Chinese artifacts at what he knew to be rock bottom prices. His buying caused him to be mentioned first in the awards at the closing ceremonies of the delegation as mentioned in the report. Leaver told the group: "Our first award is to Jerry Cohen. He receives the award for 'Best Supporter of China's Economy.' His award consists of a book of IOUs."

One of the most significant things in the comprehensive information Cohen and the Americans brought out was one of the first indications that Deng Tsao Ping was emerging as the new Chinese leader. The information was attributed to Sung Chio Chuan, member of the standing committee of the Revolutionary Committee, growing out of a meeting of Cohen and the others with him in Shanghai. Chuan pointed out that Deng had reemerged after the 11th national congress in China following the death of Mao. He called him a veteran revolutionary and said in part of him: "Deng joined the revolution during the first civil war period. His revolutionary base area was in the southwest. He was one of the earliest party members and always supported Mao against Wang Ming and the erroneous line. He was a leading member and participated in the long march. He led one of three divisions against the Japanese and fought bravely. During the war of liberation he was the leading member of one of four revolutionary field armies. After liberation, he became secretary general of the central committee.

"Veteran revolutionary cadres were a major obstacle to efforts by the Gang of Four to usurp power of the party and they fabricated slanders against Deng. Deng resisted and opposed them and Mao said Deng was able and strong in political ideology... In 1976, the Gang was in a hurry to usurp power and attacked many veteran revolutionaries, including Deng, and production declined. This worried the masses and when Chairman Hua smashed the Gang of Four the workers were overjoyed. Deng emerged again as a leading member and as a result of Hua's carrying out of Mao's behest, Deng carries out Mao's Lines: Push forward the economy, develop science and technology."

The significance of this statement by a leading party official to Americans in Shanghai became increasingly apparent as time passed. On a boat cruise around the Shanghai harbor, this same leading Shanghai Chinese communist approached Cohen and said through an interpreter that he had seen by the business card Cohen had given him that Cohen was in the duplicating equipment and computer sales field. He asked Cohen to give him some advice on computers since the mainland Chinese were just beginning to get into the field. Cohen said he spent more than an hour talking to him about computers. He said he was somewhat surprised the next morning when the same official showed up at the Shanghai airport just before the Americans were to leave China. Cohen and the official talked for more than an hour again while waiting for the plane to depart about computers. Cohen said the more he talked to the Chinese official, the more he learned that the Chinese were still quite naive about the devices. Cohen said he finally recommended to the official that the Chinese approach IBM who had the experts who could tell them what they really needed. Some weeks later back in the United States, Cohen said he learned from one of his friends at IBM that the mainland Chinese had entered into an initial 13-million-dollar contract with IBM for computers, the first such contract by an American firm.

As do most hard-working executives, Cohen liked to get away from the grind and spend some time in the open air with a group of men fishing. Just as in everything else he did, Cohen wanted to make sure it was done with style and so the society became known as the Great Society of Piscators. The members even had their own stationery, with a letterhead featuring a cartoon of fish resplendent in white tie and tails and the legend The Great Society of Piscators. On their expeditions, the members wore specially made Green Beret-style berets. They went at least annually and sometimes oftener to Canada, Alaska, Mexico, Central America and Latin America through the years to test their fishing skills, and Cohen prizes several trophy-size catches mounted on his walls. It was a result of one of these fishing expeditions to deep water lakes of the Andes Mountains in Colombia near Bogota that Cohen began another one of his international adventures. During brief stays in Bogota during the trip, Cohen's heart was touched by the sight of so many ragged youngsters begging in the street. One of his friends on the trip, James Scearce, told Cohen how he had adopted a young boy in Bogota through Foster Parents Plan, Inc. Cohen and Scearce went to have dinner with the boy, his family and a social worker for Foster Parents Plan, Hilse de Ortiz, and Cohen was so impressed he decided he would like to participate in the plan. After getting approval from his wife, Jeannette, Cohen began a 10-year period of friendship with a boy in Bogota, Pedro Nel Briceno. In the January 12, 1973, edition of The Kansas City Jewish Chronicle at the top of one of the inside pages there is a two-column headline reading "Kansas Citian 'Adopts' Foster Child." The accompanying story carries a photograph of a short, black-haired Colombian boy with the identification under the photograph reading "Pedro Nel Briceno, seven-year-old Colombian boy who was 'adopted' by Jerome Cohen, proudly poses for his foster parent." The story went on to say the following: "Jerome Cohen head of Electronic Business Equipment Co., has 'adopted' Pedro Nel Briceno, a seven-year-old Colombian boy through the Foster Parents Plan, by contributing $16 a month for the child's care. Pedro remains with his family, with every member of the family group benefitting from medical and dental care, the sustained guidance and counseling of social workers, a monthly cash grant, distribution of useful goods and the aid of special educational programs. With education a vital part of the organization's program, all foster children are able to — and must — attend school. Despite the distances between the foster parents who contribute the funds and the foster children who receive them, the two keep in touch with monthly letters translated by the organization."

For the next 10 years, beginning in December 1971, Cohen and his family continued correspondence with the small Colombia boy and his family. The thick file of correspondence is full of vignettes about what Cohen was doing and about the happenings in the family and with Pedro himself. Cohen was more than generous with the Briceno family during the 10 years, providing extra money for Christmas and birthday gifts for Pedro and members of his family, as well as for other purposes in assistance to the large family. It must have been an interesting experience for Pedro and his family to be receiving these letters from a man in Kansas City who wrote about his family, his business and his travels to all parts of the world during these 10 years. Pedro was one of 10 children, and his father was a truck driver and his mother took care of his three brothers and five sisters, two of whom were younger than he. In the early stages of the relationship, the letters were written to Cohen for Pedro from his father and sisters and as he progressed in school he took over the correspondence himself. Cohen's first letter to Pedro set the tone for the 10 years of correspondence and support. It said in part: "Have you started to school yet? It is my understanding that you start school when you are seven years old and if you have started, I want you to do a good job and study hard, so that I can be proud of you and the grades you make. Please tell your family that your new Foster Parent is a business man in the United States of America and that he lives in a big city in the state of Missouri. You may also tell them that he has two daughters. One age 30, who is married; and one age 24, who is going to get married in August. His 30-year-old daughter has presented him with two grandchildren, one grandson age 6 who is going to school here in America and a granddaughter age 3. So I feel that I know what little boys like you are interested in." In the first letter from Pedro, written by his father, there was the following message: "They informed me at the plan that you are my new foster father. I am very happy and thankful to you for choosing me as your foster child. I will try to correspond to your efforts, being a good student and being obedient with the plan. I do not have anything to tell you about myself but I tell you that I will do my first grade at school this year and I will study with much interest since I now have a person who is concerned about me. I tell you that my family is very thankful to the plan for the assistance. I have received the monthly contribution. Thanks a lot." The letters from Pedro and his family were always written in Spanish and then translated into English in typed form with Cohen getting a copy of both letters from the office in Bogota.

The regular letter correspondence is filled with details about both the family life of Cohen and from Pedro about his family. One letter from the plan official in Bogota told Cohen the family was so large it did not have enough beds and gave prices for which additional beds could be purchased. Cohen immediately sent a check for $194.40, since he had inaugurated the inquiry about the beds in response to a letter from Pedro. The purchase included three metal bunk beds with mattresses and two single size beds with accessories. Within a short time, Cohen received a letter from Pedro in which he said: "Thank you for the money you sent me. This money was used to buy beds and mattresses. We had beds but they were in bad situation." In a 1972 letter, Cohen wrote the following about the wedding of his daughter, and his religion, saying in part: "On September 26, we had a big wedding celebration for my youngest daughter, Elaine, who is 24 years old. She got married to an accountant and we had a very big wedding for her. After their wedding, they went to visit in England and France and will be living in Chicago, a big city 500 miles from where I live... My religion is Jewish and we have just finished celebrating our New Year and Day of Atonement and I want to wish you and your family a happy and prosperous new year."

In October 1972, Pedro wrote to Cohen: "Foster father, I have some sad news for you. My father was fired from his job due to political reasons and we are having a hard time even though my father tries hard." Cohen sent a letter to the social worker he had met in Bogota, Hilse de Ortiz: "In his last letter he wrote me his father was fired from his job and I have written our plant manager in Bogota to see if I can get him placed. I don't think it would be wise to tell them about this until I hear from the manager on a more positive answer from him, but I felt that you should know that I am trying to make this possible. If there is anything about the family you think I should know other than what he writes me about, I would appreciate hearing from you." A short time later the letters indicated that father was once again working.

Over the 10 years, the letters reflected increasing changes in the lives of the two correspondents, the young boy growing into manhood in Bogota and Cohen prospering in Kansas City. Finally, in early 1982, Cohen received the following letter from Pedro Nel Briceno: "I fondly greet you and hope you are enjoying good health. I tell you that I am being cancelled from Program and I am writing this letter in order to express to you my most sincere thankfulness for the help you gave me. May God help you in your business. I will pray God so you will succeed in everything you do forever. My siblings and I will continue studying hard. Please tell your daughters and my grandmother hello for me. I will think of you always and will continue loving you." A letter from the Foster Parents Plan in Bogota to Cohen said in part: "We are pleased to inform you that your foster child, Pedro Nel Briceno, has graduated from our program. After ten years of assistance, the family has established a good base for their eventual self-support... Pedro and the other children are attending school and will be able to continue with their education..Your concern, your support, helped the family to substantially improve its financial and living conditions...None of this would have been possible without your generous support—you made all the difference." Cohen wrote back to Pedro expressing his gratitude for having him for 10 years as a son and bade him farewell with a display of affection. Another era had ended.

Despite a decade in which he had traveled all over the world and made all kinds of international contacts, Cohen never lost sight of what needed doing in Kansas City. Some of his foremost civic endeavors during this period was directed toward his long-time friend and mentor, the legendary H. Roe Bartle, former mayor who had died in 1974, shortly after taking part in the ground-breaking ceremonies for the new convention center which the city was to name H. Roe Bartle Hall. Cohen had taken great delight in participating in the dedication ceremonies for Bartle Hall during the 1976 American Bicentennial Convention of the Shrine of North America on July 5, 1976. In early 1977, Cohen had launched an effort to have a 9-foot-high bronze statue of Bartle installed in the lobby of Bartle Hall as a fitting tribute to the longtime mayor and Boy Scout executive.

First he got the city council to approve the idea of allowing such a statue to be installed. The next move was to get a prominent American sculptor to do the job so that a price could be determined. Who better to do the project than the sculptor who did the highly regarded statue, the Flag Raising on Iwo Jima, commemorating the famous Joe Rosenthal photograph of World War II, Felix De Welden? De Welden, who had also done a famous bronze of Harry S. Truman for permanent display at the Harry S. Truman Museum and Library in Independence, was agreeable and estimated a cost of around $75,000 for the 9-foot bronze statue of Bartle.

Cohen also put together a committee to head the H. Roe Bartle Memorial Statue Fund consisting of himself and four other well-known Kansas Citians of the day, Jay Dillingham, Jack Whitaker, Jerry Smith and Ernie Hueter. A letter went out from the committee reading in part: "We are writing to you because of your friendship with 'Chief' Bartle. All of us who knew and admired him are pleased with the naming of the H. Roe Bartle Exhibition Center. This is a great and deserved tribute to one of the most colorful and exceptional leaders who ever gave his talents to serving Kansas City. Roe's friends are also delighted that the city council has authorized installation of a nine-foot bronze statue in the main entry hall. To create the statue, the Kansas City Arts Commission has selected Felix De Welden, a celebrated sculptor whose Raising the Flag on Iwo Jima is on display in Washington, D.C. Total cost of the project will be $75,000. All funding will come from contributions made by Kansas Citians." Costs rose and the final cost of the statue and base was $90,000.

Three years later, the dedication ceremonies for the completed statue were held on March 21, 1980, with Mayor Richard Berkley; Mrs. Margaret Bartle, widow of the late mayor; De Welden, the sculptor; Charles B. Wheeler, who was mayor when the statue project was started, and Mrs. Jimmy Bartle Taylor, his daughter, taking part. The dedication program said in part: "H. Roe Bartle served Kansas City as mayor from 1955 to 1963, a dynamic period in which the city added about 225 square miles of land, the Kansas City Chiefs football team and such capital improvement projects as the Broadway bridge. From the time he moved to Kansas City in 1928 until his death in 1974, Mr. Bartle also served his adopted home as a civic leader, speaker and one of the city's most avid boosters."

But Cohen was not through with immortalizing Bartle yet. Although he was identified in news stories as the principal fund-raiser for the statue, Cohen wanted to help his longtime friend, lawyer and civil rights activist, Sidney L. Willens, who felt there was a need for a picture mural in the Bartle lobby to supplement the bronze statue. On August 17, 1989, a letter went out over the signature of Cohen and Jay Dillingham asking for help in raising the first $15,000 to make the project a reality. The letter said in part: "All of Roe's friends and admirers felt that the statue should be a centerpiece for an exhibit display depicting the many facets of our chief's life and devotion to others... Through this impressive display exhibit, visitors and future generations can know this remarkable, colorful personality as he appeared to those of us who were privileged to know him in life. On November 18, 1989, the colorful 10-foot-high mural depicting various parts of Bartle's life was dedicated in the lobby near the statue. American Humanics Foundation, Boy Scouts, the Marching Cobras and others whose operations had been touched by Bartle took part in the 1989 dedication, including Cohen. In a memorial booklet accompanying the dedication there was this quote from Bartle: "What America needs is more lovers of children and fewer lovers of things." That kind of charity expressed by Bartle was what kept Cohen going.

COHEN HELPS MARGARET TRUMAN — *When Harry Truman became fearful his daughter, Margaret Truman, might not draw a crowd at a Kansas City concert because of earlier mixed reviews which incensed him, he turned to his friends in the Ararat Shrine, including Jerry Cohen, Frank S. (Dad) Land) and others. They ensured an enthusiastic, sell-out crowd. Cohen, fourth from left, presented a bouquet of flowers to Margaret after the concert.*

A GOLD-PLATED DUPLICATING MACHINE — *When Sir Sigmund Gestetner, the British duplicating machine magnate, presented Jerry Cohen with a landmark duplicating machine plated entirely in 14-carat gold for outstanding sales work, Cohen wanted to make sure it found a good use. He presented it to Walter Guy, left, Imperial Potentate of the Shrine of North America at the time, at the international convention in Chicago to be used to benefit the Shrine Crippled Children's Hospitals.*

17

Chances and Jackpots

Thirty years after starting the Tempo Company in the duplicating and office supply business with one other man
in 1938, Jerry Cohen was showing no signs of letting up
in a sales career that had brought him from a one-room
operation to a multi-million dollar corporation with two
headquarters buildings in Kansas City and branches in St. Joseph,
Jefferson City and Shawnee Mission in the metropolitan Kansas City
area on the Kansas side. Despite his increasing devotion to civic duty,
Cohen never let his business interests slide trying to make a name for
himself by being a park commissioner, chairman of the Mayor's Christmas Tree Fund annually or helping H. Roe Bartle form the American
Humanics Foundation to help young persons who wanted to be professional youth leaders. He was a strong believer all his life that sales work
was what had made a strong nation of the United States. He was fond of
quoting George Romney, former governor of Michigan and former Board
Chairman of American Motors and at one time a 1968 Republican presi-
dential hopeful, when Romney said, "Nothing happens until a sale is
made." To put it in his own words, Cohen gave as his reasons for continually trying to increase his annual sales volume each year from 1938
on: "We confidently tell our sales people the sales person has one of the
most responsible jobs in the nation, the economy of our country is more
dependent on their activity than on our Congressmen. When the sales

person makes a sale the factories have to make a product, to make a product the factories have to hire people, buy more materials. The worker hired to make the product in turn pays taxes, buys merchandise and the wheels of commerce turn and generate new products to be sold. So nothing happens until the sale is made. The economy of this country is more dependent on the sales person than any other. I say to anyone who is going to get into the selling profession do their part and keep America economically strong by selling more products than ever."

If selling is so important, why spend as much time as he did in contributing to the good of the community outside of the long hours required to increase sales volume? Cohen had a ready answer: "One, you help your sales ability by such work; two, you feel better for having done something to help someone else." As he put it: "I think a very important point for anyone is to remember your only justification for existence on this earth is to help another person. You will be surprised how much better you will sell. I learned through the years that you cannot help another person without helping yourself. I can give you all kinds of illustrations. You help someone who is blind or elderly or infirm cross a busy street and you are helping someone overcome a problem and giving yourself a new experience in helping that person. Remember every experience of your life is important. It stores up here in that computer that is your brain and it is there when you need it. I tell everyone never to be unkind. I don't care how low you think a person may be you must learn to treat him with respect because you never know when he may turn up to be the boss. Sales are made between persons, not companies. Kansas City has been very good to me and I feel I have an obligation to give back to the community. I do that with a lot of public service, charity, religious, community service. One part of your life and one of your basic goals should be to give some of your time to charitable or community activities because you do one of two things. One is that there is no way you can be a part of any effort without making yourself better for having done so. The other is that you are going to meet someone there with the same ideas and that person can teach you how to do some things better. You never know how you are going to use it but don't ever give up making yourself available."

The 3M Company had always had a soft spot in its heart for Cohen both for his willingness to experiment with the company in developing new duplicating products for offices and in providing the kind of sales volume Cohen did for its duplicating and paper distribution facilities. It was obvious in early 1967 that the government was going to be one of the biggest consumers of duplicating equipment and supporting paper products and so in February 1967, 3M decided to hold a conference in Washington, D. C., to acquaint its company executives and leading dealers across the nation with how to do business with the federal government, both in Washington and at the regional level. Just as he had been selected by 3M as one of its annual Turtle Club members of 15 top dealers nationwide and the 3M Business Products Association Council when it was organized, Cohen was one of 16 dealers asked to join 3M executives at the Washington conference. David Kirk, 3M manager for the conference, listed four basic findings for the conference: "(1) The conference attendance, represented in depth from every quarter, reflected a renewed interest in exploiting the tremendous government market. (2) Enthusiastic support for BPSI and growing divisional commitments to the marketing program indicate confidence in its value and effectiveness. (3) Commitments for follow up action on marketing programs and recommendations reflect agreement and support. (4) Manpower commitment to the total marketing effort in the branches, in the districts and in Washington is increasing at a significant rate which, if continued, will insure a properly balanced total marketing effort as related to the potential government business which should and will belong to us." In a published report of the conference, 3M Company devoted several pages to the fact the Vice President Hubert Humphrey was a guest at the session. Humphrey was a former mayor of Minneapolis and U. S. Senator from Minnesota where the company began and continues to maintain the corporate headquarters. There was a photograph of Vice President Humphrey with three top 3M executives with whom Cohen had long been associated. The legend with the photograph read: "Everyone present at the reception had an opportunity to talk with the Vice President during the evening. Mr. Humphrey, Ernie Boverman, Charles Bree and Roy Bruchman all are listening to the words of Jerry Cohen as we caught this candid shot of personalities at the BPSI reception."

In the late 1960s, Cohen continued to use colorful approaches to try to increase his sales through greater production by the sales staff. In

1969, for instance, Cohen unveiled what was to be known as "Jerry's Thousand Dollar Club," a method of involving wives in efforts of their husbands to qualify for $1,000 bonuses for their efforts during that sales year. The couples were invited to a breakfast at a midtown Kansas City hotel at which Cohen and his sales manager, Fred Snitz, would unveil the promotion. The invitations bore the following legend: "Rambling Thru Breakfast with Cohen. A Triple Threat — Cineram — Slice of Life Extravaganza — In EBE Living Color. An All-Star Cast Production from the Century Club Players. Produced by 'Dan Rowan' Ruoff and 'Dick Martin' Snitz. Paid for by Jerome Cohen. Special Guest Attraction: Jeannette Cohen." At the place setting for each wife was an envelope containing a check made out to her husband in the amount of $1,000. The checks were not signed and the women were told not to open the envelopes until permission was granted for them to do so. After Snitz and Ruoff explained the rules, the women were asked to open the envelopes. They were told that if their husbands made the sales quota in the Thousand Dollar Club rule book by the same time next year Cohen would sign the checks. The checks were then returned and placed on the sales board in the sales room to remind the salesmen daily of what they had promised their wives. The promotion was considered so innovative by 3M that it featured a two-page spread with reproductions of the Cohen graphics for the event, photographs of the participants at the colorful breakfast and a story in the March 1969 edition of the corporate slick paper magazine, Center Span.

Always a student of history and of his own Jewish heritage, Cohen enjoyed using examples from these two areas to try to teach members of his staff how to be good managers and how to motivate others. He used Jethro, father-in-law of Moses; Alexander the Great and Julius Caesar as examples from these areas. As he said: "Let's see how some of our ancestors managed. In the book of Exodus in the Old Testament, we find Jethro giving his son-in-law, Moses, some sound managerial advice on such time-worn organization principles as span of control—a fancy term for how many people one man can boss — and managerial decentralization and delegation of authority — still fancier terms for operating independence. Jethro laid it out in a measly 14 Biblical verses which were understandable. How about that, behavioral scientists! That Jethro! He's just got to be one of the first management theorists. His state, and his army, along with his organized religion, were the originators of managerial principles. Using a military example, Alexander the Great was one of the better-known managers of his time! He had to be good to run a big slice of the world by the time he was 26. Alex's specialty, of course, was war. An innovator of the first rank, he introduced new principles of military organization, such as the Macedonian phalanx. It sounds like a teenage dance but was something quite different. The phalanx involved the employment of human physical resources in a way not previously done. First of all, Alexander preceded the infantry with mounted noblemen, from 1,200 to 2,000 of them. Behind them, he lined up the infantry shoulder to shoulder in extended lines. The term line, as in line-and-staff organization, comes from the military. Each soldier carried a long spear which he extended in front of his shield. Arranged this way, Alexander had a moving, pointed metal wall. On the flanks, he positioned his archers and the whole thing was supported by catapults, the artillery of the day, invented by his father, King Philip. Those of the enemy who were not done in by the catapults were either by the archers, being trampled by the cavalry or speared by the infantry. Alexander was more than a military tactician, though. He, like Jethro, was a believer in managerial decentralization. When he had conquered a new territory, he put a governor in charge who had extensive management latitude. Generally, the governor was a native of the vanquished country so Alexander mixed in a bit of practical psychology with his governing policy. Julius Caesar was no slouch as a manager, either. He couldn't afford to be, having no more than eleven legions — about 66,000 men — at any one time. He invaded England with only 4,000 men. The big question, however, is how you get people to behave in such a way that they positively influence toward the goals. A lot of people along the way thought they had the answer to the question, including Julius Caesar. If the troops hadn't done too well on the battlefields and he wanted higher individual performance, Caesar would line them up on the battlefield and execute every tenth man. Maybe that is why he never had more than 66,000 men! Julius thought he was a heck of a motivator with such methods but studies have concluded that Julius' technique has short-lived results."

Nobody could have predicted the demand for paper, ink and duplicating equipment supplies when Cohen first opened his doors with one other fulltime employee in 1938 selling stencils. But his perseverance in a growing field had caused his business to grow in the first 30 years, until by 1968 he had over 250 employees, operating a headquarters in Kansas City and branches in three other cities with 60,000 square feet of space and representing over 50 national and international firms. How the paper distribution business had grown since World War II was indicated in a speech made in 1969 by Stephen D. Boudreau, manager of marketing development for one of Cohen's suppliers, the St. Regis Paper Co. He said in part: "Paper has averaged from 1947 to 1968 about 79,000 tons for every billion dollars of gross national product. Most authorities agree that GNP should grow at about four percent for the next several years. The American Paper Institute estimates a slight reduction in the paper ratio to GNP in the next few years to about 3.7 percent. Demand is estimated at 54 million tons or 540 pounds per capita for 1968 and 84 million tons or 690 pounds in 1980." Cohen could not have said it any better about his business than Boudreau said about paper distributors in his remarks: "The paper distributor is the vitally important last step in the integrated physical distribution system. If he is to satisfy that economic function — if he is willing to be imaginative, accept the new concepts and products, if he will grub in the garden for accurate market data and true costs, if he will look to develop new products and markets — then, for him, the bloom will stay on the boom for some time to come." What Boudreau said was an encapsuled form of how Cohen attempted to approach his growing business.

Cohen recognized the potential of the business he had undertaken when he said he had tried through the years to build Electronic Business Equipment so that it would emerge as "the leading source for all major products and supplies which constitute the 'electronic office,' one of the most rapidly changing environments in the history of American business." He went on to say: "The phenomenal growth EBE has enjoyed during the past decades is not easy to explain or analyze. Many companies acquire distributorships for national products. Many companies survive the change and explosion of technology. But few companies achieve such a level of success and national reputation in their industry. You ask what makes EBE different? Instead of representing a manufacturer to a customer, we represent our customer to the manufacturers. That difference creates a unique business relationship with both our customers and our manufacturers — a better relationship. Most distributors take what their manufacturers offer and sell these products to their customers. EBE has a different approach. We often pioneer the development and marketing of new office products. On hundreds of occasions, we have worked with major manufacturers to develop new products and to improve existing products. EBE has frequently contributed solutions which lower the cost of operation, improve efficiency and reduce breakdowns. Most distributors are not involved in this function. We have always viewed selecting the manufacturer, studying the product, selling the product, servicing the product and improving the product as one continuing, interrelated process. I think that's what makes us different."

Cohen always conducted his business on the basis of trying to keep the customer happy after he bought the product. In an expanding field in which rapid progress was being made in the duplicating business technology, he tried to work with his customers and eliminate their frustration with the need for equipment maintenance, service and repair and replacement parts. He said his precepts for building his company were these: "A single course for the most-wanted brands in the electronic office, an operating concept whereby EBE selects the most-reliable and long-lasting products to offer to its customers; unlimited user training which meant that the existing operators were trained now and new operators are trained as they are added, even years from today; full service with over fifty factory trained and field-experienced serving staff to minimize downtime and inconvenience; an inventory of nearly 5,000 different replacement parts; training seminars in EBE facilities or in those of the customer to insure efficient operation of all EBE-installed systems; a systems approach to the various markets served, combining hardware, training, facilities, material, service, and supplies; an attractive financing package available for purchase, lease or rental and a selling philosophy which simply states that EBE exists to serve the customer's needs."

There was one great problem for businesses, offices and industry, however, in the great proliferation of document copying and storage of documents it required. It was the sheer bulk in the ever-growing load of paper and how to find storage for it in an office atmosphere which had never before been required to face such a monumental task. Computers were coming into operation for such purposes but they were too large and bulky in the early stages to be useful to most of the customers of Cohen and his companies at the time. The 3M Company, long Cohen's mentor in research and development, had decided on reducing the documents to small scale film images in a process known as microfilm. As a result, Cohen formed a micrographic division in his companies. As he said: "This division offers a system approach to microfilm recording, storage and access to paper documents in order to create an efficient document files management system. A full range of hardware, service and suppliers are provided from complete custom microfilming to film processing and to complete in-office systems. This is in addition to a full line of state-of-the art hardware and supplies from the world's foremost manufacturers of micrographics products. Experienced personnel assist in the design or improvement of efficient information handling systems."

Cohen had originally become associated with 3M back in 1948 when the old Minnesota Mining and Manufacturing Company was beginning to get into the exploding office duplicating field on an experimental basis. By February 1973, Cohen became the first 3M dealer with a 20-year history in the duplicating field. The result was a full-page spread in the 3M company magazine, Center Span, in its May 1973 edition. There for thousands of persons across the nation to read was the article headlined "Jerry Cohen First 20-Year Dealer." Two top-ranking 3M executives in the duplicating field, Earl Bassett and Eric Darby, had flown to Kansas City to present Cohen with a beautifully-engraved antique clock. The article accompanying the photographs read like a history of 3M in the duplicating field and gave Cohen full credit for much of its success. It said in part: "Back in February of 1953, Jerry Cohen was already familiar with the 3M Company and some of its products. The founder and president of the Tempo Company had been asked in 1948 to take the 3M lab output for a year of a new product they were experimenting with and develop it. The product was a presensitized aluminum printing plate and it proved to be the first successful one in the printing industry, thanks in large part to the efforts of the Tempo Company. Thus, in 1953, because of his pioneering work on the presensitized plate, the Cohen organization was invited to become one of the seven dealers in the United States to prove a new dry copying process, infrared copying. And thus it was February of this year that Jerry Cohen became the first in the country to observe his 20th anniversary as a dealer for 3M duplicating products. Jerry recalls that back in the 1950s he and his people worked with 3M to help perfect their new infrared copying process and in 1955, the company introduced the first Thermofax 'Secretary' Copier which became the leader in the office copying field. With Thermofax Copier sales booming in 1958, 3M asked dealers to separate sales of these products from their other activities so a new corporation was formed in Kansas City — Electronic Business Equipment, Inc.

As business grew, more and more space was needed. A year after Electronic Business was formed, it was moved to a new location. In 1964, EBE again moved, this time into the spacious, functional and beautiful quarters it now occupies at 1500 Grand in Kansas City. The second part of the 3-city dealership was formed in 1959 when another corporation, Jefferson City Electronic Business Equipment, was set up to service that trade area. The third location, St. Joseph, has had an Electronic Business Equipment outlet over four years. Meanwhile, in addition to expanding its duplicating products line, 3M was also introducing microfilm products, overhead projection systems and background music systems to its line. And the Cohen organization was in the forefront in introducing them to the public. Throughout the years, Jerry Cohen has prided himself on being a pace-setter in every facet of business. Besides pioneering new products, he has been a leader in making sure that service to customers was tops; that employees had spacious, attractive and well-equipped facilities to work in, as well as good pay and fringe benefits; that advanced methods of operation in all phases of business were utilized, that sales efforts were fully supported by advertising and sales promotion. On the matter of service, Jerry said, 'We believe that if you take care of the customer, the customer will take care of you.' That's the philosophy that has kept the Cohen-3M organization on top for 20 years."

An interesting sidelight of the story was that Cohen brought in some of his longtime employees to be photographed with him and the clock in one of the pictures run with the magazine article. They included Rudy Schibler, business manager for 10 years at that time; Tony Snider, general sales manager; John Robinson, visual products manager; Jack Spotts, service manager for 25 years; Harry Cohen, Jerry's brother who had been with the company for 33 years at that time; Earl Bassett; Mildred Roofener, office manager, the Tempo Company, 22 years, and Betty Hoback, office manager, Electronic Business Equipment, 16 years. As things happen, however, two of the persons in the photograph had died in 1973 between the time the picture was taken and it was printed in the

3M magazine. One was Jerry's own brother, Harry Cohen, who had been with him in the company from the time Jerry bought out his first partner, and the other was Schibler. Cohen wanted the photograph run, however, as a tribute to the two and the caption carried with the photograph in the article identified them as "the late" before their names. Of all the businesses mentioned in the article, the only one that did not live quite up to either 3M or Cohen standards over the years was the one dealing with background music systems. With 3M heavily into the recording tape business, it looked like a good idea when it was launched but it did not fit in with the scheme of Cohen and other duplicating equipment dealers across the nation. Within three years, Cohen had sold the system, which provided the music for elevators in office buildings and hotel rooms, to a nationally known company which was devoting its time exclusively to such distribution and 3M had withdrawn from the field.

Over the years, however, Cohen had only a couple of his business investments turn sour compared to a widespread collection of gold nuggets he got from most of them. Both of these were driven by what he felt were longtime community interests rather than assessments of their business potential as he did in connection with most of them. One of these was his love for live theater for Kansas City and his investment in an ill-fated dinner theater project in the 1970s, the Palace Dinner Theater. It operated in the Uptown Theater at 36th and Broadway which had just closed as a motion picture house. It featured some good shows and performing talents which the public enjoyed. The problem developed, however, with a Chicago partner in the operation whom Cohen had learned to distrust, and so Cohen quickly withdrew without suffering substantial losses. The company quickly folded after Cohen withdrew. The second was a concept of a downtown newspaper to promote the area with the public at a time when the downtown area of Kansas City was suffering from changing American lifestyles as were those of most major metropolitan areas. Cohen never left the downtown area during his more than 50 years in business and he loved the atmosphere it had for him. He learned there was a great deal he did not know about newspaper production costs and advertising revenues even though he and others involved had respect for the man who was attempting the publishing experiment. The paper folded within a few months with a loss to Cohen of just over $10,000. Two bloopers were not bad for a man for whom his solid business hunches paid off in the millions of dollars.

18

A Jewish Centennial

While his business was growing at a phenomenal rate and his involvement in a wide variety of civic activities was taking more of his time, Jerry Cohen and his wife, Jeannette, remained just as committed to their Jewish religious heritage and as members of their Jewish reform congregation in their synagogue, Temple B'Nai Jehudah. In many respects, there was a great similarity between Cohen and his rabbi for years, Rabbi Samuel Mayerberg, in their work for civic betterment with Rabbi Mayerberg being immortalized as one of the great American Jewish leaders by Albert Vorspan in his 1960 book, Giants of Justice. In the book, Vorspan listed Rabbi Mayerberg along with such other U.S. intellectual greats as Simon Wolf, friend of Abraham Lincoln and Ulysses H. Grant; Louis Brandeis, Jewish Justice of the U.S. Supreme Court; David Dubinsky, Jewish labor leader, and Herbert H. Lehman, longtime U.S. Senator from New York.

In his introduction to the book, Vorspan could have been describing the almost parallel civic activities of Rabbi Mayerberg and Cohen in Kansas City: "What are the Jews? A nation, a religion, a nationality, a culture, a civilization, a problem? None of these or all of them? There have been countless answers — none of them fully satisfactory... The reason is that the Jew defies all the pigeonholes of language and is, in the end, a unique animal, shaped by a glorious and miserable history into something different under the sun. Slavery, Mt. Sinai, the prophets, Christianity, the Talmud, the Crusades, the Inquisition, the French Revolution, America, Hitler, Israel — all have left their special-prints upon this stiff-necked people and neither freedom nor democracy, nor science, nor suburbia have quite managed to wipe out the uniqueness. Whatever definition of the Jew is conjured up, one soon comes face to face with a characteristic which amounts almost to one of the stigmata of the Jew: a passion for justice. Judaism gave the world not only monotheism but ethical monotheism."

Although Cohen would be reluctant to place himself on the same level with Rabbi Mayerberg, there were many similarities between the two of them. Both had begun fighting the Kansas City political machine of Tom Pendergast in the late 1930s, Mayerberg from a sense of moral indignation and Cohen from being sickened by the excesses of the political machine he saw while he was working for the Missouri General Assembly before he started his own business. Both had been active in founding the Citizens Association which swept Pendergast out of City Hall in 1940. They remained committed and fought for the good government concepts of the Citizens Association in active support of the first two of its mayors, John B. Gage and William E. Kemp. Mayerberg took some flack from some of the members of his congregation who profited from their relationship with Tom Pendergast on the grounds that the rabbi of their synagogue should not be engaged in political activities but Cohen and other members of the congregation stood behind him. Irvin Fane, a Jewish lawyer who was president of the synagogue congregation in the 1940s under the first Citizens Association mayors, had supported the reform and had been named to the Board of Police Commissioners in 1953-1955.

As Rabbi Mayerberg wrote later: "While I hold the firm conviction that ministers should never engage in partisan political activities, I also cherish the unwavering belief that, where inequity runs rampant, where depraved and selfish men prey upon a community, it is not only the right but also the compelling duty of the minister to lead in the movement to eradicate such evil powers from the community. If one holds the fearless, God-intoxicated prophets of Israel as his human ideals, as I do, one is impelled by his conscience to enter the fray with all the courage and strength he can summon." When H. Roe Bartle was elected mayor in 1955, Mayerberg and Cohen both actively entered city government operations by accepting appointments to official boards. In late 1955, Bartle named Cohen to be a member of the Kansas City Board of Parks and Recreation. In 1957, Governor James T. Blair had appointed Rabbi Mayerberg to the Kansas City Board of Police Commissioners. In appointing Rabbi Mayerberg, making him the first minister in Missouri to hold such a strategic public office, Governor Blair told him: "You are the symbol of good government. You will put the fear of God in the heart of the underworld." Cohen went on to be named a member of the Board of Parks and Recreation while Mayerberg became vicepresident of the Police Board. During Bartle's second term as mayor, the old machine remnants had regained a majority of the city government and L. P. Cookingham, who had been city manager for 15 years under the Citizens Association reform movement, resigned. While still on the Police Board, Rabbi Mayerberg took an active role in going after the old political machine remnants on the city council and succeeded in forcing the resignation of Reed McKinley, who had succeeded Cookingham, for malfeasance in office. McKinley, who had been Director of Public Works under Cookingham, held a press conference. As Vorspan described what had transpired: "Grimly, he acknowledged that for months he had been under pressure from four members of the council and from political faction leaders and that he had not been free to do what was best for the city. It was a complete vindication of everything the rabbi... had contended." Rabbi Mayerberg resigned from the Police Board in 1961, citing ill health. He did accept appointment of Police Chaplain in April 1963, the first rabbi in Kansas City to be appointed to the post. Cohen continued to serve on the Board of Park Commissioners until 1963 when Bartle left the office of mayor.

Rabbi Mayerberg, who had accepted the call to serve at Temple B'Nai Jehudah on May 9, 1928, asked that he be allowed to retire just after his 68th birthday in June 1960. He asked the synagogue board to allow this just two days before the annual meeting of the congregation on May 27, 1959, when his decision became public. In his letter making his request to retire, Rabbi Mayerberg had told the congregation: "Many of my colleagues in the rabbinate have made the mistake of remaining in the active service of their congregations far beyond their years of full capacity and of full usefulness. I do not wish to make this mistake. While

I still feel young and vigorous, I cannot help but be aware that there are certain physical limitations which come with age; and I will not under any circumstances permit myself to remain in office for even a single day beyond my maximum capabilities. This would be unfair to the wonderfully generous friends who constitute this magnificent congregation. My 31 years as the Rabbi of Congregation B'Nai Jehudah are full of precious memories, and it was extremely difficult for me to call a halt to the work I love so much. But my love for this congregation compels me to step aside for a younger man and I do with full self-assurance that our Board of Trustees will choose as my successor the best man who is available in the United States. This congregation is entitled to nothing else."

Irvin Fane, who had helped Rabbi Mayerberg be persuaded to be appointed to the Kansas City Board of Police Commissioners and who was a past president of the congregation, was named to head the committee to find a successor for Mayerberg. He sent out a letter to the congregation which spelled out the status of Temple B'Nai Jehudah at that particular point in its history: "Our ritual practices are a little to the left of or to the right of center, depending on where you are sitting. Older families in the congregation are largely of the 'Classical Reform' persuasion, but today they represent a minority in interest, participation and numbers. Nevertheless our practices are not as traditional as those in many Reform congregations. Our problems are those which I believe are fairly common to the large congregation: Relatively poor attendance at Sabbath services; inadequate giving to Temple causes; inadequate ceremonial observance in the home; the children do not enjoy the Religious Schools, etc. We are looking for a man of deep spiritual dedication who also can preach well and teach well, and who can inspire a very hungry congregation."

Cohen got into the day-to-day work of the synagogue through his wife, Jeannette, by helping with the annual thrift shop sale conducted by the National Council of Jewish Women. Jeannette served as a volunteer at the thrift shop for 46 years, serving as its manager, chairman of the yearly sales and in other capacities until it closed. Cohen himself served as an advisor for the thrift shop, did publicity for it for many years, assisted in the annual fashion shows held by the shop and helped with moving merchandise to the sale. In fact, Jerry was so helpful that the council under the 1957 president, Serina Lorsch, made him an honorary member, the first temple man to be so honored. The April 1957 council newsletter, Councilgram, carried one of its biggest articles in the issue about him with his photograph. The lead of the article said of him: "Girls, don't look now, but there's a man in our midst! And we think it's time to give recognition to Mr. Jerome Cohen, who has given so generously of his time and talents, helping us whenever we have needed him. Though Mr. Cohen has served the council in many capacities, The Thrift Shop owes him the greatest debt of gratitude. Sharing the energetic enthusiasms of his wife, Jeannette, he has worked untiringly on the fashion show and sale. For over 12 years, he has helped move the merchandise from the storage basement to the site of the sale, a most tremendous task. He has handled a good part of the 'big' publicity in The Kansas City Star, and every year Jerry is seen running in and out of the sale headquarters throughout the day of the sale, helping whenever needed and available for all emergencies. Truly, a great deal of credit for the success of the annual Thrift Shop sale goes to Jerome Cohen...As the owner of a duplicating machine and supply firm he has aided the Council office, helping to solve mechanical problems and willingly assisting at no charge. Mrs. Cohen states that her husband says he was 'put on earth to help others. He helps everybody,' she asserts. And it is this humanitarian generosity coupled with dynamic energy that gives Council this wonderful friend. Truly, we owe a most genuine and heartfelt thank you to this very 'notable man in our midst.' "

For the successor to Rabbi Mayerberg, the pulpit committee headed by Fane had nearly 40 names of rabbis submitted for consideration. Of these, 10 were interviewed at length and allowed to meet with the temple board, Rabbi Mayerberg and the staff. On December 30, 1959, the committee unanimously recommended that Rabbi William Silverman, of the Temple Ohabai Solomon, Nashville, Tennessee, be selected. Rabbi Silverman had been a favorite of Rabbi Mayerberg from the beginning and Temple B'Nai Jehudah accepted the recommendation on January 8, 1960. Rabbi and Mrs. Mayerberg were honored with a civic dinner on June 22, 1960, at the Hotel Muehlebach, at which it was announced that the temple chapel would be named in honor of Mayerberg as "abiding testimony in the imperishable ideals of our faith by which our Rabbi inspired and encouraged by his devoted helpmate, has guided... the families of Congregation B'Nai Jehudah so lovingly and so well." On the following Friday, Rabbi Mayerberg conducted his final Sabbath Eve service as rabbi, using as his text for his sermon the final words of the book of Ecclesiastes: "The end of the matter, all having been heard: Revere God and keep His commandments, for this is the whole man. For God shall bring every work into the judgment concerning every hidden thing, whether it be good or whether it be evil." He said he did not want them to remember him for his civic role or for the way he had attacked corruption in local government but for his congregational ministry, saying, "If you want to remember me, try to remember me as a man of faith; a man who really believed, who had no equivocations in his belief." Rabbi Mayerberg did not live to enjoy his retirement long, however, for he died four years later on November 22, 1964.

Installation services for Rabbi Silverman were held in the synagogue at 8 p.m. September 9, 1960, under the direction of Dr. Maurice N. Eisendrath, the president of the Union of American Hebrew Congregations. Rabbi Silverman reflected the views of many of the members of his congregation at the time when he said: "The greatest threat to our civilization is not from atomic bombs or guided missiles. Rather, it is to be found in man's acquiescence to doom, his reluctance to struggle against evil, and his loss of faith in tomorrow. The adherents of the prophetic faith must challenge the pessimism of our era, insisting that man is not a cosmic orphan, alone in a parentless universe, but that he is a divinely endowed child of God, blessed with a potential of goodness, holiness and love — a potential that summons us to enter upon an exalted adventure, pioneering into the future, advancing unto untouched and untrodden vistas, struggling to establish new religious frontiers of faith."

Cohen was beginning at this point on an even greater exercise of his longtime Jewish heritage in a variety of ways. He was taking an active role in the men's organization, the Temple Brotherhood, working his way up through the ranks to being elected president of the Brotherhood for 1965-66. As president of the Brotherhood, he followed his own lifelong service dictum of trying to leave an organization better when he left it than when he took it over. In accordance with the directions taken by Rabbi Mayerberg and Rabbi Silverman in trying to promote interaction with Protestants and Roman Catholics, the Brotherhood held its first inter-faith dinner. He also instituted a luncheon series for Brotherhood members with Rabbi Silverman called "Luncheon with the Rabbi" and started a monthly Brotherhood newspaper called Kol Achim, the Voice of the Brothers. He launched a drive to collect and ship textbooks for use in Reform congregations in Europe. Among his other innovations during his term as president were organizing the men of the Brotherhood to supervise traffic in the Temple parking lot during religious school hours, getting the organization to tape the Bar Mitzvah and Bat Mitzvah of each synagogue youth for presentation to the family and began the conduct of annual retreats for Brotherhood men. Support of the Jewish Chautauqua Society, devoted to the preservation of Jewish culture, exceeded the annual quota.

As a result of his far-reaching concepts, Cohen and Temple B'Nai Jehudah were presented the highest awards of the National Federation of Temple Brotherhoods at its 1966 convention. They included the Louis Fein Jewish Layman Award for "the most outstanding service in the Brotherhoods, to the Jewish Chautauqua Society and with continued dedication to ideals of Reform Judaism." They were also presented the Abraham Reiter Memorial Award for Excellence in programming by a large temple men's club, the Temple B'Nai Jehudah having achieved 400 members in its men's club under Cohen. As a result of the organizing efforts of Cohen as president of the Brotherhood, the National Federation of Temple Brotherhoods voted to hold its 1972 convention in Kansas City. For three days in 1972, Kansas City became the center of Reform Judaism with outstanding Jewish men and rabbis coming here from all over the nation for social activities, seminars and religious activities centered on Temple B'Nai Jehudah. Cohen was also elected to serve on the National Federation Board and served for several years on the national level.

As a great admirer of both Harry S. Truman and Eddie Jacobson, the fellow member of Temple B'Nai Jehudah and a fellow businessman, a haberdasher who had once been in business with Truman, it was only natural that Cohen would become a major supporter in the Kansas City area for Bonds for Israel. Jacobson was always quiet about the important influence he had had on getting Truman as president to recognize the state of Israel as soon as it was created in 1948 but the record is clear. Towards his death, Jacobson did say. "The President always listened to me because he knew I would tell him the truth. But I want to make it clear that whatever President Truman did for Israel he did because he thought it was the best thing for this country. I had hoped that I could sit down and write up my little part in the drama from beginning to end so that history will record the fact that there would be no state of Israel today except for Harry S. Truman, whose name should daily be blessed in every temple and every synagogue the world over."

Cohen served as a member of the Kansas City governing committee from its beginning and purchased thousands of dollars worth of the securities to assist the new Jewish nation from its beginning. His work on Bonds for Israel efforts led him to serve on committees for dinners in 1964 and 1965 by the State of Israel Bond Organization in Kansas City which had honored General Lucius D. Clay, famed World War II commander and diplomat, and Vice President Hubert Humphrey, respectively. Former President Truman was present for both dinners and made the awards to each personally. The award to General Clay said "Harry S. Truman Commendation Award conferred upon General Lucius D. Clay, distinguished military leader and statesman, staunch champion of freedom in war and peace. As one of the architects of the liberation of Europe during World War II, he was instrumental in the rescue of survivors of the concentration camps and in aiding displaced persons destined to find a home in Israel. His exemplary life and career testify to the highest standards of American citizenship, humanitarian leadership, devotion to democracy and friendship for the people of Israel." That dinner also featured an address by Abraham Feinberg, president of the State of Israel Bond Organization, and a concert by Jan Peerce, famed Metropolitan Opera tenor. The award to Vice President Humphrey read: "Harry S. Truman Commendation Award presented to the Honorable Hubert H. Humphrey, Vice President of the United States, whose exemplary life and career of public service expresses the spirit, heart and substance of American democracy; whose vision and unique eloquence have helped to guide and strengthen the American people in times of difficulty and crisis; whose broad humanitarianism encompasses a deep-rooted concern for the well-being and progress of Israel and other freedom-loving nations as the means of hastening world understanding and peace." That dinner featured an address by Ephraim Evron who was Israel's minister to the United States at the time.

Cohen received numerous awards for his service and commitment to support Israel through the Bonds for Israel campaign. In 1978, he was presented with the Herbert S. Lehman Award by the State of Israel for these efforts. Lehman was the first Jew elected to the United States Senate and was one of the most highly regarded public servants in the United States. Lehman was always a role model for Cohen with the tenets that led Lehman to be named as "the Man of the Century" by all the Institutions of Reform Judaism. He tried to practice what Lehman said in one of his speeches: "America is a nation born of a great ideal and as long as the nation survives that ideal must and will be cherished and preserved. Jewish history teaches that spiritual idea, in a people, as well as in an individual, gives strength and endurance transcending material wealth and power."

For his Bonds for Israel efforts, Cohen was also honored in 1978 by Menachim Begin and other Israeli officials. Besides Begin, Cohen visited with Moshe Dayan, famed Israeli war general and minister of foreign affairs for Israel in 1978; Arnon Gafay, governor of the Bank of Israel; Simha Ehrlich, minister of finance; Mayor Teddy Kolek, of Jerusalem; General Dan Shomron, who led the daring Israeli raid on Entebbe; Shamon Peres, a future prime minister himself, and others. Yitshak Shamir, who was the speaker of the Knesset, the Israel parliament at the time and another future prime minister, introduced Cohen and other American honorees from the rostrum at the parliament, when a measure was introduced to provide a new $1 billion Israeli bond issue. Cohen was recognized by Begin and successive Israeli prime ministers each year for the next 15 years for his efforts in behalf of Bonds for Israel. As Begin told Cohen and the other Americans that first year: "I believe you will give the wholehearted support for only a strong Israel will ultimately have peace. We have to make sure that the state of Israel is preserved for generations to come. We stand on the threshold of momentous change and are aware of the enormous financial burdens that Israel will have to bear if and when the beginning of peace comes."

Cohen received accolades of the more than 1,500 members of his synagogue, Temple B'Nai Jehudah, when they accorded him with the honor of electing him to serve as president of the temple congregation for two years from 1980-1982. Cohen always wanted to repay his friends for having honored him, and in 1981 he and his wife, Jeannette, announced that they were undertaking the entire cost of a 100-acre retreat center which the synagogue had purchased in 1979. The retreat, still occupied

by the synagogue, is located about an hour's drive south of the synagogue site in Cleveland Township in Cass County. The sprawling acre-
age contains a 30-acre lake for boating and two smaller ones stocked for
fishing, hiking trails through gently rolling wooded hills and many natural clearings. The site contains a combination dining hall with complete
kitchen facilities air conditioned for use in the summer and heated for
winter; adjoining dormitory facilities for 60 with showers and toilets and
club rooms; a caretaker's residence; tennis courts and playing fields as
well as outdoor picnic tables and grills. An outdoor chapel was dedicated
on the grounds in 1994. Cohen had served as a member of a temple
brotherhood committee which had surveyed a variety of sites for such an
outdoor retreat center.

The Kansas City Jewish Chronicle reported on January 23, 1981:
"The Brotherhood's board of directors gave unanimous approval earlier
this month for recognizing 'this magnificent generosity by designating
the facility... 'The Jeannette and Jerome Cohen Retreat Center of the
Temple B'Nai Jehudah Brotherhood.' " The article went on to say: "The
retreat center is intended to broaden and intensify entire families. Some
of the most successful worship and study programs currently available
in other communities have been in retreat settings, adding significant
new dimensions to congregational enthusiasm and commitment." Rabbi
Zedek of the synagogue credited Cohen and his wife with being the driv-
ing force behind the fact that Temple B'Nai Jehudah had a retreat center
and said: "Without them, it would not have happened. They have been
most generous regarding the project."

Cohen had also played a major role in other developments that were
landmarks in the life of his synagogue. During his tenure as president of
the temple brotherhood in 1965, he had been a strong promoter of better
understanding between Catholic and Protestant Christians and Jews. In
a historic step in 1965, his commitment to brotherhood led to the Very
Reverend Joseph V. Sullivan, chancellor of the Roman Catholic Diocese
of Kansas City-St. Joseph, accepting an invitation of Rabbi Silverman to
deliver the sermon of Temple B'Nai Jehudah at Friday Sabbath services.
Following the Kaddish prayer by Rabbi Silverman signifying the conclusion of the formal sabbath service, Bishop Sullivan delivered a sermon on "Brotherhood Without Compromise." A group of Catholic nuns
joined the Jewish congregation in the services also. It was the first time

in 37 years that a Catholic prelate had taken part in the synagogue services. Cohen was also responsible for establishing an annual dinner attended by men of the synagogue, of the Country Club Christian Church and of three Roman Catholic parishes, St. Elizabeth's, St. Peter's, and Visitation.

Another of the landmarks in his long career with Temple B'Nai Jehudah was the participation in the decision to build a new synagogue at 69th Street and Holmes Road. Ground was broken for the structure February 21, 1965, and the dedication of the new sanctuary was held on May 5-6, 1967. Rabbi Maurice N. Eisendrath, president of the American Union of Hebrew Congregations, spoke at the sabbath dedication service on Friday, May 5. On Sunday, May 7, Bishop Charles W. Helmsing, of the Kansas City-St. Joseph Diocese of the Roman Catholic Church, and the Rev. Robert Meneilly, representing the Metropolitan Kansas City Council of Churches, participated with Rabbi Maurice D. Solomon, president of the Rabbinical Association of Greater Kansas City, and Mayor Ilus W. Davis in a community celebration of the dedication. In a four-page article on the new synagogue in its July 1969 issue, the Architectural Record said: "A remarkably effective religious atmosphere has been created in this sanctuary of the Temple B'Nai Jehudah complex in Kansas City... The original building, designed by Kivett and Myers, was designed to be in deliberate contrast to the other facilities—a separate space, used only for worship and with a character that states this. The sanctuary evokes one of the oldest structural forms, the tent, but translated into today's materials and methods. And the interior, punctuated by an 83-foot concrete center pole, provides a big serenely uncluttered space permeated by soft blue light from the spiraling plastic skylight. Both the shape and lighting of the interior keep the eye focused on the altar and its furnishings..." Another of the landmarks in the synagogue came on October 2, 1970 — the celebration of its centennial anniversary. It was in October 1870 that Louis Hammerslough presided over a meeting of Kansas City Jews in a second floor room over a grocery store at 4th and Walnut to form Temple B'Nai Jehudah. A total of $800 was pledged by 20 families and the Rev. Marcus R. Cohen of Chicago was hired as rabbi for the congregation.

The centennial celebration ran for a year and featured many highlights for the year, things in which Cohen and his family eagerly participated. Included was a centennial pageant with a cast of 60 members staged in two performances in the synagogue social hall at 8:30 p.m. May 2, 1970, and again at 2:30 p.m. the following day. The pageant featured two Jewish merchants who were believed to be the first Jews to settle in what is now Kansas City when they opened a trading post in Westport Landing in 1840. The two are recorded only as L. Cahn and E. Block but they prospered, trading powder, lead, tobacco, sugar, coffee, candies and beads for ponies, pelts, furs, trinkets and money. Joseph S. Chick, the first Kansas City banker, credited them with being the first to recognize the Kansas City potential when he said: "The Jews could have no higher compliment than to say that they were the first to realize Kansas City's future possibilities."

Another was a series of three concerts by the Kansas City Philharmonic Orchestra in tribute to the centennial on November 17, 18 and 19, featuring an Israeli soprano, Netania Davrath, and the world premiere of a specially commissioned work, Symphony No. 6-Day War, composed by Irwin Bazelon. Centennial convocation lecturers and guest speakers included Morris B. Abram, who was president of Brandeis University; Roland B. Gittlesohn, who was president of the Central Conference of American Rabbis; Elie Wiesel, known as "the poet of the Holocaust"; Herbert Tarr, rabbi and author; and Jacob R. Marcus, who was considered the foremost authority on American Jewish history. A giant centennial banquet was held May 23, 1970, in the grand ballroom of the Hotel Muehlebach.

At the centennial religious celebration on October 2, 1970, in the presence of descendants of 11 congregation founders on Shabbat Shuvah, the Sabbath of Return, Rabbi Silverman gave voice to the tenets by which Cohen had tried to live his life in Kansas City: "We know that science is dynamic. So is religion. Nothing can stand still. It must regress or progress. So we have advanced in time for generation through generation, amidst the tide of ceaseless tides of change to the present day. We turn our sights now to the future and we consider what binds generation to generation together. The fear of anti-Semitism? To combat prejudice? Is it interfaith understanding and brotherhood? Or is it just the will to survive? Is that why we want to preserve Judaism? There must be something more. And I believe that 'something' more may be found in one word, called 'covenant' — a sacred law; a purpose, a mission that transcends the generations, that is not rooted in time but is fluid in the timeless. In the Torah portion for Yom Kippur we read: 'Neither with you only do I make this covenant and this oath, but with him who standeth here with us this day before the Lord our God and also with him that is not here with us this day'... all the generations that are yet to be. There is no meaning to Jewish life without Torah, without a sense of mission, without God and the love of God — which means the love of God's children — without wedding oneself to a destiny to help make this a better world. Yes, even in a space age 'it is a tree of life,' but only 'to those who hold fast to it'; it is no vain thing, dear friends, it is your life, and my life, and the life of the Jewish people. And through this Torah and through this covenant you shall prolong your days upon the earth, with meaning and with sacred purpose."

ORANGUTAN LOVER JERRY COHEN — *Two orangutans from the Swope Park Zoo snuggle up to Jerry Cohen during an annual picnic of Friends of the Zoo, a support organization for the Parks and Recreation Department. Cohen headed the annual picnics to raise funds for the group annually for many years.*

A NEW HIPPO GETS A GREETING — *Elaine Cohen, daughter of Jerry Cohen, feeds some bread slices to a newly-acquired hippopotamus at the Swope Park Zoo while her proud father looks on behind her. William T.A. Cully, longtime zoo director, holds the bread while Frank Theis, longtime president of the Kansas City Parks and Recreation Board on which Cohen also served, is visible in the straw hat at the end of the cage.*

19

His Business Reaches 50

As the 1970s dawned and Jerry Cohen was looking forward to the fourth decade of his duplicating and supply business, Cohen had no second thoughts about his decision to enter the field he had selected in which to operate his business. The duplicating of records by business, industries, professional groups such as doctors and lawyers, and by the government was growing exponentially with leaps and bounds over each successive year he was in the business, increasing his sales by his original goal of 15 percent annually easily. While business was increasing by leaps and bounds, the United States was in the midst of some of its greatest domestic turmoil since the Civil War, however. Riots in black ghettoes in metropolitan areas in the wake of the assassination of Martin Luther King, Jr., the riots in the streets of Chicago in 1968 at the Democratic national convention over the U.S. war in Vietnam and creeping inflation resulting from policies of President Lyndon Johnson in trying to finance a full-scale war while at the same time expanding federal social action spending all had created an atmosphere of uneasiness on the part of Cohen and business leaders across the nation. Richard M. Nixon had been elected president in 1968, defeating Vice President Hubert Humphrey after Lyndon Johnson decided not to seek reelection.

Even in the rapidly expanding duplicating of documents, technology had reached a cross-roads in the area of how to store the mountains of documents created in offices by the growth of the need for duplicating. Solutions were varied for the problems with one group trying to develop less expensive computer storage and others concentrating on a microphotographic processing of documents and development of retrieval systems for these microfilms. As usual, Cohen was still in the forefront of trying to solve these problems with his longtime mentor, the 3M Company. Recognition of the problem was shown in a giant two-page advertisement run in the influential business publication, The Wall Street Journal, in its January 15, 1970, issue by 3M Company.

There was a photograph of Cohen in the giant advertisement along with other 3M duplicating dealers from across the nation running across the bottom of the page. Taking up the upper two-thirds of the page were the latest pieces of 3M machines in the field above the headline in large, black-faced type, "The Finders/The Keepers." The text under the headline in the advertisement expressed the direction Cohen had taken for the moment to help his customers deal with the growing mountain of documents his duplicating machines had created for them. It said: "We call 3M Microfilm Reader-Printers the finders. They find microfilmed information in seconds. Print copies at the push of a button. Get information to the people who need it. They help you find a needle in a haystack. We call 3M Microfilm Cameras and microforms the Keepers. They put 3,000 letter-size documents on 100-foot rolls of microfilm. Reduce engineering drawings to 7-3/4-inch by 3-1/4-inch microfilm aperture cards. Store a year's invoices on one small microfilm cartridge.

"The Finders and the Keepers. Compact 3M Brand Microfilm Systems that help you handle tons of information. For example: Find documents stored on microfilm aperture cards and microfilm sheets in seconds with the 3M Executive I Reader-Printer. Project them full size. Get a dry copy by pulling a lever. Pay only $280 each and you can put a new 3M Executive I Reader-Printer in every department. Could you use speed and economy like this? Reduce up to 3,000 letter-size documents to 100 feet of microfilm with the 3M 3400 Cartridge Camera. Slip a compact 3M Microfilm cartridge into the 3400 and film a few documents. Remove the cartridge. Index it on the back. Film additional documents in the same microfilm cartridge later. Find any information on 3M Microfilm Cartridges with the new 3M 400CT Reader-Printer. Project it. View it vertically or horizontally. Push a button and get a full-size copy in seconds.

"How much confusion could you eliminate with this finder and keeper system from 3M? Keep up to 10,000 documents on 3M Microfilm Cartridges. Find any one in seconds with the 3M 400 Page Search. Then print a copy. Move quickly to another document, in either direction. Rewind the microfilm automatically. Cut information retrieval time. How many hours could this incredibly fast microfilm system save your staff of paper handlers? Reduce extra-large documents to microfilm aperture cards with a 3M 2000 Series II Processor-Camera. Push a button. Expose film, process it, and mount it automatically in less than a minute. View that aperture card and make a 12-inch by 18-inch or 18-inch by 24-inch print of it with a 3M 200 Reader-Printer. Can you think of an easier way to reduce file space by 96 percent? Find all the detail of original drawings as the 3M 333 Dry Silver Printer turns out a sharp 18-inch by 24-inch print from a microfilm aperture card. Deliver these low-cost copies about twice as fast as ever before. How much time could the 333 save your engineers? How must wasted effort could it save?"

Cohen could not have said it better how he was viewing the exploding information systems that were coming onto the market in such a rapid stream. In addition to the costs of the original microfilm units outlined in the advertisement at a fairly low level as compared with computers for business at that point, Cohen could also see the microfilm system with its need for film, paper, chemicals, and other products in its information storage operations fitting well into a philosophy he had expressed since he first went into business for himself. That portion of the philosophy, he laughingly described once as follows: "I always said from the beginning that if it don't eat and drink, we don't want it." This was another way of saying that he wanted to sell basic information duplicating units which would create a continuing sales possibility by its demands for paper and other supplies in its operations. He said the same thing in a more formal note when he said: "In addition to the specialized machines offered by each EBE division, this group is a unique source of supplies and accessories for computers, word processors, copiers and related equipment. Included are major brand names of tapes, disks, diskettes, data cartridges, head cleaning supplies, anti-static products, computer supplies, copier paper, computer and multi-use labels, ribbons, correction fluid and dictating tape cassettes. A large inventory and knowledgeable staff provide for prompt and efficient service and delivery for these supplies."

Cohen also did not want to have these copy machines having any more downtime for repairs than necessary, thereby interrupting their voracious appetite for supplies or causing owners to feel that the person who supplied them the system in the first place had lost interest in them after the initial sale. As he said: "The service department provides full service for every product sold by EBE. This is accomplished by factory-trained and field-experienced personnel, through service disciplines and an inventory of over 5,000 different replacement parts to reduce customer downtime. This division has been recognized nationally for its fast response times, which are designed to minimize customer inconvenience. This is accomplished through a computer-operated order entry and dispatching system. Our service group often contributes major design changes and improvements to national manufacturers, in order to improve operating efficiency."

Cohen was also shrewd enough to recognize early in the 1970s that the final decision had not yet been made by business and industry as to how they were best to meet the record-breaking information storage explosion. The result was that he entered upon a policy getting his firms proficient in both the microfilming process and in computers. As he said: "We want this company to offer a systems approach to microfilm recording, storage and access in order to create an efficient files management system as well as to move into the rapidly changing word processing world. In the microfilm section, we want a full range of hardware, services and supplies to be provided from complete custom microfilming to film processing to complete in-office systems. This is in addition to a full line of state-of-the-art hardware and supplies from the world's foremost manufacturers of micrographic products. Experienced personnel assist in the designer improvement of efficient information handling systems. Computerized indexing and computer output microfilm is also offered. As a company moves into the rapidly changing world of computer word processing, its key concerns are flexibility for the future, compatibility with future computer innovations and ease of use. The computer word processing systems offered by EBE were rated top in the industry on these significant points. We developed a wide variety of systems 'you can't outgrow' matched with unlimited user-training, full service and supplies. EBE offered a complete product line, starting with single stand-alone unit and growing as large as a company might require, with multiple units and without ever having to change hardware. This due to the unique family of products EBE offers all compatible in hardware, software and training procedures."

With this philosophy as his guiding light, Cohen sought and established an increasingly wider circle of providers for his companies. The Japanese were beginning to enter into the document duplicating business with new innovations and Cohen had no reluctance about getting into business with them if he felt they could provide an improved service for his customers. Over the decade of the 1970s this led his company into profitable relationships with three Japanese pioneers in the field, Minolta, Canon and Ricoh.

On January 3, 1977, Cohen expanded even more by establishing a new division in Kansas, Systems and Services in Kansas with headquarters in Shawnee Mission and servicing 18 counties in northeast Kansas. The new division was an outgrowth of a relationship he had developed with a company called Control-O-Fax in 1965 in competition with another dealer for its products in the Kansas City area. As usual, Cohen was so successful that by 1976 he was able to buy out his competitor in the Kansas City area and form the basis of his new Kansas division. The new division had a staff of 18 and was placed under the direction of Sue Varner, who had been associated with Cohen in his 3M division and who had been a high performer selling Control-O-Fax products. Within a year after she took over the new division, Varner had doubled her sales staff. This kind of business acumen had always stood Cohen in good stead for the 40 years he had been in business for himself. As a 3M writer said in a three-page article on Cohen and his operations together with photographs in its company magazine, Center Span, in the 1970s: "Throughout the years, Jerry Cohen has prided himself in being a pacesetter in every facet of the business. Besides pioneering new products, he has been a leader in making sure the services to customers were tops; that employees had spacious, attractive and well-equipped facilities to work in as well as good pay and fringe benefits; that advanced methods of operation in all phases of his business were utilized; that sales efforts were fully supported by advertising and sales promotion. On the matter of service, Mr. Cohen said 'We believe that if you take care of the customer, they customer will take care of you.' Mr. Cohen said that what they provide customers is actually 'overservice' and termed it one of three factors in creating business, not waiting for business to come to the company. This has involved risk many times in the case of new products, but is worthwhile in the long run, Mr. Cohen said. The third factor is a belief in the dignity of the individual, both employees and customers. 'People buy from people,' he emphasized. 'They don't buy from companies.' "

In 1978, Cohen reached a couple of landmarks in his Kansas City business career. The first was that his businesses, which he had begun in 1938 with $300 in borrowed capital as the Tempo Company, reached its 40th anniversary of sales growth and expansion. He had gone in the business from receiving a weekly salary of $15 and weekly payment of $3 to his wife for full-time secretarial work to a company with an annual volume of $27 million with 380 employees.

The other landmark was that Cohen himself had achieved the normal retirement age of 65 but showed no signs that he was slowing down or was willing to step aside as top executive of the company. He may have begun to have some thoughts during this time about where his company was headed in the light of his advancing age but he was taking no public action. He may have secretly harbored some ideas that his youngest daughter, Elaine Cohen, who had been working on stage since she was four years old and was now operating her own company, Live Marketing, Inc., successfully in Chicago, might some day take over the helm, but that was not to be. Certainly she was probably more successful in business for her age than her father was at the same age, thanks to watching him operate from his footsteps. She has been featured with the Keebler Baking Co. in a photograph and article in The Chicago Tribune Magazine. The article began: "Talented Elaine Cohen, some 85 pounds of sheer energy, has 'em rolling out of the aisles and into exhibitors' booths at trade shows across the country with her fast-paced musical minishows. 'That's where exhibitors want prospective buyers — inside, listening to the product pitch, not just pausing to pick up a piece of literature,' says the ebullient Cohen, founder and president of Live Marketing, an Evanston-based firm that promises its trade show clients concrete results in the form of orders and leads. She gets the prospects to stop, look and listen by combining Broadway rhythm and Second City kind of patter with catchy jingles that convey product information. Costumed song-

and-dance artists, puppets and audio-visuals put the message across. 'We aim to get the audience into the act and have everyone exit smiling,' Cohen says, adding, 'there's a fine line between involving people and embarrassing them.' Her expertise has got her featured in such trade publications as Exhibit Marketing, Successful Marketing, High Tech-Marketing and Exhibitor. She has many top corporations among her clients, including 3M, IBM, Minolta, Canon, Polaroid, Kodak, Kimberly-Clark, Apple Computer, Allis Chalmers and AT&T."

This is the same Elaine Cohen who at 10 was starring at Starlight Theater in the musical, "Panama Hattie," with Julie Wilson, Paul Lynde and the comedy team of Pepper Davis and Tony Reese. She had gone on to obtain a degree in theater from Northwestern University just outside Chicago and it was as a student there that she began working at trade shows in Chicago. As the Chicago Tribune article said: " 'I passed out shopping bags and did the narrations and found the presentations deadly dull. Boring beyond belief. I was sure I could come up with something better.' She did. She began translating product information into snappy scripts, then set them to music. At the outset, she was pretty much a one-gal show, writing, singing and dancing. Today she seeks out the best writers, musicians, costume designers and performers she can find and puts them together in production spectacles for clients, who pay up to $500,000 for each production and keep coming back for more."

While his daughter was succeeding in a new business venture, Cohen continued to increase the scope of his operations. Always an innovator, he devised a system for smaller firms who did not feel they could afford an entire microfilm operation such as 3M was pushing, opening a new branch called the Custom Microfilm Lab. They could pick and choose microfilm operations to fit their needs with the new Cohen division doing the work and billing clients for it. At its height, the microfilm lab was processing roughly three million sheets of information monthly for clients and storing it in a computerized retrieval service. Cohen, always combining his business sense with trying to make a better world, found out disabled workers could do the microfilming process and hired a staff. For his efforts in helping the disabled, Cohen was named Employer of the Year by the Missouri Rehabilitation Counseling Association. Operating the microfilm business led him into another processing laboratory business to help companies develop audiovisual sales presentations. The new Cohen enterprise had the ability to duplicate any audio or video cassette, turn motion picture film into video cassettes or to put 3x5-inch transparencies into slides. As one of the first dealers, Cohen helped 3M company make its debut in the audio-visual field.

By the time the 1970s were coming to a close, Cohen still saw his business growing and continued at breakneck speed in his wide variety of civic activities such as serving as the chairman of the annual Mayor's Christmas Tree effort for the needy. Each passing year, however, found him facing up to what the future held for this company, largely a one-man operation for more than 40 years. He still wanted to keep the business in the family and wanted some kind of long-range plan in effect if, God forbid, anything should happen to him. His son-in-law, Howard Jacobson, who had married his older daughter, Rosalyn Cohen, and given him his only two grandchildren, had been so successful in investment counselling that he was a vice president of E. F. Hutton and Co. by the late 1970s.

By 1981 when he reached the age of 68, Cohen had decided that he would try to interest Jacobson in leaving Hutton and coming into Electronic Business Equipment as vice president and general manager. Some of his friends who were powerhouses in the Hutton firm through the years, such as John Latshaw, tried to raise questions for Cohen about whether he was doing the right thing when such father-son-in-law relations had often turned quickly sour and because of the success Jacobson was having with Hutton. Jacobson himself was trying to be nice in the interests of family relationships but he himself had reservations about such a move. He wasn't sure he understood the fast-paced changes he felt were in progress in the duplication business at the time; he worried about leap-frogging over executives who were in place in the firm at the time, and some of his friends were counselling him that he was too good a money manger and not a people manager. Cohen, however, was persistent: "I hated to give EBE away because my health had failed. I'd worked too hard for too long to give it up to outsiders. I really wanted someone family to come in and take over now." As always, Cohen was too good a salesman, and Jacobson agreed to come into the business after reaching agreement with Cohen on several major points. As Jacobson, who immediately became second in command to Cohen as vice president and general manager, said: "I hated to see the company get sold to a conglomerate, too. I felt I had an obligation to see the business continue as a family business. Besides, coming here was a great opportunity as well as a challenge."

Jacobson began immediately to try to improve the business rather than accepting the task as a pension until Cohen would be forced out by ill health or by recognition that he could no longer handle the reins of running the company. As Jacobson said in an interview published by Corporate Report, a Kansas City publication, of the time when he came on board: "When I came in, I redefined the organizational chart to give more authority and responsibility down the line so Jerry isn't making every day-to-day decision. I wanted to combine Jerry's entrepreneurial spirit and the corporate-type environment I was used to. Years before, Jerry had set an annual growth rate of 15 percent. I instituted long-term planning. I wanted to determine not only that we were going to grow 15 percent but how we were going to do it. I wanted to plan five to ten years out."

Within a short time, Jacobson brought in several managers from the outside to build a professional management team and broadened the decision-making powers of the managers. He instituted an on-going management-training program. He implemented an employee stock-ownership program and within a short time the employees owned eight percent of the stock compared to 92 percent held by Cohen. Cohen was cooperative in being willing to give up on some of the day-to-day decisions Jacobson was delegating to other managers he brought in, but he made it clear he was still at the helm of the company. Five years after Jacobson came into the company in October 1981, Cohen said in a published 1986 interview in answer to the question of when he planned to retire: "When I can't breathe anymore. I've got to have a reason to get up every morning — that's the way I stay healthy." There was also a large advertisement in The Kansas City Star, which featured a large photograph of Cohen leaning on a sleek 3M office copier and with the headline: " 'In 1953, we sold the first 3M copier purchased in Kansas City. Today we sell every one of them.' —Jerry Cohen, President, Electronic Business Equipment." It was obvious that he was willing to work with and share responsibility with his son-in-law but that he was not retiring and still felt in charge.

How well Cohen was doing in marketing with his businesses was officially recognized by the Kansas City business community in 1980. He was named the Marketing Man of the Year by the Sales and Marketing Executives of Kansas City. In winning the award, first presented in 1968 by the organization, Cohen had joined a distinguished group of Kansas City entrepreneurs who had previously received the award: Donald J. Hall, of Hallmark Cards, Inc.; Ewing Kauffman, of the Kansas City Royals and Marion Laboratories, Inc.; Henry and Richard Bloch, of H & R Block; Dr. Charles Kimball, of Midwest Research Institute; the Rev. Maurice Van Ackeren, of Rockhurst College; and Stanley H. Durwood, of American Multi-Cinema, Inc.

In the December edition of SME News, the official publication of the organization, there was a story across the front page with a large photograph of Cohen and headline "Marketing Man of the Year Selected." The story said: "After a thorough review of all the nominations and with the unanimous approval of the board, Jerome Cohen is the man of the year to be honored and presented the Steuben Glass Owl at our February 9th meeting. Cohen is president and chief executive officer of Electronic Business Equipment, Inc., of K. C., St. Joseph and Jefferson City and the Tempo Co. of Kansas City. Under his direction his company showed increases in '78 of 25 percent and '79 an increase of 23 percent. His company is recognized by 3M Company as one of the leading 3M business products distributors in the country... by Gestetner Co. as one of their best dealers... by NBI Word Processing as a leader in the word processing field in sales and service. Cohen's civic and charitable activities over the years include: Chairman, Mayor's Christmas Tree Association over 25 years; executive board, Starlight; past president, Friends of the Zoo; governor, American Royal Association; commissioner, K. C. Park Board, seven years. And the list goes on. His selection is welcomed by area business who know him and by all those hundreds who have benefited by his dedication and help in their good causes. He is a worthy member of the distinguished group who have received this prestigious SME award."

Despite a heavy snowstorm during the day, a capacity crowd turned out in the Ballroom of the Alameda Plaza Hotel on February 9, 1981, at the dinner at which Cohen received the coveted award. James Wietzel, president of the Advertising and Marketing Executives, presented Cohen the exquisitely crafted crystal owl by Steuben symbolizing the honor and said in part: "Jerry Cohen played an important role in the development and creation of an entire industry. Always looking for a new, improved product, he took chances on ideas that were only experimental, proved they would work in the duplicating machines in his sales region and then went on to investigate other new processes. Several of the new ideas became important milestones in the duplicating industry. Throughout the years, Jerry Cohen has prided himself on being a pacesetter in every facet of business. The Cohen organization has always been in the forefront in introducing new, better products to meet the increasing needs and demands of consumers. To mention Cohen's business accomplishments, however, is to tell only about half the man. Part of the credit for the wide recognition and fine reputation that his companies enjoy can be attributed to the many civic, fraternal and religious activities of their founder." An audio-visual show of the life and times of the honoree was presented, narrated by Walt Bodine, noted area newscaster, and closing with the tag line, "He sold copies, but Jerry is an original."

In accepting the award, Cohen paid tribute to his family and said: "I will always try to merit the dignity and honor of this award and cherish it all my life. Behind every great man there are many great people and I have always found that a great accomplishment is the result of many jobs well done. In accepting this prestigious award tonight I feel you are not only honoring me but all my loyal, dedicated employees who have had their share of accomplishments over the years and the results of their efforts make me look good." There was even a brief message from President Ronald Reagan in which he said: "You exemplify the spirit of American free enterprise. The ability to move the output of industry and find markets for our services in this country and throughout the world will always be critical to the economic vitality of our nation. Your contributions are highly valued and appreciated."

As it turned out, 1988 was a critical year for Cohen and his businesses in many ways. For one thing, it marked the 50th anniversary of his first humble beginnings of his business in 1938. For another, it marked the year Cohen was turning 75, a birthday when many successful businessmen have already been long swallowed up in the rocking chair. Cohen, however, was still going at breakneck speed to try to stay abreast of the speed of change that was occurring in the information systems of business and industry compared to those humble mimeograph beginnings in 1938. It was becoming increasingly apparent to Cohen and to Jacobson as well that keeping abreast in computers was more expensive than previous changes and a broader financial base than even their successful firm could meet. The result was that Cohen began negotiating with another rapidly growing element in the computer and duplicating field in the United States, Danka Industries. Danka had started in Tampa, Fla., in 1977 under the aegis of a group of financial management investors who had a feel for capital requirements in the field. Their growth and goals appealed to Cohen since by 1988 Danka had become the largest independent, totally integrated copier and fax machine dealer in the United States. At the 50th anniversary celebration set for October 13, 1988, for Cohen and his companies, the negotiations with Danka had moved along quietly and steadily. By the time the several hundred guests, including employees, had gathered for the golden anniversary gala on the third floor of the Kansas City Club, Cohen was able to make an announcement that caught many by surprise. EBE was merging with Danka to take advantage of its financial abilities.

After welcoming the guests and expressing his gratitude for their support over the past 50 years in building his companies into the top office equipment dealer, Cohen made his announcement: "To ensure our company's continuity and growth over the next 50 years, I have today signed a letter of intent wherein the stock of EBE will be transferred to Danka Industries and EBE will be an independent entity of that company. My purpose in doing this is to join the strengths of their successful marketing expertise and the greater buying power of Danka Industries with the EBE overall extensive knowledge of our 50 years of pioneering efforts in the office machine field. Our combined strength will let us continue to be the number one office machine dealer in the Kansas City and St. Joseph areas... There is always a reluctance to change, but we must continue to improve and this means changes. Changes are a constant process."

Although Cohen said in the original announcement that he would remain as chairman of the board and chief executive officer of EBE and Jacobson would remain as president, such was not to be. Within 18 months by April 1990, Jacobson had gone back into the investment counselling business as a vice president of the United Missouri Bank in Kansas City in charge of its foreign currency department. Cohen was still going strong. A 1991 edition of a Danka Industries in-house publication featured a full-color photograph of Cohen together with two stories about Danka in Kansas City. One was about working with the Police Department for a computerized high speed, high level image processing system. The other was how Macintosh computers and laser printers had been furnished by Danka to provide stories and results on the Senior PGA Tour at Loch Lloyd Country Club in Kansas City.

COHEN IS MAYOR'S CHRISTMAS TREE — *For 40 years, Jerry Cohen headed the Mayor's Christmas Tree Fund as chairman since Mayor H. Roe Bartle first appointed him to the post in 1955. He is shown here with one of Kansas City's top longtime celebrities, Marilyn Maye, the famed vocalist, who helped him with one of the drives. He has served as chairman under each successive mayor since Bartle — Ilus Davis, Charles Wheeler, Richard L. Berkley and the current mayor, Emanuel Cleaver II.*

CHRISTMAS EFFORT HELPS THOUSANDS — *Kansas City off-duty firemen and members of the Marine Corps Reserve load military trucks with Christmas packages provided by the Mayor's Christmas Tree Fund headed by Jerry Cohen for 40 years. Millions of dollars have been raised to help thousands of needy Kansas Citians from children to the aged, under the direction of Cohen.*

20

Patriotism Flows

"**A**ggressive young man wants part-time work to keep him from idling away his life; can give references from 71 jobs, none of which paid a thing; they include such organizations as Piscator's Society, Elmer's Fishing Club, the United States Navy, the Venerable Master Lodge of Perfection and others; willing to ride car in Soap Box Derby, act in Starlight Theater presentation, be a Santa Claus and light a fire without matches for over-24-year-old Girl Scouts; fearless and forthright, big and bold; owns Tea House, Japanese flower garden, works of Japanese art and over 50 goldfish; write Box 1973."

This pseudo newspaper classified advertisement was run in a two-column profile on Jerry Cohen at the beginning of the story in The Buzz Saw, the internal house organ of Rotary Club 13, the downtown Kansas City Rotary Club. The mock advertisement on the article, which was rare for its size in reference to members who made worthwhile contributions to the city, in a way expressed the wonder of the author and other Kansas Citians about how Cohen was able to make so many civic contributions and at the same time operate four highly successful business enterprises. The article which followed the pseudo advertisement carried this awe of the many civic contributions Cohen made all his life in Kansas City. It read in part: "Any Club 13 Rotarian who doesn't immediately identify this personality as Jerry Cohen should be appointed to a committee of which Jerry is chairman, where he will quickly learn the meaning of Rotary's 'Get Involved... Enthusiastically' policy. Jerry Cohen, in person, not only is the president of four successful electronic business equipment companies of his own, but in his years in Kansas City, he has been associated with, given trouble to, messed up, helped grow or organized 71 different civic enterprises — none of which pay him one cent. Not only that, he has been a board member, an executive, committeeman, a second, third or first vice president, a secretary and a treasurer of just about half of them and a full-time hard-working president of a dozen or so of the 71 groups... His horoscope reads that he is 'bold and warlike in nature.' One observer pointed out that anybody who is big can be bold and... 'Besides, Cohen is really not so big. He is just well-rounded'... On the truly, truly human side of Jerry Cohen, a beautiful rainbow of compassion and charity shines through all of his efforts and results... and whether he checks out of life through the B'nai B'rith or the DeMolay route, he won't even have to show any of his 71 membership cards. The folks Up There keep good books on Everybody Down Here... and they know all about Club 13's Jerry Cohen."

Such accolades in the Rotary Club publication were deserved because Cohen regarded his membership in Rotary Club 13 as one of his greatest civic duties. His principal mentor in Rotary had been a longtime friend and former mayor who had named him to the Kansas City Board of Parks and Recreation, H. Roe Bartle. Bartle took Rotary seriously and so did Cohen, who thoroughly enjoyed the fellowship. He was a regular weekly participant in the luncheons in Rotary Club 13, which had a reputation for having one of the most lax meeting attendance requirement regulations in the movement. Whenever he was traveling both at home and abroad, Cohen would seek out the local Rotary Club to attend. He loved to talk about meetings he had attended in out-of-the-way clubs in Europe, Asia and Latin America. Whenever he was asked to take on a committee chairmanship, he went about it with gusto. He was elected to the board of Rotary Club 13, but not as an officer. He loved serving on the speakers committee and The Kansas City Star carried a photograph of him with H. Lamar Hunt, the owner of the Kansas City Chiefs, whom he got to speak and introduced at one of the weekly luncheons. He got one of the top officers of the 3M Company to come on a regular basis in the 1980s and early 1990s to speak in what came to be one of the most popular annual meetings of the club. It was the financial forecasts that the officer made for each calendar year and which proved over time to be so successful in their accuracy. He was John McDivitt, a vice president of 3M who was responsible for its corporate fiscal projections. Cohen always had a soft spot in his heart for the Rotary Youth Camp which the club operated on a wooded track on the shores of Lake Jacomo and was a willing contributor to meet its financial needs.

During his membership in Rotary Club 13, the club also reached a major landmark in 1985 when it played host to the Rotary International convention just as Ararat Shrine had done in 1976 when it hosted the American Bicentennial international convention. It was the second time that the Kansas City club, one of the oldest in the nation, had played host to an international convention of the organization, the first having been in 1918 just as World War I was coming to a close and peace was the major theme then. Some 4,500 members from the U.S. and Canada attended the 1918 convention which had as its headquarters the old Orpheum Theater in Kansas City. Besides commenting on the extensive coverage of the event by Kansas City newspapers, an historical account of the 1918 convention said: "One of the greatest accomplishments of the convention according to that week's Buzz Saw was the automobile ride. One thousand three cars were employed to take visitors on a 35-mile tour of Kansas City's 'dustless boulevards,' and Wednesday night's Bean Supper proved to be a huge success. Thirty-five committees made up of local Rotarians from both Kansas Cities handled the activities."

The 1985 convention was a much larger affair, however, drawing some 15,000 guests from Rotary Clubs around the world headed by Carlos Conseco of Mexico, who was the international president at the time. Cohen was named as a member of the Rotary Club 13 host steering committee for the convention and served as chairman of one of the major committees, that which directed what was known as the House of Friendship. Its primary function was to provide a warm, entertaining area in Bartle Hall where delegates could rest and relax. As usual with all things he undertook, the House of Friendship proved to be one of the most popular features of the 1985 convention, featuring a large Western-style bar, a backdrop of Western memorabilia, tables covered with red checkered tablecloths in the Western bar area, another area replete with writing desks equipped with stationery and postcards, living room style furniture for quiet conversation, a wall of club banners from around the world, continuous entertainment of singers, dancers and musicians, and light snacks and soft drinks. Large numbers of Rotarians and their wives were recruited from the Kansas City club and other Rotary clubs in the metropolitan area to serve as hosts and hostesses during all the hours the hospitality rooms were open.

In addition to seeing that all these operations ran smoothly to rave acclamations from the delegates, Cohen and his wife, Jeannette, entertained delegates from Taiwan clubs in their Oriental-decor home when delegates from other nations had been guests at home visits in other homes in the area. To prepare for their roles at the 1985 Rotary International convention in Kansas City, Mr. and Mrs. Cohen had joined other Kansas City couples in attending the 1984 convention and were guests of two British couples in their homes during the convention in Birmingham, England.

The one thing which Cohen kept doing year after year in civic activities was another project in which Bartle as mayor had gotten him involved in 1955, serving as chairman of the Mayor's Christmas Tree Fund to help make the holidays a little merrier for the less fortunate in Kansas City. Cohen was originally tapped by Bartle for the job because Bartle wanted to change the way the program operated. After Bartle left the Mayor's office after eight years of service, Cohen continued to work at the task under each successive mayor right up through 1994 when he served his 39th year in the job under Mayor Emanuel Cleaver II and showed every sign of serving his 40th year in 1995 if he was able and whoever was mayor continued to want his services.

One of the biggest boosts to his efforts came when Joyce C. Hall, the founder and chief executive of Hallmark Cards, decided in the early 1970s to build the Crown Center complex with its two hotels, shopping center and restaurants as well as theaters and as one of its Christmas promotions to have a giant tree-lighting ceremony on the day after Thanksgiving and donating it to the kickoff of the Mayor's Christmas Tree Fund drive. Hallmark also made annual Christmas ornaments from the old trees and sold them annually with the funds going to the Christmas Tree effort. Cohen was always looking for new ideas to keep the Mayor's Christmas Tree Fund before the public yearly to draw attention for the needy.

Some of his greatest successes were achieved under Mayor Richard Berkley who went all out to support him during his 12 years in the office. It was during the term of Mayor Berkley that Cohen observed his 26th year. Berkley held a breakfast to honor Cohen at the Hyatt Regency Hotel in Crown Center and presented him with a colorful framed certificate in commemoration of the occasion. The certificate said in part: "Mr. Jerome Cohen has served his fellow man with distinction and dedication for the past quarter century as an officer of the Mayor's Christmas Tree Association, a benevolent organization which has raised and distributed funds over the past 70 years to provide Christmas cheer in the form of toys, food, clothing, toilet and personal articles and entertainment to those needy persons whose holidays would otherwise be bleak and dreary, including children, welfare recipients, persons in various public institutions and the ill and elderly in nursing and convalescent homes. Mr. Cohen has raised more than $900,000 to help make Christmas merrier during his service as chairman, vice chairman and chairman of the finance committee of the organization. His superb leadership and selfless devotion of his time, his unique talents and his boundless energy on behalf of his less fortunate neighbors have, over a quarter of a century, touched the lives of succeeding generations of Kansas Citians by spreading holiday cheer among the needy and by assuring contributors that their gifts for the worthy purposes of the association would be faithfully applied in such a manner as to provide the maximum benefits to the ultimate recipients with the minimum of administrative costs." At that point in reality, Cohen had raised over $10 million in goods, services and cash.

Although Cohen was not active in the political arena outside of the Citizens Association as he was in the late 1950s and early 1960s, he continued to be actively interested in the political issues of the day. Not the least of his worries was the double-digit inflation of the latter stages of the administration of President Jimmy Carter, ranging from 15 to 20 percent at times, and the effect it was having on businesses such as his. He fired off a letter to President Carter supporting the initiatives by Carter against the increasing inflation but urging him to do more. For his efforts, Cohen received a specially signed letter from Alfred E. Kahn, who had served as chairman of the President's Council of Economic Advisors and had now been elevated to a virtual economic czar as advisor to the President on inflation.

In the letter to Cohen, Kahn declared: "I speak for the President as well as myself in thanking you for your recent letter expressing support for the President's anti-inflation program. I know how unnecessary it is to tell you how important a strong and broad commitment by American business is to our anti-inflation program. We renew our pledge to do our part by holding down government spending and the budget deficit, and by injecting economic sense into regulation. It is the combination of price and wage compliance by business and labor with self-restraint by government that will bring us success. Your continued commitment to the anti-inflation program is an act of civic responsibility in which you may take pride. It is important not only in its own, but in the example it sets for others. If you were to publicize it, it would help reassure others that if they support the program and adhere to the standards, they will not be acting alone." Cohen continued to support Republicans after Ronald Reagan swept Carter out of office in the 1980 elections which also saw a friend of Cohen, Christopher (Kit) Bond, a lawyer, become governor of Missouri.

In 1982, when the increasing number of Republican governors accepted an invitation from Bond to hold a meeting of the Republican Governors Association in Kansas City, Cohen served on a committee helping host the conference and provided some of the gifts given each of the governors. As Bond, who went on to become U.S. Senator from Missouri, said in a letter to Cohen after the conference: "I am most grateful to you for making them available for us. Many of the other governors, as well as national media representatives and Republican Governors Club members from other states, told me how much they appreciated the hospitality and generosity of Kansas City. Clearly, your generosity was an important factor in that overall perception. It was a most enjoyable conference for us and I am sure Kansas City has improved its already fine reputation as a good place to visit and do business. Thank you again for your help." In November 1975 elections, Cohen also joined with other civic leaders in pushing a bond issue to improve the metropolitan junior colleges at their Penn Valley, Longview and Maple Woods campuses. In the action, Cohen was joining many prominent Kansas Citians, including Charles B. Wheeler, Richard Berkley, Sarah Snow, Fred Arbanas, Emanuel Cleaver, Ilus W. Davis, William Deramus III, William H. Dunn, Judge Leonard S. Hughes, Jr., Herman Johnson, Sister Olive Louise

Dallavis, Morgan Maxfield and W. W. Hutton.

One of the biggest patriotic outdoor celebrations in Kansas City history was held on September 15, 1990, in Swope Park when more than 200,000 persons turned out for a Celebration of Youth to commemorate the 100th anniversary of the founding of the Kansas City Department of Parks and Recreation. Who else could have been chosen to serve as general chairman in planning and directing such a giant celebration, in which more than 20,000 Boy Scouts and Girl Scouts alone participated, than Jerry Cohen, who had served as a member of the Kansas City Board of Parks and Recreation and a longtime friend of the veteran scout executive for years of the Heart of America Council of the Boy Scouts, the late H. Roe Bartle? Carl Di Capo, himself a downtown booster through his Italian Gardens restaurant, had become president of the Parks and Recreation Board under Mayor Richard Berkley and had conceived the youth conference to commemorate the 100th anniversary of the beautiful Kansas City park system with his two fellow park commissioners at the time, Anita Gorman and Ollie Gates.

As Di Capo said later: "I conceived the idea of such a celebration because of all the negative things that were being said about the youth of the day. I wanted to have the community to see a statement of the positive things many of our area youths were doing even in the face of drugs and crime. Who would be better for the job than Jerry Cohen, who always made sure that anything in which he played a major role was a success and was a native Kansas Citian who had demonstrated his love for the youth through the years in many of his philanthropic works. We were delighted when he agreed to accept the post because we knew if there was somebody who could accomplish what we wanted do to it was Jerry."

For 12 months prior to the big event, Cohen devoted much of his time to meeting with Boy Scout and Girl Scout executives, members of the steering committee serving under him and representatives of the Kansas City Parks and Recreation Department, headed by Terry Dopson, as superintendent. Detailed plans called for more than 10,000 area Cub Scouts, Eagle Scouts and Girl Scouts to camp out in specially designated areas beginning the night of September 14, 1990; all day the main day of the celebration September 15 and all that night into mid-morning September 16. To ensure the success of the event, the parks and recreation department through the Starlight Theater Association entered into a contract with one of the hottest country music singers of the time noted for his patriotic songs, Lee Greenwood, to be featured at the closing spectacle of the day-long youth pageant. Greenwood had become a national sensation following his being featured at the 1989 inauguration of President George Bush, the bicentennial of the American presidency and taking of the oath by the first president in 1789, George Washington.

With Cohen's eye for detail, the giant event proved successful beyond the fondest dreams of the promoters in pointing up the positive sign of the lives of young people in the United States at the time. Colorful Revolutionary and Civil War recreational groups in authentic uniforms together with Missouri fur trapper and trader reenactment groups set up camp and staged demonstrations throughout the day. Student ambassadors had been selected from the Girl and Boy Scouts groups and were utilized by Kansas City advertising agencies in radio and television commercials promoting the event in advance. On the Swope Park lagoon there was a colorful race of makeshift floating rafts by the Scout groups called "The Anything that Floats but a Boat Race" that drew widespread media attention. Zoo animals were paraded along the big celebration midway at various times during the day, leading stars of the Kansas City professional sports franchises, the Royals, the Chiefs, the Blades and the Comets, made appearances all day; Arthur Ashe, the tennis star who later died from AIDS from a non-sexual source, staged a tennis exhibition; Girl Scout rock climbing champions across the nation climbed the stone towers at Starlight Theater; there was an Indian village of 25 full-size tepees where Scout Indian dancers in authentic costumes performed throughout the day. Military helicopters added to the noise and excitement with regular landing and take-offs and formation fly-bys; hot air balloons landed and took off from the park; birds of prey such as eagles, peregrine falcons and red tailed hawks appeared with their trainers and did flying demonstrations. If you couldn't find something to occupy your time from sunup until Lee Greenwood performed, you were dead. Cohen saw to that.

To open the festival, Cohen, Di Capo and the Girl Scout and Boy Scout executives had made arrangements for several hundred police-escorted Scout runners to carry a lighted torch from the site of the Eagle Scout Tribute Fountain, which had been built in tribute to Bartle when

Cohen was on the Park Board, at 39th Street and Gillham Road, to the main entrance of the Swope Park grounds where the thousands of Scouts camping at the park had been drawn in formations in a specially built amphitheater. Phil Witt, news anchorman from WDAF-TV, Channel 4, who had been a Boy Scout, and Anne Peterson, news anchor woman from KCTV-5, Channel 5, who had been a Girl Scout, served as members of the ceremony for the torch lighting and other opening ceremonies in which Cohen and Di Capo participated. Witt told the assembled Scouts: "The reason I still consider myself a Boy Scout these many years later is that what I learned in Scouting has stuck with me and helped me." Peterson said on the occasion: "For me, Girl Scouting opened a whole new world — I learned to speak my mind, trust my judgment, and become truly confident in who I am and what I'm capable of."

As the torch lighters entered the arena to light the torch to burn throughout the day, ranks of Eagle Scouts and Gold Scouts from the Girl Scouts marched into the arena. Witt and Peterson then introduced Cohen who told the hundreds of Scouts and spectators: "We are today celebrating the kind of positive influences our youth need to combat today's negative pressures. Most of today's events will be unlike any I experienced as a Boy Scout or as an Eagle Scout. Many of the skills I learned — such as cooking, signalling and knot tying — Scouts still learn today. But programs like computer studies, space exploration, cinematography and no trace camping were not options in my day. Today's Scouts, however, will enter adulthood with the same values I learned — the ones we heard in the Scout oath and promise. They will have a strong sense of who they are, what they can do and how to lead others. Ultimately, I know these boys and girls will give back to their communities and be an example for others to follow."

When Di Capo was introduced following Cohen, the Kansas City Parks and Recreation Board president told the huge crowd: "You are now in one of the largest parks within city limits in the United States of America and that's what parks and recreation is all about — planning the use of our urban space to bring beauty and natural setting to Kansas City. When you consider the 13,000 Boy Scouts and Girl Scouts camped out last night right here in Kansas City — not only is Swope Park a beautiful park within a city but with our campers there's a city within the park as well." To help the thousands of spectators who turned out for the

Lee Greenwood concert get a better view of the proceedings in the finale, two giant 30x40-foot television screens were placed in the area. Bagpipers played, there was a concert by a Barber Shop Quartet, Girl Scout choruses and Greenwood, himself a former Boy Scout, doing his patriotic hits, including "I Am an American." With a spectacular fireworks display lighting the night sky as Greenwood finished singing, there was hardly a spine without a patriotic chill among the thousands. Cohen and Di Capo had proved what was best about an American city and its youth.

Cohen always carried within his heart a genuine and true sense of patriotism for the United States throughout his life. He had learned firsthand as a second generation Jewish immigrant the opportunity America really offered its citizens. Like thousands of other Americans, he was saddened by the division created by American war efforts to try to keep South Vietnam from falling to Communist aggressors in the late 1960s and early 1970s. He was appalled that 45,000 American lives were lost in the military effort while thousands of radical left students and draft resistors were labelling the Pentagon and U.S. military forces as "totalitarian" and "fascist."

To combat the negativism of the minority toward the U.S. military establishment, Cohen had been one of the founders of the Richards-Gebaur Air Force Base Community Council and had served as its second president in 1961 and 1962. The air base encompassed more than 2,000 acres approximately 18 miles south of the headquarters of EBE in downtown Kansas City. At the height of the buildup and the Vietnam war, the base, Richards-Gebaur, was a major unit in the North American Air Defense, housing one of its largest radar sites, the so-called SAGE system, an anachronism for semi-automatic ground environment and ground control intercept, as well as the 328th fighter wing of the U.S. Air Force flying F-102 Delta Dagger fighters "providing an around the clock, all-weather shield against manned bomber attack." A variety of other defense-related units were also housed at the sprawling base.

As Col. James H. Wood, one of the base commanders during Cohen's active association with the group, said of the community council and the efforts of Cohen: "The purpose of this group is to identify the common interests of the civilian and military communities with the view of recognizing the problem areas and supporting constructive efforts of mutual benefits. Another goal of the group is to provide continuity in the common relationships with the base despite frequent changes of personnel. Each year the council also sponsored and assisted in the annual base open house program. Through the efforts of this outstanding group of civic leaders, Richards-Gebaur has enjoyed a community relations atmosphere second to none."

During his term as president of the council shortly after it was initiated, Cohen instituted a program which continued throughout the Vietnam war with the Air Force of recognizing the outstanding air man of the month and of the year as selected by commanding officers of the various units at the base. As an Air Force press release said: "The personnel at Richards-Gebaur Air Force Base have benefitted greatly from this program and are deeply appreciative of the sponsorship of the base community council in making the Airman of the Year possible. It is through programs such as this that the real spirit of base community relations comes forth. Through the unselfish efforts of community and civic leaders in the Greater Kansas City Area, the awards given to these airmen have added greatly to the program. Without this feeling of cooperation between the base and surrounding communities, programs such as the airman of the year would not be possible."

A three-day festival to celebrate the 10th anniversary of the base was sponsored by the council and featured such things as the Thunderbirds USAF precision flying team, skydiving exhibitions, displays of the latest military aircraft and weapons, night flare parachute drops, fireworks and the first display of the Gemini four-man space capsule outside the Seattle World's Fair. As an Air Force press release said: "The base community council is sponsoring the event to further enhance the already-exceptional civilian-military community relations, to acquaint close to a quarter million visitors with the United States Air Force and to provide financial support for base welfare projects."

Whenever youth was involved, Cohen could be counted upon to go all out in support. When Kansas City instituted a program to have business and civic leaders support the annual National Association of Intercollegiate Athletics basketball tournament by serving as honorary coaches for the various teams, Cohen was in the forefront. There are some great photographs of Cohen on the sidelines at the Municipal Auditorium with the cheerleaders for the Western Carolina College team. He provided gifts and entertainment for the team members, the coaches and the cheerleaders during their stay. As Jim Gudger, the Western Carolina team coach, wrote Cohen after the team returned home: "On behalf of the basketball team, the athletic department of Western Carolina and myself, I want to thank you for your most gracious consideration and the kindness shown to our club during our stay in Kansas City. Our boys mention you quite often and certainly talk about the fine dinner at Lucian's following the final game. Several of my boys have never had an experience like that. Our trip back was very good and we had quite a reception on our campus honoring the basketball team on our return. Mel Gibson, who I am sure you remember, returned to Kansas City the week after the tournament and played in the Pan American trials. He was selected over many of the outstanding big college stars as one of the representatives of the United States in the Pan American Games now being staged in Sao Paulo, Brazil. He will go on from there to Rio de Janeiro to play in the world tournament on the completion of these games. The professional clubs are very much interested in this boy and it looks like he has a lucrative basketball career ahead. Bill Gustafson, who you will remember as 'Gus,' asked to be remembered to you and, of course, you can't forget the way he can eat. Again let me say that we are most appreciative of your most generous consideration during our visit to Kansas City." Once again — as in everything else seemingly he touched — Cohen's generosity turned to gold.

21

His Faith Shines

After his affiliation with Danka Corporation in 1988, Jerry Cohen found the duplicating business with which he had been associated for over 50 years changing even more rapidly. He still headed Electronic Business Equipment division of Danka and he was in the office every day keeping up his civic work and staying in touch with his employees of many years but much of the day-to-day business operations were being controlled by Danka managers.

Cohen still kept an eye out for small business opportunities to keep him busy and one of the most successful of these into which he ventured was the operation of a Kansas City radio station, KNHN Radio, AM 1340. He was instrumental in getting into that business because of a longtime association with a Kansas Citian named Bill Johnson. Cohen had first become acquainted with Johnson when Johnson was a radio advertising salesman with KCMO Radio 81 and Cohen began promoting his business on the radio station. Johnson moved on up to the television associate of KCMO Radio, a television station known as KCMO-TV, Channel 5, now known as KCPT-5, Channel 5. This was in the mid-1950s when 3M came out with its first small, desktop-size copier, the Thermofax, and Johnson put Cohen on the night television news live promoting the units. Cohen gave the television promotion and advice from Johnson credit for the tremendous sales success he had. Johnson moved on to an advertising agency and continued to handle the Cohen accounts on radio and television. Johnson began looking at buying a radio station in Kansas City and persuaded Cohen to invest in the operation on a large scale.

Once again the Cohen gold touch he had demonstrated for more than 50 years came through with the radio station. Johnson decided to convert the station into the city's first 24-hour news station and entered into an agreement with the radio news affiliate of the Ted Turner television news network, CNN Radio. The time could not have been more fortuitous. Saddam Hussein invaded the oil-rich kingdom of Kuwait with the armed forces of Iraq and President George Bush moved immediately to begin an American military buildup in the Persian Gulf to stop Hussein from rolling on to invade Saudi Arabia and Israel. The building of American forces and the eventual military action known as the Gulf War to defeat Iraq kept Kansas Citians glued to KNHN 1340 Radio and its CNN News affiliation when they could not watch television.

As Cohen said of Johnson: "I had always considered him a clean, honest, moral, hardworking man. He knew the radio business and it took a lot of imagination and ingenuity to me, at least, to do what he did. I guess all my life in my business I tried to stay a step ahead of the industry, and Bill became the same kind of pioneer in the radio industry here in Kansas City with his decision to go with an all news station. I feel like we are pioneers again in the radio industry, and I am looking forward to the growth of radio as it becomes more and more important as a means of direct contact with the people. I guess the other thing I like about being in KNHN is that we get the prominent and important people of our area on this station to let them express their views and then respond to questions from listeners."

In the years after his affiliation with Danka in 1988, he saw the changes in operations bring about the closing of his branch offices such as the one in the Missouri state capital, Jefferson City. The building which housed the division in Jefferson City had been built especially for that purpose by Cohen in 1960 at 401 Madison, within walking distance of the state capitol building and at a highly visible location in the central Jefferson City business district. After the decision to close the two-story modern brick structure as an EBE branch, Cohen began looking around for a buyer for the property. When it did not move quickly, Cohen began thinking of possibilities for its use. The National Society of Professional Engineers was to hold its national meeting in the summer of 1994 in Kansas City in connection with the 60th anniversary of the Missouri Society of Professional Engineers. In honor of the occasion, Cohen conceived the idea of donating the building and property on which it sits to the Missouri Society for its state headquarters as a gift by him to its nonprofit foundation, the MSPE Educational Foundation, Inc. It was quickly accepted by the state group and on July 13, 1994, hundreds of engineers from across the nation attended a luncheon at the Hyatt Regency hotel given by the Chamber of Commerce of Greater Kansas City where Cohen officially turned over the property to Gerald J. Reihsen, engineer and head of the state society. In remarks, Cohen told the large luncheon crowd: "Over the years, I have always found a great accomplishment or achievement is the result of many jobs well done. What I am about today is a testimonial to the partnership between professional engineers and businessmen. Since I started in business over five decades ago, I have come to respect and admire the role engineers have played in designing and developing a quality product for me to market. When quality products are designed, it perpetuates our economy. Factories have to hire people and buy raw materials to make the products and marketing people, like me, to distribute. Then everyone involved causes the wheels of commerce to turn and generate new sales and growth. The philosophies for any success I have achieved in my marketing career and in my life are these very simple basics: God created every person equal. He gives each of us 24 hours a day, what we do with these 24 hours is the difference between success and failure. What you get on this earth you get from people. Treat them accordingly. My only justification for existence on this earth is to help someone else. You cannot help another person without helping yourself. Today, I have chosen to help the Missouri Society of Professional Engineers by making a donation to their educational foundation. Frankly, since this week is the National Society of Professional Engineers 60th anniversary annual meeting and it's being held in my native town, I could think of no better time than now to make this presentation." In reply, Reihsen said to Cohen: "Thank you for your very generous donation. On behalf of the foundation officers and our society members, we look forward to the day when we can invite you to gather with us in Jefferson City to dedicate 'your' building to serve the foundation and society's goals and objectives. I'm certain this building will be transformed into a lasting tribute to the profession it exemplifies."

Cohen and his wife have never ceased giving to Kansas City throughout their lives. There was always something new for them to give. Along with all the other things they gave through the years to Temple B'Nai Jehudah, their synagogue, they gave a newly remodeled stainless steel kitchen. They were recognized in the August 21, 1989, issue of the Temple Bulletin with a picture of Jeannette looking over one of the new kitchen ovens on the front page with a headline which read: "Newly-remodeled kitchen a gift from Jeannette Cohen." Underneath the photograph was the caption: "Sisterhood and Temple are very appreciative of the magnificent new stainless steel state-of-the-art kitchen now open for use. Recently remodeled, upon the completion, Jeannette Cohen, Sisterhood's benefactor, checks out the new ovens, refrigerators, counter tops with flat surfaces offering much more work space and sinks." There were more photographs inside about the Cohen gift. Thanks to Cohen, the National Federation of Temple Brotherhoods at its meeting in Kansas City arranged by Cohen, Harry S. Truman was presented a life membership in the Jewish Chautauqua Society for this service to Jews. Others who had received the honor previously were Rabbi Samuel Mayerberg, Joyce Hall, Walter J. Berkowitz, E. B. Berkowitz, Henry Talge and Leo Wertgame.

In return for his efforts in giving so much for the 50 years to the community he operated his businesses, Cohen in the later years of his life received increasing recognition for his efforts. They came from a wide variety of sources. When the first William Gillis awards were established by the Gillis Home for Children to be presented annually to Kansas Citians who best represented the Kansas City Spirit portrayed in the 1951 post-flood painting by Norman Rockwell, Cohen was among five outstanding citizens of the area to receive one. Others who were selected to receive that coveted first award were Joyce C. Hall, founder of Hallmark Cards and originator of the Crown Center redevelopment project; R. Crosby Kemper, chairman of the United Missouri Bancshares and civic philanthropist who had given time and effort to the construction of Kemper Arena and the now Marriott Downtown Hotel; Ilus W. Davis, noted lawyer who served as Mayor of Kansas City during eight of its most crucial years, and Joan Dillon, a founder of the Performing Arts

Foundation and the leader of the effort to preserve the historic Folly Theater. Cohen received one of the first Thomas Jefferson Awards for public service in 1984 after WDAF-TV, Channel 4, began the practice of selecting such winners.

In 1985, Cohen was named Corporate Volunteer of the Year at a luncheon given by the Corporate Volunteer Council and received a citation which read: "Jerome Cohen, president of Electronic Business Equipment, Inc., has always been a believer in helping all of the people of Kansas City and has been a leader in almost every organization which he belongs. He has served on the board of directors of the Starlight Theater and has been an officer since its inception. He is a past president of the Friends of the Zoo and has served as chairman of the annual picnic for more than 25 years. One of his favorite projects, and by far the most time consuming, is the Mayor's Christmas Tree Association. Jerry has been chairman of this event for more than 30 years. He has also found time to be vice president, president and chairman of the board of Temple B'Nai Jehudah. He has also served on the board of the McCoy House, is a committee chairman of the Rotary Club 13 and has been chairman of the Soap Box Derby for many years. Jerry has not only committed his own life to helping others but has been instrumental in getting literally hundreds of other people to do volunteer work for 56 organizations in Greater Kansas City."

Jerry Lewis, the famed motion picture, stage and television comedian who received the Nobel Peace Prize in 1977, the only entertainer ever so honored, came to Kansas City in 1993 to perform at the Jewish Community Center of Greater Kansas City Sportsnite at which Cohen was one of three honorees along with Bobby Bell, All-American football player and linebacker for the Kansas City Chiefs, and Denny Matthews, voice of the Kansas City Royals for more than 25 years. Cohen was presented the Ervin Feld Award for Outstanding Civic Contribution. In 1982, Cohen was chosen to receive the Civic Award of the Heart of America lodge of B'nai B'rith "in recognition of his long and devoted services to the Jewish community and the general community as well."

Of all the awards Cohen received for his civic service, the three that probably came closest to his heart as representing how he had tried to live for more than 80 years was receiving the Guardian of the Menorah Award from B'nai B'rith, being selected as the Jewish honoree at the annual banquet of the National Conference of Christians and Jews and being selected to be the featured speaker at the annual Mayors' Prayer Breakfast of Kansas City in 1990. He received the Guardian of the Menorah Award at the annual fund-raising luncheon for B'nai B'rith youth services at the Hotel Muehlebach presided over by Joseph Solsky, noted Kansas City businessman and Jewish philanthropist. Cohen became the 16th recipient of the coveted Jewish award, joining the distinguished company of Rabbi Gershon Hadas, Louis A. Cumonow, H. Roe Bartle, Earl J. Tranin, Daniel J. Brenner, Morten Brown, Abraham E. Margolin, William J. Klein, Richard A. Bloch, Barney A. Karbank, Judge John W. Oliver, Jay B. Dillingham, Louis Pozes, Dr. George A. Russell and Hy Vile. As Solsky said: "The Guardian of the Menorah Tribute is given each year to the outstanding Kansas Citian who has shown, through service and commitment, their devotion to the cause of youth and community. Jerome Cohen, exceptionally well-known in the Greater Kansas City area for his activity in a variety of endeavors, exemplifies the spirit of the Guardian of the Menorah. Jerry Cohen's efforts on behalf of youth include association with Camp Fire, Girl Scouts, American Humanics Foundation, Metropolitan Junior College, Hyman Brand Hebrew Academy and institutions for the handicapped.

"He has served as president of Temple B'Nai Jehudah, as well as supporting the Israel Bond organization, Jewish Vocational Service and the Greater Kansas City Region, National Conference of Christians and Jews. Mr. Cohen has served as a member of the Kansas City, Missouri, Park Board and president of Friends of the Zoo, as well as the executive committee of the Starlight Theater. Since 1955, he has been the chairman of the Mayor's Christmas Tree Fund, the community drive to provide for those in need during the holiday season. For all these reasons and more, Jerome Cohen deserves our praise and thanks." It was fitting in the case of Cohen that for the first time a Jewish youth who was a recipient of the B'nai B'rith youth funds raised by the luncheon spoke. Reed Lowenstein told the luncheon how much his Jewish heritage has meant to him, particularly as it related to family.

Rabbi Michael Zedek of Temple B'Nai Jehudah presented the Menorah, symbol of the award, to Cohen saying: "It is particularly fitting to present a Menorah to the honoree because the candelabra that is lit during Hanukkah has a servant candle that is higher than the others.

Today we honor one of our best servants. His service takes us to greater heights." Cohen said in accepting the honor in part: "It is with deep humility and gratitude that I accept this B'nai B'rith Guardian of the Menorah Tribute benefitting the B'nai B'rith youth activities. To have my name added to the illustrious list of former recipients of this coveted tribute is a very meaningful honor to me... Thank you for the happiness and feeling of accomplishment this tribute has given me this afternoon. I will always try to merit the dignity and honor of this award... Kansas City and the Jewish community have been very good and meaningful to me and my family. We always feel that we have an obligation to repay both of them through service that perpetuates them for generations to come. Again, ladies and gentlemen, I want to thank you for the accolade you have given me by bestowing this honor on me this afternoon, and I want to thank my partner of 50 years who has made many sacrifices to make me look good — my wife, Jeannette. I would like to close with a theme we practice at our companies — You never get rich selling; you get rich serving."

As he was receiving these three prestigious awards, his correspondence from friends indicated why they meant so much to him. There was this example in a letter from Cantor Paul E. Silbersher of Temple B'Nai Jehudah: "The room was full with people and the people were full of praise for you... a most worthy and deserving human being and an example for anyone to follow who wants to know what it means to be a mentsch. We are also proud that you are such an important part of B'Nai Jehudah as you are of the community of Kansas City in general. You are one of the kind of individuals...of whom there are too few...who inspire us to continue to believe that man's better nature can triumph over his darker side." Or this from Carl Puritz, the president of the Hyman Brand Hebrew Academy of Greater Kansas City: "Your career has spanned a multitude of activities and services generously shared for the benefit of so many deserving causes and organizations. You have always shared your expertise, time, resources and warm personality for the benefit of others and the entire community has been enriched by your willingness to serve and your many accomplishments. On behalf of our board of trustees, as well as the parents and students of our day school, I convey our congratulations to you for this honor."

The National Conference of Christians and Jews was an organization created in New York to help promote brotherhood by creating understanding rather than animosity among two such powerful forces in national life as the Christians and the Jews and in the Kansas City area a dedicated Jewish woman worker, Evelyn Wasserstrom, had built the Kansas City organization into one of the premiere groups when Cohen was selected to be recognized as the Jewish honoree. Cohen was being honored at the same time as three of his longtime friends, Sen. John C. Danforth, Missouri Republican; Jerry Smith, antique car collector and the Catholic honoree, and Vic Swyden, powerful veteran member of the Kansas City city council who was the Protestant honoree. Senator Danforth was being named the Midwest Citizen of the Year, an award created in 1975 with the honoring of Sen. Stuart Symington and had included such other luminaries as Walter Cronkite, the CBS television news analyst; Bill Vaughan, humor writer for The Kansas City Star, and Sen. Thomas F. Eagleton.

The citation for Cohen presented at the dinner in the 20th Century Ballroom of the Westin Crown Center Hotel read as follows: "Representing the Jewish community is Jerry Cohen, president of Temple B'Nai Jehudah. His community involvement includes the Hyman Brand Hebrew Academy, Israel Bonds, Jewish Chautauqua Society, Jewish Vocational Services and Jewish Community Center. He has also served as Chairman of the Mayor's Christmas Tree Fund, Soap Box Derby, Camp Fire Girls, People-to-People, Starlight Theater, Friends of the Zoo, Kansas City Park Board and the Sister Cities Commission."

In accepting the award, Cohen said: "It is with deep humility and gratitude that I accept this National Conference of Christians and Jews citation award. To have my name added to the illustrious list of recipients of this coveted award is a very meaningful honor to me. I want to extend my sincere thanks to the National Conference of Christians and Jews executives who believed in me enough to name me to receive this citation tonight. Being honored by this great humanitarian organization is one of the greatest accolades one can receive. I want to especially thank all the people who worked to make this beautiful citation dinner successful. It is hard for me to express in words my gratitude for the happiness and feeling of accomplishment you have given me tonight. I will always try to merit the dignity and honor of this award and cherish it all my life."

Cohen felt particularly honored to be chosen to be selected as the speaker at the 1990 Mayor's Prayer Breakfast since he had been in on the events annually since their beginning. Sen. Frank Carlson, Kansas Republican, had created the concept of holding prayer breakfasts by public officials by convincing his fellow Kansan, President Dwight D. Eisenhower, to hold the first one in Washington, D.C., in 1957. In 1961, Mayor H. Roe Bartle had asked Cohen, who was then on the Kansas City Parks and Recreation Board, to serve on a committee of civic leaders to plan a Mayor's Prayer Breakfast in Kansas City that year. Bartle wanted it held on George Washington's birthday in honor of the founder of the country, and Senator Carlson was selected to be honored as the first speaker for his part in having started the movement. From then until he was named the speaker, Cohen had attended every such breakfast held in Kansas City.

In remarks made at the 1990 breakfast, Cohen has what is probably the greatest and most moving account he has ever given of how he has tried to live his life of more than 80 years. It is worth repeating at length in this slightly shortened version: "My philosophy for any success I may have achieved in my business career and in my daily life are very simple basics acquired over the years in my association with the many business, civic, religious, regular and Masonic organizations. When I tried to find the purpose for my being on this earth, I found that you are only put on this earth to help someone else and when you can't do that you have no real justification for being here. In the various organizations I have been involved with over the years, I have always given them my best efforts. One of my goals when I join an organization is to help that organization achieve its goals. I always hope that any organizations I work with are better because I have served. Einstein says it another way when he says man can find meaning in life only through devoting himself to society and that only a life lived for others is worthwhile. Much has been given us and much will rightfully be expected from us. We have duties to others and duties to ourselves and we can't shirk either. One of the things I learned the hard way was that it doesn't pay to get discouraged. Keeping busy and making optimism a way of life can restore your faith in yourself. You must sell yourself on yourself first. The real competition in life is with yourself first, then with others.

"I have always tried to follow optimism with strong affirmations for good. I find a person who begins his day with affirmations lives each hour with confidence and assurance. To me affirmations, which are my beliefs, are tiny seeds that contain unlimited possibilities for greatness, achievement and fulfillment. Men and women of every age, those who scales the heights of spiritual, professional, physical or political attainment, are the individuals who believed in and practiced the wisdom of affirmation. A few of the affirmations I use in my daily life are: God needs me to do his work and His other children need me to be an example of kindness and unselfishness. The important thing about any challenge, whether you succeed or fail is what you learn from the experience and share that knowledge with others so that they too may learn. The Good Lord has provided me a good life up to now and there is no reason for Him to forsake me now or in the future. Everything I attempt I always do with the idea of succeeding for I have always believed that God rests in action and that nothing is impossible with God's help.

"One of the most important lessons of life is that success must continuously be won and is never fully achieved. Every day is one of test and every day puts at risk all that has been gained. It is not worthwhile to think of the end of a period for you are always at the beginning of a new one. You cannot rest content. There are numerous books and artists portrayals of the life and accomplishments of George Washington. As we study these, one fact is consistent — he would always be classified as a hero of his day. Because the contemporary American hero cannot live a life identical to that of George Washington, we need to determine a measure that will take these differences into account. As a result, the new hero of our day can be either a man or a woman — a person who believed in liberty and freedom, who supports public education and who speaks up when the principles of our constitution are threatened. In short, the contemporary American hero is you. Yes, you! Each of you, like George Washington, care about the future as well as today. We must care about the future as well as today. Work for a stronger America based upon the guidelines set forth in our great document of freedom. Oppose those who feel the individual should be the slave of the state. And, of greater significance, fight for what is right because it is right. Conversely, as America's contemporary hero, you are a crusader against those who attempt to take what is wrong and try to make it right. Our success as a nation is based upon our legacy from men like George Washington. It is through this strong foundation that America has been able to grow and expand to the benefit of many people from many different lands, including each one of us. Honesty, integrity and adherence to the foundation of our government — that is what is required for Americans who will preserve the principles of America.

"Today, like others who have followed in the footsteps of George Washington, we must be leaders and set good examples for those who will follow us. As the baton has been passed to us, we must preserve it and pass it on to future generations. Albert Pike said: 'What we do for ourselves alone dies with us; what we do for others and the world remains and is immortal.' Somehow this seems appropriately to apply to George Washington who did all that a man can do in service to his country. He made sacrifices; he fought; he died. On the sands of time, he left great footprints for others to follow. To his countrymen, he gave a great gift — individual liberty. We must protect our legacy and insure its bequest for the next generation. Thus, we form a link, a chain of union of sorts, with the ideals of our founding fathers. We cannot depend upon others to do what we must do. Let us walk side by side; let us work together. Let us actively strive to promote our principles and, in this way, build a stronger America. If it is to be, it us up to me and each one of you."

Cohen had given his living testament. He believed every word of it. It was the way he lived.

HIS FAMILY ALWAYS CAME FIRST — *Whatever success Jerry Cohen may achieve, he has always put his family first as his most precious gift. In this recent photograph taken in their Oriental-style home on Ward Parkway, Cohen and his wife, Jeannette, share their pride in their family, left to right, Arlen Rubin, Chicago, a son-in-law; Elaine Cohen Rubin, a daughter; Richard Jacobson, a grandson; Mrs. Cohen; Cohen; Rosalyn Cohen Jacobson, Kansas City, a daughter; Howard Jacobson, a son-in-law, and Shari Jacobson, a granddaughter.*

HE SUPPORTED HIS SYNAGOGUE — *Jerry Cohen has served his Jewish faith well through his synagogue, Temple B'Nai Jehudah, 69th and Holmes, and he and his wife have made numerous generous gifts to the synagogue, including a 100-acre retreat center south of Kansas City. Cohen is shown here with the current rabbi of Temple B'Nai Jehudah, Rabbi Michael Zedek.*

Epilogue

During his active life with Temple B'Nai Jehudah, Jerry Cohen was instrumental in getting Albert Vorspan, the author of a book on Jewish leaders in the U.S. called Giants of Justice, in which Rabbi Samuel Mayerberg had been immortalized, to come to speak in Kansas City and the author was well received. The admiration of Vorspan, whose book was published by the Union of American Hebrew Congregations, and the way in which Vorspan had immortalized Cohen's rabbi, Mayerberg, with whom Cohen had worked in the Citizens Association, is worthy of note when one looks back on the life of Cohen in Kansas City. Cohen sensed in the way he had tried to live his own life some of the spirit of the Jew in what Vorspan had written in his book.

Although he would be reluctant to say it personally, Cohen's life was reflected in what Vorspan had written in his book: "The desire to build a better world has sunk deep into the chromosomes, the bones, the blood, the memory and soul of the Jew. An ancient tradition, which exalts this world and invests man with a spark of God, has been tested by centuries of persecution, and the totality of all this has made the Jew not only a barometer of civilization but also a symbol of a divine discontent and a messenger of a brighter tomorrow. Only in America, to borrow from Harry Golden, has the Jew in the modern world been free to accept this social vision. Somebody has described the Jewish adventure in

America as 'History without tears.' Here, where cultural and religious groups are encouraged to maintain their distinctive identities, here Jews have been able to contribute the group values of their heritage to the building of a great democracy. America is founded on basic concepts which stem from the Bible and which undergird both Judaism and Christianity: The equal dignity of all men created in the image of God. It is no accident that Jews and Judaism have flourished in America as in no other place upon the globe. And it is no accident that Jews have contributed their full share of leaders in all walks of American life and that the greatest Jews in America have also been among the greatest of Americans."

During many of the years of service Cohen was contributing to Kansas City, there was a small cabal of other Jewish leaders surrounding him who were also contributing much to the support of cultural, civic and charitable aspects of city life. In addition to Cohen, the roll of the more prominent Jewish leaders in such a category in the post-World War II era were Isaac and Michael Katz, the Ike and Mike Katz of Katz Drug Co.; Fred and George Goldman, brothers in the jewelry business; Les Milgram, of the Milgram Food Stores; Charles Hipsh, of the hotel and entertainment business; Henry Talge, manufacturer of small appliances; Eddie Jacobson, the haberdasher and former partner of Harry Truman; Irvin Fane, a lawyer; Phil Small, of the Parkview Drug Stores; and Hy Vile, founder of a large printing company. There were a couple of catalysts around whom this group made their contributions during the period: Harry Truman, who had gone from senator to vice president and eventually president and whom they were always trying to cultivate on behalf of the creation of Israel, and H. Roe Bartle, the rotund Boy Scout and civic leader who went on to become mayor and who served on many of the company boards of the men.

There is a great photograph of Bartle sitting before a large birthday cake in the presence of Cohen, Milgram and Hipsh. One by one, they died off, leaving the torch finally only in the hands of Cohen, the sole surviving member of this once-influential coterie. Of the two, Truman and Bartle, Cohen knew, admired and worked with Truman but Bartle was his real mentor with whom he worked much more closely and knew much more intimately as their correspondence indicated. It was Bartle with whom he organized and planned the American Humanics Foundation to help talented young persons with whom he worked in city politics and saw that he was named a member of the Kansas City Parks and Recreation Board for the eight years Bartle was mayor.

As early as 1957, Bartle had written Cohen a letter in which he said: "As far as I am concerned, I do not know of anyone I would rather have helping me row my boat than one Jerry Cohen. Keep that eagle eye and your strong muscles prepared to pull the oars for a long, long time to come." Or one in 1961: "I do not believe the good Lord ever gave to me a finer, a truer, or a better friend that Jerry Cohen. Certainly your fidelity, loyalty, helpfulness and devotion to me both personally and officially have been stimulating. There are times when I am sure you do not feel I am grateful but such is not the case for I know I can ever count upon you when the count is down. With all good wishes, please know me ever to be devotedly your friend." One in 1970 from Bartle to Cohen addressed "My richly beloved friend": "You will never know the terrific thrill that was mine when I had the privilege of reading the September 1970 issue of Center Span. The way in which your good company was spotlighted and the splendid comments made relative to my wonderfully fine and proven friend, Jerry Cohen, pleased me immensely. Your personal story and that of the development of the Electronic Business Equipment Company reads like an Alger story and is filled with romance. It pleased me more than I can proclaim that the story as it related to your own personal life and the many contributions you have made to the worthwhileness of living in the Heart of America rekindled the relationships which have been ours on an official though a very personal basis. The comment relative to your more than seven years as a commissioner of the Kansas City Park Board and the further mention of the nine years you have given so liberally of your time, thought, energy, talents and substance to the Mayor's Christmas Tree Association has proven conclusively that my judgement of the character, the capacity and the ability of Jerome Cohen was fully justified. This communication is being dictated on the eve of Thanksgiving Day and affords me an opportunity to proclaim sincerely that I am deeply grateful to the almighty God for the very rich friendship which you have extended to me for, lo, these many years. I pray that you, your dear wife, and all who are a part of the inner circle of your affections have a blessed and meaningful Thanksgiving season. You deserve the best, Jerry, and I want it to come your way in full measure."

In December 1971: "It was most pleasurable to have had the opportunity of being out at the Municipal Farm with you yesterday. Your loyalty, fidelity and devotion to many is as well known to others as it is to me. If we had a few more men like Jerry Cohen in Kansas City I am sure it would be a greater and finer place in which to live and enjoy the richness and fullness of life." One of the last letters from Bartle to Cohen came dated February 3, 1974, only a few weeks before he died, and was addressed to 'My richly beloved son, Jerry,' It related how his wife, whom he affectionately called "Miss Maggie," was still recuperating and that he was back in St. Luke's hospital with pain therapy. Bartle concluded the letter by writing: "I pray that 1974 will be a great year for Jerry and all of those who are a part of the inner circle of his affections. I want you and them to have good health with happiness supreme and the satisfaction that comes when you are bringing hope, cheer, helpfulness and love to those around and about you. That is your pattern of life, Jerry, for, lo, these many years and I know you'll keep it up."

Cohen had no hesitance about letting Bartle know how he felt about him as this letter he wrote Bartle testifies: "I will always count one of my greatest blessings in life the privilege of knowing you intimately and associating with you in the many worthwhile causes that have been the creation of your wonderful mind and generous heart. When I was young I read all about the great men in history books, but I feel that I have been blessed in observing a great American create history through his acts of kindness and benevolence to his fellow man. Through my association with you, I feel that I have grown immensely to be a bigger person with greater vision and a better understanding of the problems of fellow human beings." Under the Indian name, Chief Lone Bear, which he took in Mic-O-Say, the Indian-oriented Scout honor society he had created in the Boy Scouts of America, Bartle wrote a poem which could serve as an epitaph for himself and had the spirit by which Cohen had tried to live his life:

> "My work is done;
> Though brief has been life's span
> I have known brotherhood,
> And man to man
> Have felt the stirring kinship of the tried,
> The nobleness of sacrifice, the pride,

That causes man to taste the bitter with the sweet
And, tasting, lift his head above defeat
And strongly brave his tasks:
For, serving thus, he gives to life and to eternity
That spark bequeathed to him
By her who gave him life,
Who faced the grim dark valley of ordeal,
That he might live,
That he might guide mankind freely to give.
And I have stood beside a sacred place
And there with fellow tribesmen made my vows,
Have searched myself, and sought my inner strength,
Have goaded mine own spirit
To enshrine
Within my heart a long-enduring goal
That on the morrow might have more avail
Than just the mem'ry of a totem pole
Or white-washed rock.
Yes, these things have I known in mine own heart,
And they are good.
And this I know when my race is run,
When starlight falls o'er oak-clad hills,
And setting sun bespeaks the end of my life span
I have been challenged to the best in me,
I have been strengthened by Eagle's Claw.
I go, Great Spirit, answering Thy call
For it well — my brothers carry on."

Another Jewish man who contributed much to Kansas City himself in community betterment and was a close personal friend of Cohen was Hy Vile. Vile and Cohen worked together in many civic projects through the years and in 1981. Shortly before Vile died, he wrote Cohen a letter to express his feelings toward him: "Hello, Jerry. You deserve every honor that has ever been given to you. Few people in this community are as unselfish in the projects they work on as Jerry Cohen. Wherever there is an activity to help people, usually you will find Jerry Cohen... wherever there is work, where the compensation is just the satisfaction of helping people, you'll find Jerry Cohen... whenever there is a tough job that most people won't tackle, look up Jerry Cohen. And that's a wonderful legacy to leave to all those that you care about. In the years ahead, the heritage that you bequeath to those that follow will bring fruit. And that, Jerry, is the greatest feeling in the world. If Roe Bartle were around today, I think he would say: Jerry, I'm proud of you. Just keep on working like you are. You do me great honor knowing that I had a bit to do with helping you get started in community work.' And that, too, Jerry, is something to be proud of. So, congratulations, and may all the years ahead be good and healthy ones for you and your family." Vile also included a copy of a poem he had printed for Jerry. Its author was unknown, but its four stanzas give poetic expression to the way Cohen tries to lead his life. Entitled "Reasons for Life," it reads:

> "I don't know how to say it but sometimes it seems to me
> That maybe we are stationed where God wanted us to be;
> That the little place I'm filling is the reason for my birth,
> And just to do the work I do — He sent me down to earth.
> If God had wanted otherwise, I reckon He'd have made
> just a little different, of a worse or better grade.
> And since God knows and understands all things of land and sea
> I fancy that he knows He placed me just where He wanted me.
> Sometimes I get to thinking, as my labors I review
> That I should like a higher place with greater tasks to do;
> But I come to the conclusion, when the envying is stilled
> That the post to which God sent me is the post He wanted filled.
> So I plod along and struggle in the hope when day is through
> That I'm really necessary to the things God wants to do.
> And there isn't any service I can give which I should scorn
> For it may be just the reason God allowed me to be born."

In 1994, Cohen shows no signs of going out to pasture. Even as he finishes his 39th year as chairman of the Mayor's Christmas Tree Drive in Kansas City, he has his eye on the 40th one. In his more than 80 years of life, Cohen just keeps going... and going... and going. His life of service in Kansas City in that period has meaning on its own but even more meaning as a part of an epoch in human existence, the story of how Jews across America have been freed from centuries of persecution by coming to the United States and what their coming has meant to the U.S. from one end of the nation to the other. As Stanley Fieldstein has said in the conclusion to his monumental best seller, This Land That I Show You: "The passage of the Jew into American life is a saga of the deepest human experience. It afforded dignity and safety and psychological space to a homeless, embattled people who had been strangers in many lands for much of history. America changed the Jew, as it changed every immigrant, but America was more profound than the process of acculturation. The Jew in America could become human and various in all the ways Walt Whitman sang. Identity cards, restrictive laws, the murderous passion of mobs, the rights of lords — the old fears and humiliations remained, then receded, like some dark legend that loses its potency in the telling, vestiges of suffering no longer valid. The Jew spans the whole of American existence, sharing the marvelous incongruity of each citizen: his pride in his origins, his success as an American and his simultaneous worship of Jehovah, Lincoln and Babe Ruth." In the case of Cohen, make that Harry Truman and George Brett.

ALWAYS A CHEERLEADER FOR KANSAS CITY — *Jerry Cohen has loved help-ing Kansas City grow, and one of his ways of doing that was to serve as a sponsor of one of the teams at the annual National Intercollegiate Athletic Association basket-ball championships here. Always a cheerleader at heart, Cohen is shown serving with the cheerleaders for the team he sponsored. The coach wrote him later, "You gave those kids experiences they never would have had otherwise."*

ANYTHING FOR A SALE — *Jerry Cohen, although you'd never know it, is the man striding up at right in the 3M Batman costume. Cohen had just arrived in a helicopter at a picnic directed at souping up his employees to greater sales efforts in the duplicating field. All of his employees, some of whom are shown here greeting him, got free helicopter rides as a part of the sales encouragement effort.*

Index

About the Author

Ray Morgan is a veteran of 50 years as a working journalist. He spent 35 years working for the Kansas City Star and its now defunct morning edition, The Kansas City Times. It was during his newspaper career in Kansas City, including writing the About Town column in The Times, that he first began covering the activities of Jerry Cohen and became interested in doing a book about Cohen. His journalism career has also included doing political news analysis on KCTV-5, Johnson County and KCPT-19 as well as on such radio stations as KNHN 1340, KCMO 81 and KMBZ 98. His writings have appeared in The New York Times, The Washington Post, Newsweek and Business Week. He has received numerous awards on his news coverage. He is listed in the current editions of Who's Who in America and Who's Who in the World.

CITIZEN JERRY COHEN